## Why do you need this new edition?

### Here are some of the updates and new discussions found in the seventh edition:

1. Completely updated with new data from the 2010 Census and American Community Survey

2. Hate crimes are now covered as a form of discrimination

3. Discussion of the policy to conduct business audits to identify illegal immigrants

4. A feature titled "Spectrum of Intergroup Relations" addresses the unique social circumstances of individual racial and ethnic groups

5. Discussion of the birthright citizenship controversy

6. Relevant scholarly findings in a variety of disciplines, including economics, anthropology, law, and communication sciences, have been incorporated.

# Seventh Edition

# Race and Ethnicity in the United States

## Richard T. Schaefer
*DePaul University*

**PEARSON**

Boston   Columbus   Indianapolis   New York   San Francisco   Upper Saddle River
Amsterdam   Cape Town   Dubai   London   Madrid   Milan   Munich   Paris   Montreal   Toronto
Delhi   Mexico City   São Paulo   Sydney   Hong Kong   Seoul   Singapore   Taipei   Tokyo

Editor in Chief: Dickson Musslewhite
Publisher: Karen Hanson
Associate Editor: Mayda Bosco
Editorial Assistant: Joseph Jantas
Director of Marketing: Brandy Dawson
Executive Marketing Manager: Kelly May
Marketing Assistant: Diane Griffin
Director of Production: Lisa Iarkowski
Production Editor: Barbara Reilly
Production Project Manager: Maggie Brobeck

Manager, Central Design: Jayne Conte
Cover Designer: Suzanne Duda
Cover Image: © Brian J. Abela/Shutterstock
Media Director: Brian Hyland
Lead Media Project Manager: Tom Scalzo
Editorial Production and Composition
    Service: Sneha Pant/PreMediaGlobal
Printer/Binder: R. R. Donnelly/Harrisonburg
Cover Printer: R. R. Donnelly/Harrisonburg
Text Font: 10/12 ITC Garamond Std Light

Credits and acknowledgments borrowed from other sources and reproduced, with permission, in this textbook appear on page 241.

**Library of Congress Cataloging-in-Publication Data**

Schaefer, Richard T.
  Race and ethnicity in the United States / Richard T. Schaefer. — 7th ed.
    p. cm.
  Includes bibliographical references and index.
  ISBN-13: 978-0-205-21633-8
  ISBN-10: 0-205-21633-1
  1. Minorities—United States.  2. Prejudices—United States.  3. United States—Ethnic relations.  4. United States—Race relations.  I. Title.
  E184.A1S25 2013
  305.800973—dc23

2011049073

10 9 8 7 6 5 4 3 2 1

ISBN-10: 0-205-21633-1
ISBN-13: 978-0-205-21633-8

*To the students in my classes as well as those readers who communicate with me from afar. They all help me to grasp the complexity of race and ethnicity in the United States.*

# Contents

# Preface

Race and ethnicity are an important part of the national agenda. And they are not static phenomena. The results of the 2010 Census confirm what we see on our streets and hear in our classrooms; nearly half of the population under age 18 are members of racial or ethnic minorities. Results show that 11 percent of the country's 3,143 counties already have become "majority minority"—less than 50 percent non-Hispanic white. And another 225 counties will have reached the "tipping point" toward becoming majority minority sometime in the next decade: Between 40 percent and 50 percent of the population in those counties are minorities. The Latino population increased 43 percent since 2000 and has more than doubled since 1990. Overall, minorities accounted for 92 percent of the total U.S. population growth during the past decade with Hispanics accounting for over half of the increase.

Immigration continues to be a major force. *Every day* on the average arrive 3,100 people who have received immigrant visas that allow them to settle and become naturalized citizens after five years. Another 2,000 unauthorized foreigners a day settle in the United States with the majority eluding apprehension by authorities (Martin and Midgley 2010; Mather, Pollard and Jacobsen 2011).

President Barack Obama called for a national discussion on race. He did so first as a candidate when his relationship to an outspoken African American minister was called into question and then just a year later when, as president, he weighed in on a confrontation between a police officer and a respected professor who was Black. The first non-White president speaks to the issue on a national stage in a personal way not seen with his predecessors in the Oval Office is noteworthy in its own right.

Race has always been a part of the social reality. Specific issues may change over time; however, they continue to play out against a backdrop of discrimination that is rooted in the social structure and changing population composition, as influenced by immigration patterns and reproduction patterns.

We continue to be reminded about the importance of the social construction of many aspects of racial and ethnic relations. What constitutes a race in terms of identity? What meaning do race and ethnicity have amid the growing number of interracial marriages and marriages across cultural boundaries? Beyond the spectrum of race and ethnicity, we see the socially constructed meaning attached to all religions as members debate who is the "true" keeper of the faith. The very issue of national identity is also a part of the agenda. The public and politicians alike ask, "How many immigrants can we accept?" and "How much should be done to make up for past discrimination?" We are also witnessing the emergence of race, ethnicity, and national identity as global issues.

## Changes in the Seventh Edition

As with all previous editions, every line, every source, and every number have been rechecked for their currency. We pride ourselves on providing the most current information possible to document the patterns in intergroup relations in the United States.

Relevant scholarly findings in a variety of disciplines, including economics, anthropology, law, and communication sciences, have been incorporated. Previous users of this book will notice the addition of the Spectrum of Intergroup Relations, which has been given new representation, in three chapters.

The seventh edition includes the following additions and changes:

### Chapter 1
- New opening examples
- Retitled section "Ranking Groups"
- "Multiracial Identity" section expanded and relocated to give more attention
- Census 2010 and American Community Survey 2010 data update all statistics
- 2009 metropolitan segregation data for African Americans, Hispanics, and Asian Americans
- 2010 census multiple-race data
- 2010 map of minority population by counties
- Racial and ethnic population projections for 2050

### Chapter 2
- Research Focus: Islamophobia
- "White Privilege" section moved to this chapter to give better social context

- 2010 map of change in minority population by county
- 2011 data on ethnic and racial profiling
- 2010 survey data on perception that President Obama is a Muslim

## Chapter 3

- Hate crimes (updated to 2010) now covered as a form of discrimination
- Explanation of reasons presented for designating offenses hate crimes
- Income and wealth inequity data updated to 2010 studies
- Tables and figure on income by race and sex, holding education constant updated
- Listen to Our Voices: Randall Kennedy's *The Enduring Relevance of Affirmative Action*
- Spectrum of Intergroup Relations added

## Chapter 4

- Research Focus: Challenge to Pluralism: The Shark's Fin
- "The Environment and Immigration" section
- Voters caught as "illegals" while registering to vote
- Two figures on immigration updated through 2010
- Table on refugees updated to 2010
- Coverage of refugees from 2010 earthquake in Haiti
- Listen to Our Voices: Galina Espinoza's *That Latino "Wave" Is Very Much American*
- Birthright citizenship controversy
- Current policy to conduct business audits to identify illegal immigrants
- Updated languages most frequently spoken at home
- Map from American Community Survey on percent of people who are foreign born by country
- Spectrum of Intergroup Relations added

## Chapter 5

- Chinese outnumber Italians in Manhattan's Little Italy
- Research Focus: Self-Identifying as "Arab American"
- "Ethnic paradox" coverage expanded
- Listen to Our Voices: *Asian America Still Discovering Elusive Identity*, by Jean Han
- Table on churches with more than a million members updated
- Controversy over National Day of Prayer

**Chapter 6**
- Updated comparison of schooling, health, and income measures
- Figure: Changes in Minority Population 2000–2010, Under Age 18
- Spectrum of Intergroup Relations covering entire textbook added

## Features to Aid Students

Several features are included in the text to facilitate student learning. A chapter outline appears at the beginning of each chapter and is followed by "Highlights," a short section alerting students to important issues and topics to be addressed. To help students review, each chapter ends with a conclusion and summary. The key terms are highlighted in bold when they are first introduced in the text and are listed with corresponding page numbers at the end of each chapter. The Spectrum of Intergroup Relations first presented in Chapter 1 also appears in Chapters 4, 5, and 6 to reinforce major concepts while addressing the unique social circumstances of individual racial and ethnic groups.

In addition, there is an end-of-book glossary with full definitions referenced by page numbers. This edition includes both "Review Questions" and "Critical Thinking Questions." The Review Questions are intended to remind the reader of major points, whereas the Critical Thinking Questions encourage students to think more deeply about some of the major issues raised in the chapter. Updated Internet exercises allow students to do some critical thinking and research on the Web. An Internet Resource Directory has been expanded to allow access to the latest electronic sources. An extensive illustration program, which includes maps and political cartoons, expands the text discussion and provokes thought.

## Ancillary Materials

The ancillary materials that accompany this textbook have been carefully created to enhance the topics being discussed.

### For the Instructor

**Instructor's Manual and Test Bank** (ISBN 020521634X). This carefully prepared manual includes chapter overviews, key term identification exercises, discussion questions, topics for class discussion, audiovisual resources, and test questions in both multiple-choice and essay format. The Instructor's Manual and Test Bank is available to adopters at www.pearsonhighered.com.

**MyTest** (ISBN 0205216366). This computerized software allows instructors to create their own personalized exams, to edit any or all of the existing test questions and to add new questions. Other special features of this program include random generation of test questions, creation of alternate versions of the same test, scrambling question sequence, and test preview before printing. The MyTest is available to adopters at www. pearsonhighered.com.

**PPTs** (ISBN 0205216374). The Lecture PowerPoint slides follow the chapter outline and feature images from the textbook integrated with the text. The slides are uniquely designed to present concepts in a clear and succinct manner. They are available to adopters at www.pearsonhighered.com.

## For the Student

**MySearchLab** is a dynamic website that delivers proven results in helping individual students succeed. Its wealth of resources provides engaging experiences that personalize, stimulate, and measure learning for each student. Many accessible tools will encourage students to read their text, improve writing skills, and help them improve their grade in their course.

Features of MySearchLab

Writing

- Step by step tutorials present complete overviews of the research and writing process.

Research and citing sources

- Instructors and students receive access to the EBSCO ContentSelect database, census data from Social Explorer, Associated Press news feeds, and the Pearson bookshelf. Pearson SourceCheck helps students and instructors monitor originality and avoid plagiarism.

Etext and more

- Pearson eText—An e-book version of *Race and Ethnicity in the United States*, 7th Edition, is included in MySearchLab. Just like the printed text, students can highlight and add their own notes as they read their interactive text online.
- Chapter quizzes and flashcards—Chapter and key term reviews are available for each chapter online and offer immediate feedback.
- Primary Source Documents—A collection of documents, organized by chapter, are available on MySearchLab. The documents include head notes and critical thinking questions.
- Gradebook—Automated grading of quizzes helps both instructors and students monitor their results throughout the course.

## Acknowledgments

The seventh edition benefited from the thoughtful reaction of my students in classes. Jessica Chiarella and Kathleen Talmadge, students at DePaul University, assisted with special tasks related to the preparation of the manuscript. Professor James Burnett of Idaho State University also provided improved suggestions for the seventh edition.

I would also like to thank my publisher, Karen Hanson, and my associate editor, Mayda Bosco, who both worked closely with me on this book.

The truly exciting challenge of writing and researching has always been an enriching experience for me, mostly because of the supportive home I share with my wife, Sandy. She knows so well my appreciation and gratitude, now as in the past and in the future.

Richard T. Schaefer
*schaeferrt@aol.com*
*www.schaefersociology.net*

# About the Author

Richard T. Schaefer grew up in Chicago at a time when neighborhoods were going through transitions in ethnic and racial composition. He found himself increasingly intrigued by what was happening, how people were reacting, and how these changes were affecting neighborhoods and people's jobs. In high school, he took a course in sociology. His interest in social issues caused him to gravitate to more sociology courses at Northwestern University, where he eventually received a B.A. in sociology.

"Originally as an undergraduate I thought I would go on to law school and become a lawyer. But after taking a few sociology courses, I found myself wanting to learn more about what sociologists studied and was fascinated by the kinds of questions they raised," Dr. Schaefer says. "Perhaps most fascinating and, to me, relevant to the 1960s was the intersection of race, gender, and social class." This interest led him to obtain his M.A. and Ph.D. in sociology from the University of Chicago. Dr. Schaefer's continuing interest in race relations led him to write his master's thesis on the membership of the Ku Klux Klan and his doctoral thesis on racial prejudice and race relations in Great Britain.

Dr. Schaefer went on to become a professor of sociology. He has taught sociology and courses on multiculturalism for 30 years. He has been invited to give special presentations to students and faculty on racial and ethnic diversity in Illinois, Indiana, Missouri, North Carolina, Ohio, and Texas.

Dr. Schaefer is the author of *Racial and Ethnic Groups* thirteenth edition (Pearson Prentice Hall, 2012). Dr. Schaefer is the general editor of the three-volume *Encyclopedia of Race, Ethnicity, and Society* (2008). He is also the author of the thirteenth edition of *Sociology* (2012), the ninth edition of *Sociology: A Brief Introduction* (2011), *Sociology: A Modular Approach* (2011), and the fifth edition of *Sociology Matters* (2011). Schaefer coauthored with William Zellner the ninth edition of *Extraordinary Groups* (2011).

His articles and book reviews have appeared in many journals, including *American Journal of Sociology, Phylon: A Review of Race and Culture, Contemporary Sociology, Sociology and Social Research, Sociological Quarterly,* and *Teaching Sociology*. He served as president of the Midwest Sociological Society from 1994 to 1995. In recognition of his achievements in undergraduate teaching, he was named Vincent de Paul Professor of Sociology in 2004.

# 1 Exploring Race and Ethnicity

## CHAPTER OUTLINE

⟨ HIGHLIGHTS ⟩

Minority groups are subordinated in terms of power and privilege to the majority, or dominant group. A minority is defined not by being outnumbered but by five characteristics: unequal treatment, distinguishing physical or cultural traits, involuntary membership, awareness of subordination, and in-group marriage. Subordinate groups are classified in terms of race, ethnicity, religion, and gender. The social importance of race is derived from a process of racial formation; any biological significance is relatively unimportant to society. The theoretical perspectives of functionalism, conflict theory, and labeling offer insights into the sociology of intergroup relations.

Immigration, annexation, and colonialism are processes that may create subordinate groups. Other processes such as extermination and expulsion may remove the presence of a subordinate group. Significant for racial and ethnic oppression in the United States today is the distinction between assimilation and pluralism. Assimilation demands subordinate-group conformity to the dominant group, and pluralism implies mutual respect among diverse groups.

Minority women are more likely to be poor, which creates what sociologists have termed the matrix of domination. Although dominant groups seek to define the social landscape, groups who experience unequal treatment have in the past resisted power and sought significant social change and continue to do so today.

The United States has a Black president but when his parents were married in 1961 in Hawaii, the marriage of a White person and Black African would have been illegal in 22 of the other states. Shoppers in supermarkets readily find seasonings of chili peppers, cumin, ginger, and roasted coriander, reflecting

Barack Obama's historic campaign and his elevation to becoming the 44th president of the United States in January 2009 marks a significant moment in U.S. history. The fact that he is the first African American (and also the first non-White person) to serve as president demonstrates how much progress has been achieved in race relations in this country. It also serves to underscore both how long it has taken and how much more needs to be accomplished for the United States to truly be "a more perfect union" as stated in the Constitution.

the influx of immigrants and their food tastes being accepted by more and more Americans. Yet recent research shows that if a person with a strong accent says, "Ants do sleep," we are less likely to believe it than if said by someone with no accent.

Race and ethnicity is exceedingly complex in the United States. A Methodist church in Brooklyn founded by European immigrants more than a century ago is now operated by Latino parishioners whose numbers have dwindled to 30. To keep the church going they lease space to a growing Chinese Methodist church, which numbers over a thousand. Meanwhile, in nearby Queens, a Methodist church split between Latin Americans and Caribbean immigrants has just made room for a separate Pakistani Methodist congregation.

Also consider the racial and ethnic stereotypes that are shamelessly exhibited on Halloween, when many young adults view the festivities as a "safe" way to defy social norms. College students report seeing fellow White students dressed in baggy jeans wearing gold chains and drinking malt liquor to represent "gangstas." Some add blackface makeup to complete the appearance. Such escapades are not limited to misguided youth. National retailers stock a "Kung Fool" ensemble complete with Japanese kimono and a buck-toothed slant-eyed mask. Also available is "Vato Loco," a stereotyped caricature of a bandana-clad, tattooed Latino gang thug.

Racial and ethnic tensions are not limited to the real world; they are also alive and well in the virtual world. Hate groups, anti-Jewish organizations, and even the Ku Klux Klan thrive on Web sites. Such fringe groups, enjoying their First Amendment rights in the United States, spread their messages in many languages globally via the Internet, whereas the creation of such hate sites is banned in Canada, Europe, and elsewhere.

Facebook has emerged as a significant way in which people interact, but it also is a means to learn about others by their online profile. Already by 2007, colleges and universities cited Facebook as the major source of prospective students (or their parents) requesting roommate changes even before arriving on campus, because of the intended roommate's race, religion, or sexual orientation (Collura 2007; Dolnick 2010; Lev-Ari and Keysar 2010; Mueller, Dirks, and Picca 2007; Working 2007).

The United States is a very diverse nation and is becoming even more so, as shown in Table 1.1. In 2010, approximately 24 percent of the population was members of racial minorities, and another 16 percent or so were Hispanic.

**Table 1.1 Racial and Ethnic Groups in the United States**

| Classification | Number in Thousands | Percentage of Total Population |
|---|---|---|
| Racial Groups | | |
| Whites (non-Hispanic) | 194,553 | 63.0 |
| Blacks/African Americans | 34,658 | 11.2 |
| Native Americans, Alaskan Natives | 2,476 | 0.8 |
| Asian Americans | 14,229 | 4.6 |
| Chinese | 3,106 | 1.0 |
| Asian Indians | 2,602 | 0.8 |
| Filipinos | 2,476 | 0.8 |
| Vietnamese | 1,482 | 0.5 |
| Koreans | 1,336 | 0.4 |
| Japanese | 767 | 0.2 |
| Pacific Islanders, Native Hawaiians, and other Asian Americans | 2,460 | 0.8 |
| Ethnic Groups | | |
| White ancestry (single or mixed, non-Hispanic) | | |
| Germans | 50,708 | 16.5 |
| Irish | 36,915 | 12.0 |
| English | 27,658 | 9.0 |
| Italians | 18,085 | 5.9 |
| Poles | 10,091 | 3.3 |
| Scottish and Scotch-Irish | 9,417 | 3.1 |
| French | 9,412 | 3.1 |
| Jews | 6,452 | 2.1 |
| Hispanics (or Latinos) | 50,478 | 16.3 |
| Mexican Americans | 31,798 | 10.3 |
| Puerto Ricans | 4,624 | 1.5 |
| Cubans | 1,785 | 0.6 |
| Salvadorans | 1,648 | 0.5 |
| Dominicans | 1,415 | 0.5 |
| Guatemalans | 1,044 | 0.3 |
| Other Hispanics | 8,164 | 2.6 |
| TOTAL (ALL GROUPS) | 308,746 | |

*Note:* All data for 2009 except three racial groups listed at top, Hispanic total and subgroups, and total population figure, which are for 2010. Percentages do not total 100 percent, and subheads do not add up to totals in major categories because of overlap between groups (e.g., Polish American Jews or people of mixed ancestry such as Irish and Italian).

*Source:* 2009 data from American Community Survey 2010:Tables B02006, B03001, C04006; 2010 data from Davidson and Pyle 2011:117; Ennis et al. 2011; Humes et al. 2011.

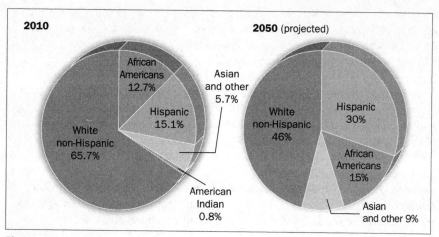

**Figure 1.1**    Population of the United States by Race and Ethnicity, 2010 and 2050 (Projected)

According to projections by the Census Bureau, the proportion of residents of the United States who are White and non-Hispanic will decrease significantly by the year 2050. By contrast, there will be a striking rise in the proportion of both Hispanic Americans and Asian Americans.

*Source*: Bureau of the Census 2010b.

These percentages represent four out of ten people in the United States, without counting White ethnic groups or foreign-born Whites. As shown in Figure 1.1, between 2010 and 2050, the Black, Hispanic, Asian, and Native American portion of the population in the United States is expected to increase from about 40 percent to 54 percent. Although the composition of the population is changing, problems of prejudice, discrimination, and mistrust remain.

## Ranking Groups

In every society not all groups are treated or viewed equally. Identifying a subordinate group or a minority in a society seems to be a simple task. In the United States, the groups readily identified as minorities—Blacks and Native Americans, for example—are outnumbered by non-Blacks and non–Native Americans. However, minority status is not necessarily the result of being outnumbered. A social minority need not be a mathematical one. A **minority group** is a subordinate group whose members have significantly less control or power over their own lives than do the members of a dominant or majority group. In sociology, *minority* means the same as *subordinate*, and *dominant* is used interchangeably with *majority*.

Confronted with evidence that a particular minority in the United States is subordinate to the majority, some people respond, "Why not? After all, this is a democracy, so the majority rules." However, the subordination of a minority involves more than its inability to rule over society. A member of a subordinate or minority group experiences a narrowing of life's opportunities—for success, education, wealth, the pursuit of happiness—that goes beyond any personal shortcoming he or she may have. A minority group does not share in proportion to its numbers what a given society, such as the United States, defines as valuable.

Being superior in numbers does not guarantee a group control over its destiny and ensure majority status. In 1920, the majority of people in Mississippi and South Carolina were African Americans. Yet African Americans did not have as much control over their lives as did Whites, let alone control of the states of Mississippi and South Carolina. Throughout the United States today are counties or neighborhoods in which the majority of people are African American, Native American, or Hispanic, but where White Americans are the dominant force. Nationally, 50.7 percent of the population is female, but males still dominate positions of authority and wealth well beyond their numbers.

A minority or subordinate group has five characteristics: unequal treatment, distinguishing physical or cultural traits, involuntary membership, awareness of subordination, and in-group marriage (Wagley and Harris 1958):

1. Members of a minority experience unequal treatment and have less power over their lives than members of a dominant group have over theirs. Prejudice, discrimination, segregation, and even extermination create this social inequality.

2. Members of a minority group share physical or cultural characteristics such as skin color or language that distinguish them from the dominant group. Each society has its own arbitrary standard for determining which characteristics are most important in defining dominant and minority groups.

3. Membership in a dominant or minority group is not voluntary: people are born into the group. A person does not choose to be African American or White.

4. Minority-group members have a strong sense of group solidarity. William Graham Sumner, writing in 1906, noted that people make distinctions between members of their own group (the in-group) and everyone else (the out-group). When a group is the object of long-term prejudice and discrimination, the feeling of "us versus them" often becomes intense.

5. Members of a minority generally marry others from the same group. A member of a dominant group often is unwilling to join a supposedly inferior minority by marrying one of its members. In addition, the minority group's sense of solidarity encourages marriage within the group and discourages marriage to outsiders.

Although "minority" status is not about numbers, there is no denying that the White American majority is diminishing in size relative to the growing diversity of racial and ethnic groups, as illustrated in Figure 1.2.

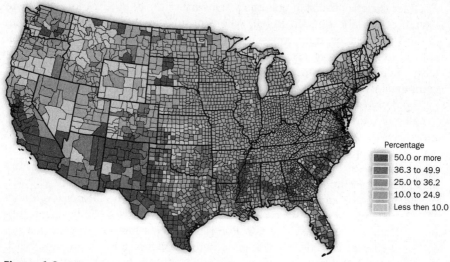

**Figure 1.2**   Minority Population by County
In four states (California, Hawaii, New Mexico, and Texas) and the District of Columbia, as well as in about one-tenth of all counties, minorities constitute the numerical majority.

*Source*: Bureau of the Census 2011d.

## Types of Groups ✓

There are four types of minority or subordinate groups. All four, except where noted, have the five properties previously outlined. The four criteria for classifying minority groups are race, ethnicity, religion, and gender.

### Racial Groups

The term **racial group** is reserved for minorities and the corresponding majorities that are socially set apart because of obvious physical differences. Notice the two crucial words in the definition: *obvious* and *physical*. What is obvious? Hair color? Shape of an earlobe? Presence of body hair? To whom are these differences obvious, and why? Each society defines what it finds obvious.

In the United States, skin color is one obvious difference. On a cold winter day when one has clothing covering all but one's head, however, skin color may be less obvious than hair color. Yet people in the United States have learned informally that skin color is important and hair color is unimportant. We need to say more than that. In the United States, people have traditionally classified themselves as either Black or White. There is no in-between state except for people readily identified as Native Americans or Asian Americans. Later in this chapter, we explore this issue more deeply and see how such assumptions have very complex implications.

Other societies use skin color as a standard but may have a more elaborate system of classification. In Brazil, where hostility between races is less than in the United States, numerous categories identify people on the basis of skin color. In the United States, a person is Black or White. In Brazil, a variety of terms such as *cafuso, mazombo, preto,* and *escuro* are used to describe various combinations of skin color, facial features, and hair texture.

The designation of a racial group emphasizes physical differences as opposed to cultural distinctions. In the United States, minority races include Blacks, Native Americans (or American Indians), Japanese Americans, Chinese Americans, Arab Americans, Filipinos, Hawaiians, and other Asian peoples. The issue of race and racial differences has been an important one, not only in the United States but also throughout the entire sphere of European influence. Later in this chapter, we examine race and its significance more closely. We should not forget that Whites are a race too. As we consider in Chapter 5, who is White has been subject to change over time as certain European groups historically were felt not to deserve being considered White. Partly to compete against a growing Black population, the "Whiting" of some European Americans has occurred.

Some racial groups may also have unique cultural traditions, as we can readily see in the many Chinatowns throughout the United States. For racial groups, however, the physical distinctiveness and not the cultural differences generally prove to be the barrier to acceptance by the host society. For example, Chinese Americans who are faithful Protestants and know the names of all the members of the Baseball Hall of Fame may be bearers of American culture. Yet these Chinese Americans are still part of a minority because they are seen as physically different.

## Ethnic Groups

Ethnic minority groups are differentiated from the dominant group on the basis of cultural differences such as language, attitudes toward marriage and parenting, and food habits. **Ethnic groups** are groups set apart from others because of their national origin or distinctive cultural patterns.

Ethnic groups in the United States include a grouping that we call *Hispanics* or *Latinos* and include Mexican Americans, Puerto Ricans, Cubans, and other Latin Americans in the United States. Hispanics can be either Black or White, as in the case of a dark-skinned Puerto Rican who may be taken as Black in central Texas but may be viewed as Puerto Rican in New York City. The ethnic group category also includes White ethnics such as Irish Americans, Polish Americans, and Norwegian Americans.

The cultural traits that make groups distinctive usually originate from their homelands or, for Jews, from a long history of being segregated and prohibited from becoming a part of the host society. Once in the United States, an immigrant group may maintain distinctive cultural practices through associations, clubs, and worship. Ethnic enclaves such as a Little Haiti or a Greektown in urban areas also perpetuate cultural distinctiveness.

## LISTEN TO OUR VOICES

### Problem of the Color Line

*W. E. B. Du Bois*

In the metropolis of the modern world, in this the closing year of the nineteenth century, there has been assembled a congress of men and women of African blood, to deliberate solemnly upon the present situation and outlook of the darker races of mankind. The problem of the twentieth century is the problem of the color line, the question as to how far differences of race—which show themselves chiefly in the color of the skin and the texture of the hair—will hereafter be made the basis of denying to over half the world the right of sharing to their utmost ability the opportunities and privileges of modern civilization. . . .

To be sure, the darker races are today the least advanced in culture according to European standards. This has not, however, always been the case in the past, and certainly the world's history, both ancient and modern, has given many instances of no despicable ability and capacity among the blackest races of men.

In any case, the modern world must remember that in this age when the ends of the world are being brought so near together, the millions of black men in Africa, America, and Islands of the Sea, not to speak of the brown and yellow myriads elsewhere, are bound to have a great influence upon the world in the future, by reason of sheer numbers and physical contact. If now the world of culture bends itself towards giving Negroes and other dark men the largest and broadest opportunity for education and self-development, then this contact and influence is bound to have a beneficial effect upon the world and hasten human progress. But if, by reason of carelessness, prejudice, greed, and injustice, the black world is to be exploited and ravished and degraded, the results must be deplorable, if not fatal—not simply to them, but to the high ideals of justice, freedom and culture which a thousand years of Christian civilization have held before Europe. . . .

Let the world take no backward step in that slow but sure progress which has successively refused to let the spirit of class, of caste, of privilege, or of birth, debar from life, liberty, and the pursuit of happiness a striving human soul.

Let not color or race be a feature of distinction between White and Black men, regardless of worth or ability. . . .

Thus we appeal with boldness and confidence to the Great Powers of the civilized world, trusting in the wide spirit of humanity, and the deep sense of justice of our age, for a generous recognition of the righteousness of our cause.

*Source*: From W. E. B. Du Bois 1900 [1969a], *ABC of Color*, pp. 20–21, 23. Copyright 1969 by International Publishers.

Ethnicity continues to be important, as recent events in Bosnia and other parts of Eastern Europe have demonstrated. More than a century ago, African American sociologist W. E. B. Du Bois, addressing an audience at a world anti-slavery convention in London in 1900, called attention to the overwhelming importance of the color line throughout the world. In "Listen to Our Voices," we read the remarks of Du Bois, the first Black person to receive a doctorate from Harvard, who later helped to organize the National Association for the Advancement of Colored People (NAACP). Du Bois's observations give us a historic perspective on the struggle for equality. We can look ahead, knowing how far we have come and speculating on how much further we have to go.

## Religious Groups

Association with a religion other than the dominant faith is the third basis for minority-group status. In the United States, Protestants, as a group, outnumber members of all other religions. Roman Catholics form the largest minority religion. Chapter 5 focuses on the increasing Judeo–Christian–Islamic diversity of the United States. For people who are not a part of the Christian tradition, such as followers of Islam, allegiance to the faith often is misunderstood and stigmatizes people. This stigmatization became especially widespread and legitimated by government action in the aftermath of the attacks of September 11, 2001.

Religious minorities include groups such as the Church of Jesus Christ of Latter-Day Saints (the Mormons), Jehovah's Witnesses, Amish, Muslims, and Buddhists. Cults or sects associated with practices such as animal sacrifice, doomsday prophecy, demon worship, or the use of snakes in a ritualistic fashion would also constitute minorities. Jews are excluded from this category and placed among ethnic groups. Culture is a more important defining trait for Jewish people worldwide than is religious dogma. Jewish Americans share a cultural tradition that goes beyond theology. In this sense, it is appropriate to view them as an ethnic group rather than as members of a religious faith.

## Gender Groups

Gender is another attribute that creates dominant and subordinate groups. Males are the social majority; females, although numerous, are relegated to the position of the social minority. Women are considered a minority even though they do not exhibit all the characteristics outlined earlier (e.g., there is little in-group marriage). Women encounter prejudice and discrimination and are physically distinguishable. Group membership is involuntary, and many women have developed a sense of sisterhood.

Women who are members of racial and ethnic minorities face a special challenge to achieving equality. They suffer from greater inequality because they belong to two separate minority groups: a racial or ethnic group plus a subordinate gender group. We explore this aspect of domination–subordination later in this chapter.

## Other Subordinate Groups

This book focuses on groups that meet a set of criteria for subordinate status. People encounter prejudice or are excluded from full participation in society for many reasons. Racial, ethnic, religious, and gender barriers are the main ones, but

Given the diversity in the nation, it is not always self-evident how people view themselves in terms of ethnic and racial background, as cartoonist Tak Toyoshima humorously points out.

*Source:* Secret Asian Man © Tak Toyoshima, distributed by United Features Syndicate, Inc.

there are others. Age, disability status, physical appearance, and sexual orientation are among some other factors that are used to subordinate groups of people.

## Does Race Matter?

We see people around us—some of whom may look quite different from us. Do these differences matter? The simple answer is no, but because so many people have for so long acted as if difference in physical characteristics as well as geographic origin and shared culture do matter, distinct groups have been created in people's minds. Race has many meanings for many people. Often these meanings are inaccurate and based on theories discarded by scientists generations ago. As we will see, race is a socially constructed concept (Young 2003).

### Biological Meaning

The way the term *race* has been used by some people to apply to human beings lacks any scientific meaning. We cannot identify distinctive physical characteristics for groups of human beings the same way that scientists distinguish one animal species from another. The idea of **biological race** is based on the mistaken notion of a genetically isolated human group.

**Absence of Pure Races** Even among past proponents who believed that sharp, scientific divisions exist among humans, there were endless debates over what the races of the world were. Given people's frequent migration, exploration, and invasions, pure genetic types have not existed for some time, if they ever did. There are no mutually exclusive races. Skin color among

African Americans varies tremendously, as it does among White Americans. There is even an overlapping of dark-skinned Whites and light-skinned African Americans. If we grouped people by genetic resistance to malaria and by fingerprint patterns, then Norwegians and many African groups would be of the same race. If we grouped people by some digestive capacities, some Africans, Asians, and southern Europeans would be of one group and West Africans and northern Europeans of another (Leehotz 1995; Shanklin 1994).

Biologically there are no pure, distinct races. Research as a part of the Human Genome Project mapping human deoxyribonucleic acid (DNA) has only served to confirm genetic diversity, with differences within traditionally regarded racial groups (e.g., Black Africans) much greater than that between groups (e.g., between Black Africans and Europeans). Contemporary studies of DNA on a global basis have determined that about 90 percent of human genetic variation is within "local populations," such as within the French or within the Afghan people. The remaining 10 percent of total human variation is what we think of today as constituting races and accounts for skin color, hair form, nose shape, and so forth (Feldman 2010).

Research has also been conducted to determine whether personality characteristics such as temperament and nervous habits are inherited among minority groups. It is no surprise that the question of whether races have different innate levels of intelligence has led to the most explosive controversies (Bamshad and Olson 2003; El-Haj 2007).

**Intelligence Tests**   Typically, intelligence is measured as an **intelligence quotient (IQ)**, which is the ratio of a person's mental age to his or her chronological age, multiplied by 100, with 100 representing average intelligence and higher scores representing greater intelligence. It should be noted that there is little consensus over just what intelligence is, other than as defined by such IQ tests. Intelligence tests are adjusted for a person's age so that 10-year-olds take a very different test from someone 20 years old. Although research shows that certain learning strategies can improve a person's IQ, generally IQ remains stable as one ages.

A great deal of debate continues over the accuracy of these tests. Are they biased toward people who come to the tests with knowledge similar to that of the test writers? Skeptics argue that such test questions do not truly measure intellectual potential. The issue of cultural bias in tests remains an unresolved concern. The most recent research shows that differences in intelligence scores between Blacks and Whites are almost eliminated when adjustments are made for social and economic characteristics (Brooks-Gunn, Klebanov, and Duncan 1996; Herrnstein and Murray 1994:30; Kagan 1971; Young 2003).

In 1994, an 845-page book unleashed a new national debate on the issue of IQ. This research effort of psychologist Richard J. Herrnstein and social scientist Charles Murray, published in *The Bell Curve* (1994), concluded that 60 percent of IQ is inheritable and that racial groups offer a convenient means to generalize about any differences in intelligence. Unlike most other proponents of the race–IQ link, the authors offered policy suggestions that included ending welfare to discourage births among low-IQ poor women and changing immigration laws so that the IQ pool in the United States is not diminished. Herrnstein and Murray even made generalizations about IQ levels among Asians and Hispanics in the United States, groups subject to even more intermarriage. It is not possible to generalize about absolute differences between groups, such as Latinos versus Whites, when almost half of Latinos in the United States marry non-Hispanics.

More than a decade later, the mere mention of the "bell curve" still signals to many people a belief in a racial hierarchy, with Whites toward the top and Blacks near the bottom. The research present then and repeated today points to the difficulty in definitions: What is intelligence, and what constitutes a racial group, given generations (if not centuries) of intermarriage? How can we speak of definitive inherited racial differences if there has been intermarriage between people of every color? Furthermore, as people on both sides of the debate have noted, regardless of the findings, we would still want to strive to maximize the talents of each individual. All research shows that the differences within a group are much greater than any alleged differences between group averages.

Why does such IQ research reemerge if the data are subject to different interpretations? The argument that "we" are superior to "them" is very appealing to the dominant group. It justifies receiving opportunities that are denied to others. We can anticipate that the debate over IQ and the allegations of significant group differences will continue. Policymakers need to acknowledge the difficulty in treating race as a biologically significant characteristic.

## Social Construction of Race

If race does not distinguish humans from one another biologically, then why does it seem to be so important? It is important because of the social meaning people have attached to it. The 1950 (UNESCO) Statement on Race maintains, "for all practical social purposes 'race' is not so much a biological phenomenon as a social myth" (Montagu 1972:118). Adolf Hitler expressed concern over the "Jewish race" and translated this concern into Nazi death camps. Winston Churchill spoke proudly of the "British race" and used that pride to spur a nation to fight. Evidently, race was a useful political tool for two very different leaders in the 1930s and 1940s.

Race is a social construction, and this process benefits the oppressor, who defines who is privileged and who is not. The acceptance of race in a society as a legitimate category allows racial hierarchies to emerge to the benefit of the dominant "races." For example, inner-city drive-by shootings have come to be seen as a race-specific problem worthy of local officials cleaning up troubled neighborhoods. Yet, schoolyard shootouts are viewed as a societal concern and placed on the national agenda.

People could speculate that if human groups have obvious physical differences, then they could have corresponding mental or personality differences. No one disagrees that people differ in temperament, potential to learn, and sense of humor. In its social sense, race implies that groups that differ physically also bear distinctive emotional and mental abilities or disabilities. These beliefs are based on the notion that humankind can be divided into distinct groups. We have already seen the difficulties associated with pigeonholing people into racial categories. Despite these difficulties, belief in the inheritance of behavior patterns and in an association between physical and cultural traits is widespread. It is called **racism** when this belief is coupled with the feeling that certain groups or races are inherently superior to others. Racism is a doctrine of racial supremacy that states one race is superior to another (Bash 2001; Bonilla-Silva 1996).

We questioned the biological significance of race in the previous section. In modern complex industrial societies, we find little adaptive utility in the presence or absence of prominent chins, epicanthic folds of the eyelids, or the comparative amount of melanin in the skin. What is important is not that people are genetically different but that they approach one another with dissimilar perspectives. It is in the social setting that race is decisive. Race is significant because people have given it significance.

Race definitions are crystallized through what Michael Omi and Howard Winant (1994) called **racial formation**, a sociohistorical process by which racial categories are created, inhabited, transformed, and destroyed. Those in power define groups of people in a certain way that depends on a racist social structure. The Native Americans and the creation of the reservation system for Native Americans in the late 1800s is an example of this racial formation. The federal American Indian policy combined previously distinctive tribes into a single group. No one escapes the extent and frequency to which we are subjected to racial formation.

With rising immigration from Latin America in the latter part of the twentieth century, the fluid nature of racial formation is evident. As if it happened in one day, people in the United States have spoken about the Latin Americanization of the United States or that the biracial order of Black and White was now replaced with a triracial order. It is this social context of the changing nature of diversity that we examine to understand how scholars have sought to generalize about intergroup relations in the United States and elsewhere (Bonilla-Silva and Dietrich 2011; Frank et al. 2010).

In the southern United States, the social construction of race was known as the "one-drop rule." This tradition stipulated that if a person had even a single drop of "Black blood," that person was defined and viewed as Black. Today, children of biracial or multiracial marriages try to build their own identities in a country that seems intent on placing them in some single, traditional category—a topic we look at next.

# Biracial and Multiracial Identity: Who Am I?

People are now more willing to accept and advance identities that do not fit neatly into mutually exclusive categories. Hence, increasing numbers of people are identifying themselves as biracial or multiracial or, at the very least, explicitly viewing themselves as reflecting a diverse racial and ethnic identity. Barack Obama is the most visible person with a biracial background. President Obama has explicitly stated he sees himself as a Black man, although his mother was White. This led him to comment in his post-election press conference to a question about his promise to his children that they could have a dog in the White House. Obama said the dog would most likely be a "mutt," just like himself (Fram 2008).

The diversity of the United States today has made it more difficult for many people to place themselves on the racial and ethnic landscape. It reminds us that racial formation continues to take place. Obviously, the racial and ethnic landscape, as we have seen, is constructed not naturally but socially and, therefore, is subject to change and different interpretations. Although our focus is on the United States, almost every nation faces the same problems.

The United States tracks people by race and ethnicity for myriad reasons, ranging from attempting to improve the status of oppressed groups to diversifying classrooms. But how can we measure the growing number of people whose ancestry is mixed by anyone's definition? In "Research Focus" we consider how the U.S. Bureau of the Census dealt with this issue.

## RESEARCH FOCUS

## Multiracial Identity ✓

Approaching Census 2000, a movement was spawned by people who were frustrated by government questionnaires that forced them to indicate only one race. Take the case of Stacey Davis in New Orleans. The young woman's mother is Thai and her father is Creole, a blend of Black, French, and German. People seeing Stacey confuse her for a Latina, Filipina, or Hawaiian. Officially, she has been "White" all her life because she looked White. The census in 2000 for the first time gave people the option to check off one or more racial groups. "Biracial" or "multiracial" was not an option because pretests showed very few people would use it. This meant that the government recognized in Census 2000 different social constructions of racial identity—that is, a person could be Asian American and White.

Most people did select one racial category in Census 2000 and again in 2010. Overall, approximately 9 million people, or 2.9 percent of the total population, selected two or more racial groups in 2010. This was a smaller proportion than many observers had anticipated. In fact, not even the majority of mixed-race couples identified their children with more than one racial classification. As shown in Figure 1.3, White and African Americans were the most common multiple identity, with 1.8 million people or so selecting that response. As a group, American Indians were most likely to select a second category and Whites least likely. Race is socially defined.

*(continued)*

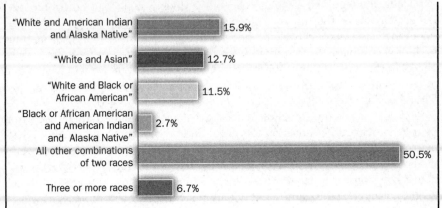

**Figure 1.3** Multiple-Race Choices in Census 2010
This figure shows the percentage distribution of the 9 million people who chose two or more races (out of the total population of 309 million).
*Source*: Humes et al. 2011:10.

Complicating the situation is that people are asked separately whether they are Hispanic or non-Hispanic. So a Hispanic person can be any race. In the 2010 census, 94 percent indicated they were one race, but 6 percent indicated two or more races; this proportion was twice as high than among non-Hispanics. Therefore, Latinos are more likely than non-Hispanics to indicate a multiracial ancestry.

The Census Bureau's decision does not necessarily resolve the frustration of hundreds of thousands of people such as Stacey Davis, who daily face people trying to place them in some racial or ethnic category that is convenient for them. However, it does underscore the complexity of social construction and trying to apply arbitrary definitions to the diversity of the human population. Symbolic of this social construction of race can be seen in President Barack Obama, born of a White woman and a Black immigrant from Kenya. Although he has always identified himself as a Black man, it is worthy to note he was born in Hawaii, a state in which 23.6 percent of people see themselves as more than one race, compared to the national average of 2.9 percent.

*Sources*: DaCosta 2007; Grieco and Cassidy 2001; Humes 2011 et al.:2–11; Jones and Smith 2001; Saulny 2011; Welch 2011; Williams 2005.

Besides the increasing respect for biracial identity and multiracial identity, group names undergo change as well. Within little more than a generation during the twentieth century, labels that were applied to subordinate groups changed from *Negroes* to *Blacks* to *African Americans*, from *American Indians* to *Native Americans* or *Native Peoples*. However, more Native Americans prefer the use of their tribal name, such as *Seminole*, instead of a collective label. The old 1950s statistical term of "people with a Spanish surname" has long been discarded, yet there is disagreement over a new term: *Latino* or *Hispanic*. Like Native Americans, Hispanic Americans avoid such global terms and prefer their native names, such as *Puerto Ricans* or *Cubans*. People of Mexican ancestry indicate preferences for a variety of names, such as *Mexican American*, *Chicano*, or simply *Mexican*.

In the United States and other multiracial, multiethnic societies, **panethnicity**, the development of solidarity between ethnic subgroups, has emerged. The coalition of tribal groups as Native Americans or American Indians to confront outside forces, notably the federal government, is one example of panethnicity. Hispanics or Latinos and Asian Americans are other examples of panethnicity. Although it is rarely recognized by dominant society, the very term *Black* or *African American* represents the descendants of many different ethnic or tribal groups, such as Akamba, Fulani, Hausa, Malinke, and Yoruba (Lopez and Espiritu 1990).

Is panethnicity a convenient label for "outsiders" or a term that reflects a mutual identity? Certainly, many people outside the group are unable or unwilling to recognize ethnic differences and prefer umbrella terms such as *Asian Americans*. For some small groups, combining with others is emerging as a useful way to make them heard, but there is always a fear that their own distinctive culture will become submerged. Although many Hispanics share the Spanish language and many are united by Roman Catholicism, only one in four native-born people of Mexican, Puerto Rican, or Cuban descent prefers a panethnic label to nationality or ethnic identity. Yet the growth of a variety of panethnic associations among many groups, including Hispanics, continued into the twenty-first century (de la Garza, DeSipio, Garcia, Garcia, and Falcon 1992; Espiritu 1992; Steinberg 2007).

Another challenge to identity is **marginality**: the status of being between two cultures, as in the case of a person whose mother is a Jew and father a Christian. Du Bois (1903) spoke eloquently of the "double consciousness" that Black Americans feel—caught between being a citizen of the United States but viewed as something quite apart from the dominant social forces of society. Incomplete assimilation by immigrants also results in marginality. Although a Filipino woman migrating to the United States may take on the characteristics of her new host society, she may not be fully accepted and may, therefore, feel neither Filipino nor American. Marginalized individuals often encounter social situations in which their identities are sources of tension, especially when the expression of multiple identities are not accepted, finds him- or herself being perceived differently in different environments, with varying expectations (Park 1928; Stonequist 1937; Townsend, Markos, and Bergsieker 2009).

As we seek to understand diversity in the United States, we must be mindful that ethnic and racial labels are just that: labels that have been socially constructed. Yet these social constructs can have a powerful impact, whether self-applied or applied by others.

## Sociology and the Study of Race and Ethnicity

Before proceeding further with our study of racial and ethnic groups, let us consider several sociological perspectives that provide insight into dominant–subordinate relationships. **Sociology** is the systematic study of social behavior and human groups, so it is aptly suited to enlarge our understanding of inter-group relations. There is a long, valuable history of the study of race relations in sociology. Admittedly, it has not always been progressive; indeed, at times it has reflected the prejudices of society. In some instances, scholars who are members of racial, ethnic, and religious minorities, as well as women, have not been permitted to make the kind of contributions they are capable of making to the field.

### Stratification by Class and Gender

All societies are characterized by members having unequal amounts of wealth, prestige, or power. Sociologists observe that entire groups may be assigned less or more of what a society values. The hierarchy that emerges is called **stratification**. Stratification is the structured ranking of entire groups of people that perpetuates unequal rewards and power in a society.

Much discussion of stratification identifies the **class**, or social ranking, of people who share similar wealth, according to sociologist Max Weber's classic definition. Mobility from one class to another is not easy. Movement into classes of greater wealth may be particularly difficult for subordinate-group members faced with lifelong prejudice and discrimination (Banton 2008; Gerth and Mills 1958).

Recall that the first property of subordinate-group standing is unequal treatment by the dominant group in the form of prejudice, discrimination, and segregation. Stratification is intertwined with the subordination of racial, ethnic, religious, and gender groups. Race has implications for the way people are treated; so does class. One also has to add the effects of race and class together. For example, being poor and Black is not the same as being either one by itself. A wealthy Mexican American is not the same as an affluent Anglo American or as Mexican Americans as a group.

Public discussion of issues such as housing or public assistance often is disguised as a discussion of class issues, when in fact the issues are based primarily on race. Similarly, some topics such as the poorest of the poor or the working poor are addressed in terms of race when the class component should be explicit. Nonetheless, the link between race and class in society is abundantly clear (Winant 2004).

Another stratification factor that we need to consider is gender. How different is the situation for women as contrasted with men? Returning again to the first property of minority groups—unequal treatment and less control—treatment of women is not equal to that received by men. Whether the issue is jobs or poverty, education or crime, the experience of women typically is more difficult. In addition, the situation faced by women in areas such as healthcare and welfare raises different concerns than it does for men. Just as we need to consider the role of social class to understand race and ethnicity better, we also need to consider the role of gender.

## Theoretical Perspectives

Sociologists view society in different ways. Some see the world basically as a stable and ongoing entity. The endurance of a Chinatown, the general sameness of male–female roles over time, and other aspects of intergroup relations impress them. Some sociologists see society as composed of many groups in conflict, competing for scarce resources. Within this conflict, some people or even entire groups may be labeled or stigmatized in a way that blocks their access to what a society values. We examine three theoretical perspectives that are widely used by sociologists today: the functionalist, conflict, and labeling perspectives.

**Functionalist Perspective**    In the view of a functionalist, a society is like a living organism in which each part contributes to the survival of the whole. The **functionalist perspective** emphasizes how the parts of society are structured to maintain its stability. According to this approach, if an aspect of social life does not contribute to a society's stability or survival, then it will not be passed on from one generation to the next.

It seems reasonable to assume that bigotry between races offers no such positive function, and so we ask, Why does it persist? Although agreeing that racial hostility is hardly to be admired, the functionalist would point out that it serves some positive functions from the perspective of the racists. We can identify five functions that racial beliefs have for the dominant group:

1. Racist ideologies provide a moral justification for maintaining a society that routinely deprives a group of its rights and privileges.
2. Racist beliefs discourage subordinate people from attempting to question their lowly status and performing "the dirty work"; to do so is to question the very foundation of the society.

3. Racial ideologies not only justify existing practices but also serve as a rallying point for social movements, as seen in the rise of the Nazi party or present-day Aryan movements.

4. Racist myths encourage support for the existing order. Some argue that if there were any major societal change, the subordinate group would suffer even greater poverty, and the dominant group would suffer lower living standards.

5. Racist beliefs relieve the dominant group of the responsibility to address the economic and educational problems faced by subordinate groups.

As a result, racial ideology grows when a value system (e.g., that underlying a colonial empire or slavery) is being threatened (Levin and Nolan 2011:115–145; Nash 1962).

There are also definite dysfunctions caused by prejudice and discrimination. **Dysfunctions** are elements of society that may disrupt a social system or decrease its stability. There are six ways in which racism is dysfunctional to a society, including to its dominant group:

1. A society that practices discrimination fails to use the resources of all individuals. Discrimination limits the search for talent and leadership to the dominant group.

2. Discrimination aggravates social problems such as poverty, delinquency, and crime and places the financial burden of alleviating these problems on the dominant group.

3. Society must invest a good deal of time and money to defend the barriers that prevent the full participation of all members.

4. Racial prejudice and discrimination undercut goodwill and friendly diplomatic relations between nations. They also negatively affect efforts to increase global trade.

5. Social change is inhibited because change may assist a subordinate group.

6. Discrimination promotes disrespect for law enforcement and for the peaceful settlement of disputes.

That racism has costs for the dominant group as well as for the subordinate group reminds us that intergroup conflict is exceedingly complex (Bowser and Hunt 1996; Feagin, Vera, and Batur 2000; Rose 1951).

**Conflict Perspective**   In contrast to the functionalists' emphasis on stability, conflict sociologists see the social world as being in continual struggle. The **conflict perspective** assumes that the social structure is best understood in terms of conflict or tension between competing groups. The result of this conflict is significant economic disparity and structural inequality in education,

From the conflict perspective, the emphasis should not be primarily on the attributes of the individual (i.e., "blaming the victim") but on structural factors such as the labor market, affordable housing, and availability of programs to assist people with addiction or mental health issues.

the labor market, housing, and healthcare delivery. Specifically, society is a struggle between the privileged (the dominant group) and the exploited (the subordinate group). Such conflicts need not be physically violent and may take the form of immigration restrictions, real estate practices, or disputes over cuts in the federal budget.

The conflict model often is selected today when one is examining race and ethnicity because it readily accounts for the presence of tension between competing groups. According to the conflict perspective, competition takes place between groups with unequal amounts of economic and political power. The minorities are exploited or, at best, ignored by the dominant group. The conflict perspective is viewed as more radical and activist than functionalism because conflict theorists emphasize social change and the redistribution of resources. Functionalists are not necessarily in favor of inequality; rather, their approach helps us understand why such systems persist.

Those who follow the conflict approach to race and ethnicity have remarked repeatedly that the subordinate group is criticized for its low status. That the dominant group is responsible for subordination is often ignored. William Ryan (1976) calls this an instance of **blaming the victim**: portraying the problems of racial and ethnic minorities as their fault rather than recognizing society's responsibility.

Conflict theorists consider the costs that come with residential segregation. Besides the more obvious cost of reducing housing options, racial and social class isolation reduces for people (including Whites) all available options in schools, retail shopping, and medical care. People can travel to access services and businesses, and it is more likely that racial and ethnic minorities will have to make that sometimes costly and time-consuming trip (Carr and Kutty 2008).

**Labeling Approach**    Related to the conflict perspective and its concern over blaming the victim is **labeling theory**, a concept introduced by sociologist Howard Becker to explain why certain people are viewed as deviant and others engaging in the same behavior are not. Students of crime and deviance have relied heavily on labeling theory. According to labeling theory, a youth who misbehaves may be considered and treated as a delinquent if he or she comes from the "wrong kind of family." Another youth from a middle-class family who commits the same sort of misbehavior might be given another chance before being punished.

The labeling perspective directs our attention to the role that negative stereotypes play in race and ethnicity. The image that prejudiced people maintain of a group toward which they hold ill feelings is called a **stereotype**. Stereotypes are unreliable generalizations about all members of a group that do not take individual differences into account. The warrior image of Native American (American Indian) people is perpetuated by the frequent use of tribal names or even names such as "Indians" and "Redskins" for sports teams. In Chapter 2, we review some of the research on the stereotyping of minorities. This labeling is not limited to racial and ethnic groups, however. For instance, age can be used to exclude a person from an activity in which he or she is qualified to engage. Groups are subjected to stereotypes and discrimination in such a way that their treatment resembles that of social minorities. Social prejudice exists toward ex-convicts, gamblers, alcoholics, lesbians, gays, prostitutes, people with AIDS, and people with disabilities, to name a few.

The labeling approach points out that stereotypes, when applied by people in power, can have very negative consequences for people or groups identified falsely. A crucial aspect of the relationship between dominant and subordinate groups is the prerogative of the dominant group to define society's values. U.S. sociologist William I. Thomas (1923), an early critic of racial and gender discrimination, saw that the "definition of the situation" could mold the personality of the individual. In other words, Thomas observed that people respond not only to the objective features of a situation (or person) but also to the meaning these features have for them. So, for example, a lone walker seeing a young Black man walking toward him may perceive the situation differently than if the oncoming person is an older woman. In this manner, we can create false images or stereotypes that become real in their social consequences.

In certain situations, we may respond to negative stereotypes and act on them, with the result that false definitions become accurate. This is known as a **self-fulfilling prophecy**. A person or group described as having particular characteristics begins to display the very traits attributed to him or her. Thus, a child who is praised for being a natural comic may focus on learning to become funny to gain approval and attention.

Self-fulfilling prophecies can be devastating for minority groups (Figure 1.4). Such groups often find that they are allowed to hold only low-paying jobs with little prestige or opportunity for advancement. The rationale of the dominant society is that these minority people lack the ability to perform in more important and lucrative positions. Training to become scientists, executives, or physicians is denied to many subordinate-group individuals (SGIs), who are then locked into society's inferior jobs. As a result, the false definition becomes real. The subordinate group has become inferior because it was defined at the start as inferior and was, therefore, prevented from achieving the levels attained by the majority.

Because of this vicious circle, a talented subordinate-group person may come to see the worlds of entertainment and professional sports as his or her only hope for achieving wealth and fame. Thus, it is no accident that successive waves of Irish, Jewish, Italian, African American, and Hispanic performers and athletes have made their mark on culture in the United States.

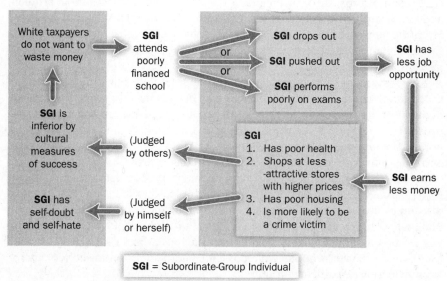

**Figure 1.4** Self-Fulfilling Prophecy
The self-validating effects of dominant-group definitions are shown here. The subordinate-group individual attends a poorly financed school and is left unequipped to perform jobs that offer high status and pay. He or she then gets a low-paying job and must settle for a standard of living far short of society's standards. Because the person shares these societal standards, he or she may begin to feel self-doubt and self-hatred.

Unfortunately, these very successes may convince the dominant group that its original stereotypes were valid—that these are the only areas of society in which subordinate-group members can excel. Furthermore, athletics and the arts are highly competitive areas. For every LeBron James and Jennifer Lopez who makes it, many, many more SGIs will end up disappointed.

## The Creation of Subordinate-Group Status

Three situations are likely to lead to the formation of a relationship between a subordinate group and the dominant group. A subordinate group emerges through migration, annexation, and colonialism.

### Migration

People who emigrate to a new country often find themselves a minority in that new country. Cultural or physical traits or religious affiliation may set the immigrant apart from the dominant group. Immigration from Europe, Asia, and Latin America has been a powerful force in shaping the fabric of life in the United States. **Migration** is the general term used to describe any transfer of population. **Emigration** (by emigrants) describes leaving a country to settle in another; **immigration** (by immigrants) denotes coming into the new country. From Vietnam's perspective, the "boat people" were emigrants from Vietnam to the United States, but in the United States they were counted among this nation's immigrants.

Although people may migrate because they want to, leaving the home country is not always voluntary. Conflict or war has displaced people throughout human history. In the twentieth century, we saw huge population movements caused by two world wars; revolutions in Spain, Hungary, and Cuba; the partition of British India; conflicts in Southeast Asia, Korea, and Central America; and the confrontation between Arabs and Israelis.

In all types of movement, even the movement of a U.S. family from Ohio to Florida, two sets of forces operate: push factors and pull factors. Push factors discourage a person from remaining where he or she lives. Religious persecution and economic factors such as dissatisfaction with employment opportunities are possible push factors. Pull factors, such as a better standard of living, friends and relatives who have already emigrated, and a promised job, attract an immigrant to a particular country.

Although generally we think of migration as a voluntary process, much of the population transfer that has occurred in the world has been involuntary. The forced movement of people into another society guarantees a subordinate role. Involuntary migration is no longer common; although enslavement has a long history, all industrialized societies today prohibit such practices. Of course, many contemporary societies, including the United States, bear the legacy of slavery.

Migration has taken on new significance in the twenty-first century partly because of **globalization**, or the worldwide integration of government policies, cultures, social movements, and financial markets through trade and the exchange of ideas. The increased movement of people and money across borders has made the distinction between temporary and permanent migration less meaningful. Although migration has always been fluid, people in today's global economy are connected across societies culturally and economically as never before. Even after they have relocated, people maintain global linkages to their former country and with a global economy (Richmond 2002).

## Annexation

Nations, particularly during wars or as a result of war, incorporate or attach land. This new land is contiguous to the nation, as in the German annexation of Austria and Czechoslovakia in 1938 and 1939 and in the U.S. Louisiana Purchase of 1803. The Treaty of Guadalupe Hidalgo that ended the Mexican–American War in 1848 gave the United States California, Utah, Nevada, most of New Mexico, and parts of Arizona, Wyoming, and Colorado. The indigenous peoples in some of this huge territory were dominant in their society one day, only to become minority-group members the next.

When annexation occurs, the dominant power generally suppresses the language and culture of the minority. Such was the practice of Russia with the Ukrainians and Poles and of Prussia with the Poles. Minorities try to maintain their cultural integrity despite annexation. Poles inhabited an area divided into territories ruled by three countries but maintained their own culture across political boundaries.

## Colonialism

Colonialism has been the most common way for one group of people to dominate another. **Colonialism** is the maintenance of political, social, economic, and cultural dominance over people by a foreign power for an extended period (Bell 1991). Colonialism is rule by outsiders but, unlike annexation, does not involve actual incorporation into the dominant people's nation. The long-standing control that was exercised by the British Empire over much of North America, parts of Africa, and India is an example of colonial domination (see Figure 1.5).

Societies gain power over a foreign land through military strength, sophisticated political organization, and investment capital. The extent of power may also vary according to the dominant group's scope of settlement in the colonial land. Relations between the colonial nation and the colonized people are similar to those between a dominant group and exploited subordinate groups. The colonial subjects generally are limited to menial jobs and the wages from their labor. The natural resources of their land benefit the members of the ruling class.

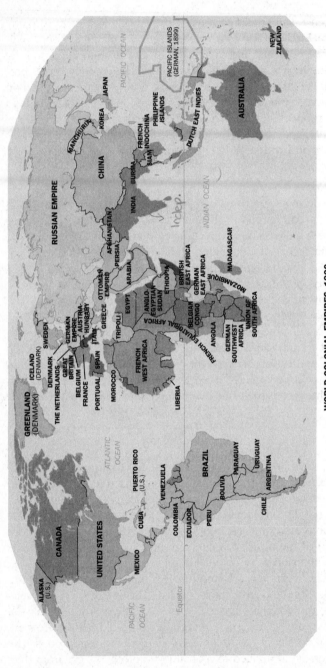

**WORLD COLONIAL EMPIRES, 1900**

- Belgium
- France
- German Empire
- Great Britain
- Italy
- The Netherlands
- Portugal
- Spain
- United States
- Other independent states

**Figure 1.5** World Colonial Empires (1900)

Events of the nineteenth century increased European dominance over the world. By 1900, most independent African nations had disappeared, and the major European powers and Japan took advantage of China's internal weakness to gain both trading ports and economic concessions.

*Source:* H. W. Brands et al. 2009:582.

26

By the 1980s, colonialism, in the sense of political rule, had become largely a phenomenon of the past, yet industrial countries of North America and Europe still dominated the world economically and politically. Drawing on the conflict perspective, sociologist Immanuel Wallerstein (1974) views the global economic system of today as much like the height of colonial days. Wallerstein has advanced the **world systems theory**, which views the global economic system as divided between nations that control wealth and those that provide natural resources and labor. The limited economic resources available in developing nations exacerbate many of the ethnic, racial, and religious conflicts noted at the beginning of this chapter. In addition, the presence of massive inequality between nations only serves to encourage immigration generally and, more specifically, the movement of many of the most skilled from developing nations to the industrial nations.

# The Consequences of Subordinate-Group Status

There are several consequences for a group with subordinate status. These differ in their degree of harshness, ranging from physical annihilation to absorption into the dominant group. In this section, we examine six consequences of subordinate-group status: extermination, expulsion, secession, segregation, fusion, and assimilation. The figure below illustrates how these consequences can be defined using the Spectrum of Intergroup Relations.

### Extermination

The most extreme way of dealing with a subordinate group is to eliminate it. Today, the term **genocide** is used to describe the deliberate, systematic killing of an entire people or nation. This term is often used in reference to the Holocaust, Nazi Germany's extermination of 12 million European Jews and other ethnic minorities during World War II. The term **ethnic cleansing** refers to the forced deportation of people, accompanied by systematic violence. The term was introduced in 1992 to the world's vocabulary as ethnic Serbs instituted a policy intended to "cleanse"—eliminate—Muslims from parts of Bosnia. More recently,

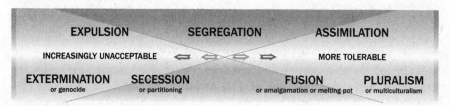

**Spectrum of Intergroup Relations**

a genocidal war between the Hutu and Tutsi people in Rwanda left 300,000 school-age children orphaned (Chirot and Edwards 2003; Naimark 2004).

However, genocide also appropriately describes White policies toward Native Americans in the nineteenth century. In 1800, the American Indian population in the United States was approximately 600,000; by 1850, it had been reduced to 250,000 through warfare with the U.S. Army, disease, and forced relocation to inhospitable environments.

In 2008, the Australian government officially apologized for past treatment of its native people, the Aboriginal population. Not only did this involve brutality and neglect, but also a quarter of their children, the so-called lost generation, were taken from their families until the policy was finally abandoned in 1969 (Johnston 2008).

## Expulsion

Dominant groups may choose to force a specific subordinate group to leave certain areas or even vacate a country. Expulsion, therefore, is another extreme consequence of minority-group status. European colonial powers in North America and eventually the U.S. government itself drove almost all Native Americans out of their tribal lands and into unfamiliar territory.

More recently, beginning in 2009, France expelled over 10,000 ethnic Roma (or Gypsies) back to their home countries of Bulgaria and Romania. This appeared to violate the European Union's (EU) ban against targeting ethnic groups as well as Europe's policy of "freedom of movement." In 2011, the EU withdrew its threat of legal action against France when the government said it would no longer expel Roma in particular but only those living in "illegal camps," which many observers felt was only a technical way for the country to get around long-standing human rights policies.

## Secession

A group ceases to be a subordinate group when it secedes to form a new nation or moves to an already established nation, where it becomes dominant. After Great Britain withdrew from Palestine, Jewish people achieved a dominant position in 1948, attracting Jews from throughout the world to the new state of Israel. Similarly, Pakistan was created in 1947 when India was partitioned. The predominantly Muslim areas in the north became Pakistan, making India predominantly Hindu. Throughout this century, minorities have repudiated dominant customs. In this spirit, the Estonian, Latvian, Lithuanian, and Armenian peoples, not content to be merely tolerated by the majority, all seceded to form independent states after the demise of the Soviet Union in 1991. In 1999, ethnic Albanians fought bitterly for their cultural and political recognition in the Kosovo region of Yugoslavia.

Some African Americans have called for secession. Suggestions dating back to the early 1700s supported the return of Blacks to Africa as a solution to racial problems. The settlement target of the American Colonization Society was Liberia, but proposals were also advanced to establish settlements in other areas. Territorial separatism and the emigrationist ideology were recurrent and interrelated themes among African Americans from the late nineteenth century well into the 1980s. The Black Muslims, or Nation of Islam, once expressed the desire for complete separation in their own state or territory within the modern borders of the United States. Although a secession of Blacks from the United States has not taken place, it has been proposed.

## Segregation

**Segregation** is the physical separation of two groups in residence, workplace, and social functions. Generally, the dominant group imposes segregation on a subordinate group. Segregation is rarely complete; however, intergroup contact inevitably occurs even in the most segregated societies.

Sociologists Douglas Massey and Nancy Denton wrote *American Apartheid* (1993), which described segregation in U.S. cities on the basis of 1990 data. The title of their book was meant to indicate that neighborhoods in the United States resembled the segregation of the rigid government-imposed racial segregation that prevailed for so long in the Republic of South Africa.

Analysis of census data shows continuing segregation despite racial and ethnic diversity in the nation. Scholars use a segregation index to measure separation. This index ranges from 0 (complete integration) to 100 (complete segregation), where the value indicates the percentage of the minority group that needs to move to be distributed exactly like Whites. So a segregation index of 60 for Blacks–Whites would mean that 60 percent of all African Americans would have to move to be residing just like Whites were.

Using census data for the five years ending in 2009 shows the following metropolitan areas with the highest segregation indexes:

Black–White
   Milwaukee (81), Detroit (80), New York (79), Chicago (78)

Hispanic–White
   Springfield, MA (64), New York (63), Los Angeles (63), Providence (62)

Asian–White
   Pittsburgh (60), Youngstown (59), Buffalo (59), Birmingham, AL (59)

Generally there has been a very modest decline in residential segregation for African Americans since 2000; it has generally increased for Asian Americans and Latinos. Regardless, the racial isolation remains dramatic. The typical White lives in a neighborhood 79 percent White; the typical African American resides in an area 46 percent Black. The corresponding figures for Latinos and Asian Americans are 45 percent and 20 percent, respectively. Even when we consider social class, the patterns of minority segregation persist (Bureau of the Census 2010b; Krysan, Farley, and Couper 2008; Frey 2011; Wilkes and Iceland 2004).

This focus on metropolitan areas should not cause us to ignore the continuing legally sanctioned segregation of Native Americans on reservations. Although the majority of our nation's first inhabitants live outside these tribal areas, the reservations play a prominent role in the identity of Native Americans. Although it is easier to maintain tribal identity on the reservation, economic and educational opportunities are more limited in these areas, which are segregated from the rest of society.

A particularly troubling pattern has been the emergence of **resegregation**, or the physical separation of racial and ethnic groups reappearing after a period of relative integration. Resegregation has occurred in both neighborhoods and schools after a transitional period of desegregation. For example, in 1954, only one in 100,000 Black students attended a majority White school in the South. Thanks to the civil rights movement and a series of civil rights measures, by 1968, this was up to 23 percent and then 47 percent by 1988. But after White households relocated or alternatives reemerged through private schools and homeschooling, the proportion had dropped back to 27 percent in 2004. The latest analysis shows continuing, if not increasing, racial isolation (Orfield 2007; Orfield and Lee 2005; Rich 2008).

Given segregation patterns, many Whites in the United States have limited contact with people of other racial and ethnic backgrounds. In one study of 100 affluent powerful White men that looked at their experiences past and present, it was clear they had lived in a "White bubble"—neighborhoods, schools, elite colleges, and workplaces were overwhelmingly White. The continuing pattern of segregation in the United States means our diverse population grows up in very different nations (Bonilla-Silva and Embrick 2007; Feagin and O'Brien 2003).

While still not typical, more couples are crossing racial and ethnic boundaries in the United States today than any generation before. Clearly this will increase the potential for their children to identify as biracial or multiracial rather than in a single category.

## Fusion

**Fusion** occurs when a minority and a majority group combine to form a new group. This combining can be expressed as $A + B + C \longrightarrow D$, where A, B, and C represent the groups present in a society and D signifies the result, an ethno-cultural-racial group sharing some of the characteristics of each initial group. Mexican people are an example of fusion, originating as they do out of the mixing of Spanish and indigenous Indian cultures. Theoretically, fusion does not entail intermarriage, but it is very similar to

**amalgamation** or the process by which a dominant group and a subordinate group combine through intermarriage into a new people. In everyday speech, the words *fusion* and *amalgamation* are rarely used, but the concept is expressed in the notion of a human **melting pot** in which diverse racial or ethnic groups form a new creation, a new cultural entity (Newman 1973).

The analogy of the cauldron, the "melting pot," was first used to describe the United States by the French observer Crèvecoeur in 1782. The phrase dates back to the Middle Ages, when alchemists attempted to change less-valuable metals into gold and silver. Similarly, the idea of the human melting pot implied that the new group would represent only the best qualities and attributes of the different cultures contributing to it. The belief in the United States as a melting pot became widespread in the early twentieth century. This belief suggested that the United States had an almost divine mission to destroy artificial divisions and create a single kind of human. However, the dominant group had indicated its unwillingness to welcome such groups as Native Americans, Blacks, Hispanics, Jews, Asians, and Irish Roman Catholics into the melting pot. It is a mistake to think of the United States as an ethnic mixing bowl. Although there are superficial signs of fusion, as in a cuisine that includes sauerkraut and spaghetti, most contributions of subordinate groups are ignored (Gleason 1980).

Marriage patterns indicate the resistance to fusion. People are unwilling, in varying degrees, to marry outside their own ethnic, religious, and racial groups. Until relatively recently interracial marriage was outlawed in much of the United States. As noted earlier, at the time that President Barack Obama's parents married in Hawaii, their union would have been illegal and unable to occur in 22 other states. Surveys show that 20–50 percent of various White ethnic groups report single ancestry. When White ethnics do cross boundaries, they tend to marry within their religion and social class. For example, Italians are more likely to marry Irish, who are also Catholic, than they are to marry Protestant Swedes.

Although it may seem that interracial matches are everywhere, there is only modest evidence of a fusion of races in the United States. Racial intermarriage has been increasing. In 1980, there were 651,000 interracial couples, but by 2009, there were 2.4 million. That is still less than 4 percent of married couples.

Among couples in which at least one member is Hispanic, marriages with a non-Hispanic partner account for 28 percent. Taken together, all interracial and Hispanic–non-Hispanic couples account for 8 percent of married couples today. But this includes decades of marriages. Among new ones, about 15 percent of marriages are between people of different races or between Hispanics and non-Hispanics (Bureau of the Census 2010a:Table 60; Taylor et al. 2010).

## Assimilation

**Assimilation** is the process by which a subordinate individual or group takes on the characteristics of the dominant group and is eventually accepted as part of that group. Assimilation is a majority ideology in which A + B + C ⟶ A. The majority (A) dominates in such a way that the minorities (B and C) become

One aspect of assimilation is when immigrants seek to learn the language of the host society, as shown in this adult English as a Second Language class in Minneapolis, Minnesota.

indistinguishable from the dominant group. Assimilation dictates conformity to the dominant group, regardless of how many racial, ethnic, or religious groups are involved (Newman 1973:53).

To be complete, assimilation must entail an active effort by the minority-group individual to shed all distinguishing actions and beliefs and the unqualified acceptance of that individual by the dominant society. In the United States, dominant White society encourages assimilation. The assimilation perspective tends to devalue alien culture and to treasure the dominant. For example, assimilation assumes that whatever is admirable among Blacks was adapted from Whites and that whatever is bad is inherently Black. The assimilation solution to Black–White conflict has been typically defined as the development of a consensus around White American values.

Assimilation is very difficult. The person must forsake his or her cultural tradition to become part of a different, often antagonistic culture. However, assimilation should not be viewed as if immigrants are extraterrestrials. Cross-border movement is often preceded by adjustments and awareness of the culture that awaits the immigrant (Skrentny 2008).

Assimilation does not occur at the same pace for all groups or for all individuals in the same group. Typically, assimilation is not a process completed by the first generation. Assimilation tends to take longer under the following conditions:

- The differences between the minority and the majority are large.
- The majority is not receptive, or the minority retains its own culture.

- The minority group arrives over a short period of time.
- The minority-group residents are concentrated rather than dispersed.
- The arrival is recent, and the homeland is accessible.

Assimilation is not a smooth process (Warner and Srole 1945).

Assimilation is viewed by many as unfair or even dictatorial. However, members of the dominant group see it as reasonable that people shed their distinctive cultural traditions. In public discussions today, assimilation is the ideology of the dominant group in forcing people how to act. Consequently, the social institutions in the United States—the educational system, economy, government, religion, and medicine—all push toward assimilation, with occasional references to the pluralist approach.

## The Pluralist Perspective

Thus far, we have concentrated on how subordinate groups cease to exist (removal) or take on the characteristics of the dominant group (assimilation). The alternative to these relationships between the majority and the minority is pluralism. **Pluralism** implies that various groups in a society have mutual respect for one another's culture, a respect that allows minorities to express their own culture without suffering prejudice or discrimination. Whereas the assimilationist or integrationist seeks the elimination of ethnic boundaries, the pluralist believes in maintaining many of them.

There are limits to cultural freedom. A Romanian immigrant to the United States cannot expect to avoid learning English and still move up the occupational ladder. To survive, a society must have a consensus among its members on basic ideals, values, and beliefs. Nevertheless, there is still plenty of room for variety. Earlier, fusion was described as A + B + C → D and assimilation as A + B + C → A. Using this same scheme, we can think of pluralism as A + B + C → A + B + C, with groups coexisting in one society (Manning 1995; Newman 1973; Simpson 1995).

In the United States, cultural pluralism is more an ideal than a reality. Although there are vestiges of cultural pluralism—in the various ethnic neighborhoods in major cities, for instance—the rule has been for subordinate groups to assimilate. Yet as the minority becomes the numerical majority, the ability to live out one's identity becomes a bit easier. African Americans, Hispanics, American Indians, and Asian Americans already outnumber Whites in most of the largest cities. The trend is toward even greater diversity. Nonetheless, the cost of cultural integrity throughout the nation's history has been high. The various Native American tribes have succeeded to a large extent in maintaining their heritage, but the price has been bare subsistence on federal reservations.

In the United States, there is a reemergence of ethnic identification by groups that had previously expressed little interest in their heritage. Groups that make up the dominant majority are also reasserting their ethnic heritages. Various nationality groups are rekindling interest in almost forgotten languages, customs, festivals, and traditions. In some instances, this expression of the past has taken the form of a protest against exclusion from the dominant society. For example, Chinese youths chastise their elders for forgetting the old ways and accepting White American influence and control.

The most visible expression of pluralism is language use. As of 2008, nearly one in every five people (19.1 percent) over age five speaks a language other than English at home. Later, in Chapters 4 and 5, we consider how language use figures into issues relating to immigration and education (American Community Survey 2009:Table S1601).

Facilitating a diverse and changing society emerges in just about every aspect of society. Yet another nod to pluralism, although not nearly so obvious as language to the general population, has been the changes within the funeral industry. Where Christian and Jewish funeral practices have dominated, funeral homes are now retraining to accommodate a variety of practices. Latinos often expect 24-hour viewing of their deceased, whereas Muslims may wish to participate in washing the deceased before burial in a grave pointing toward Mecca. Hindu and Buddhist requests to participate in cremation are now being respected (Brulliard 2006).

## Resistance and Change

By virtue of wielding power and influence, the dominant group may define the terms by which all members of society operate. This is particularly evident in a slave society, but even in contemporary industrialized nations, the dominant group has a disproportionate role in shaping immigration policy, the curriculum of the schools, and the content of the media.

Subordinate groups do not merely accept the definitions and ideology proposed by the dominant group. A continuing theme in dominant–subordinate relations is the minority group's challenge to its subordination. Resistance by subordinate groups is well documented as they seek to promote change that will bring them more rights and privileges, if not true equality. Often traditional notions of racial formation are overcome not only through panethnicity but also because Black people, along with Latinos and sympathetic Whites, join in the resistance (Moulder 1996; Winant 2004).

Resistance can be seen in efforts by racial and ethnic groups to maintain their identity through newspapers and organizations and in today's technological age through cable television stations, blogs, and Internet sites. Resistance manifests itself in social movements such as the civil rights movement, the feminist movement, and gay rights efforts. The passage of such legislation as the Age Discrimination Act or the Americans with Disabilities Act marks the success of oppressed groups in lobbying on their own behalf.

Through recent efforts of collective action, African American farmers successfully received Congressional approval in 2010 for compensation denied them in the latter 1900s by the Department of Agriculture.

Resistance efforts may begin through small actions. For example, residents of a reservation question why a toxic waste dump is to be located on their land. Although it may bring in money, they question the wisdom of such a move. Their concerns lead to further investigations of the extent to which American Indian lands are used disproportionately to house dangerous materials. This action in turn leads to a broader investigation of the way in which minority-group people often find themselves "hosting" dumps and incinerators. As we discuss later, these local efforts eventually led the Environmental Protection Agency to monitor the disproportionate placement of toxic facilities in or near racial and ethnic minority communities. There is little reason to expect that such reforms would have occurred if we had relied on traditional decision-making processes alone.

Change has occurred. At the beginning of the twentieth century, lynching was practiced in many parts of the country. At the beginning of the twenty-first century, laws punishing hate crimes were increasingly common and embraced a variety of stigmatized groups. Although this social progress should not be ignored, the nation needs to focus concern ahead on the significant social inequalities that remain. It is too easy to look at the accomplishments of Barack Obama and Hillary Clinton and conclude "mission accomplished" in terms of racial and gender injustices (Best 2001).

An even more basic form of resistance is to question societal values. In this book, we avoid using the term *American* to describe people of the United States because geographically Brazilians, Canadians, and El Salvadorans are Americans as well. It is very easy to overlook how our understanding of today has been shaped by the way institutions and even the very telling of history have been presented by members of the dominant group. African American studies scholar Molefi Kete Asante (2007, 2008) has called for an **Afrocentric perspective** that emphasizes the customs of African cultures and how they have pervaded the history, culture, and behavior of Blacks in the United States and around the world. Afrocentrism counters Eurocentrism and works toward a multiculturalist or pluralist orientation in which no viewpoint is suppressed. The Afrocentric approach could become part of our school curriculum, which has not adequately acknowledged the importance of this heritage.

The Afrocentric perspective has attracted much attention in education. Opponents view it as a separatist view of history and culture that distorts both past and present. Its supporters counter that African peoples everywhere can come to full self-determination only when they are able to overthrow White or Eurocentric intellectual interpretations (Conyers 2004).

The remarkable efforts by members of racial and ethnic minorities working with supportive White Americans beginning in the 1950s through the early 1970s successfully targeted overt symbols or racist and sexist actions. Today's targets are more intractable and tend to emerge from institutional discrimination. Sociologist Douglas Massey (2011) argued that a central goal must be to reform criminal justice by demanding repeal of the three-strikes law, mandatory minimum sentencing, and harsher penalties for crack than for powdered cocaine. Such targets are quite different from laws that prevented Blacks and women from serving on juries.

In considering the inequalities present today, as we do in the chapters that follow, it is easy to forget how much change has taken place. Much of the resistance to prejudice and discrimination in the past, either to slavery or to women's prohibition from voting, took the active support of members of the dominant group. The indignities still experienced by subordinate groups continue to be resisted as subordinate groups and their allies among the dominant group seek further change.

## Matrix of Domination: Minority Women

Many women experience differential treatment not only because of their gender but also because of race and ethnicity. These citizens face a subordinate status twice defined. A disproportionate share of this low-status group also is poor. African American feminist Patricia Hill Collins (2000) has termed this the **matrix of domination** (Figure 1.6). Whites dominate non-Whites, men dominate women, and the affluent dominate the poor.

Gender, race, and social class are not the only systems of oppression, but they do profoundly affect women and people of color in the United States. Other forms of categorization and stigmatization can also be included in this matrix, such as sexual orientation, religion, disability status, and age. If we turn to a global stage, we can add citizenship status and being perceived as a "colonial subject" even after colonialism has ended (Winant 2006).

Feminists have addressed themselves to the needs of minority women, but the oppression of these women because of their sex is overshadowed by the subordinate status that both White men and White women impose on them because of their race or ethnicity. The question for the Latina (Hispanic woman), African American woman, Asian American woman, Native American woman, and so on appears to be whether she should unify with her brothers against racism or challenge them for their sexism. The answer is that society cannot afford to let up on the effort to eradicate sexism and racism as well as

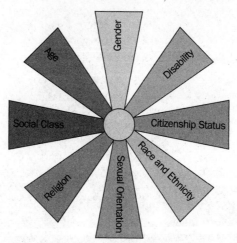

**Figure 1.6**  The Matrix of Domination
The matrix of domination illustrates how several
social factors—including gender, social class,
and race and ethnicity—intersect to create a
cumulative impact on a person's social standing.

other forces that stigmatize and oppress (Beisel and Kay 2004; Coontz 2010;
Epstein 1999; MacLean and Williams 2008).

The discussion of gender roles among African Americans has always provoked controversy. Advocates of Black nationalism contend that feminism only
distracts women from full participation in the African American struggle. The
existence of feminist groups among Blacks, in their view, simply divides the
Black community and thereby serves the dominant White society. By contrast,
Black feminists such as bell hooks (1984) argue that little is to be gained by
accepting the gender-role divisions of the dominant society that place women
in a separate, subservient position. African American journalist Patricia Raybon
(1989) has noted that the media commonly portray Black women in a negative light: as illiterates, as welfare mothers, as prostitutes, and so forth. Black
feminists emphasize that it is not solely Whites and White-dominated media
that focus on these negative images; Black men (most recently, Black male
rap artists) have also been criticized for the way they portray African American
women (Threadcraft 2008).

Native Americans stand out as a historical exception to the North American patriarchal tradition. At the time of the arrival of the European settlers,
gender roles varied greatly from tribe to tribe. Southern tribes, for reasons
unclear to today's scholars, usually were matriarchal and traced descent
through the mother. European missionaries sought to make the native peoples
more like the Europeans, and this aim included transforming women's role.
Some Native American women, like members of other groups, have resisted
gender stereotypes (Marubbio 2006).

Few women head a Fortune 500 corporation and almost no minority women reach those rarified heights. Xerox Corporation's Ursula Burns is the only African American woman to head such a corporation. Educated as a mechanical engineer, she began at Xerox as a summer intern in 1980 and rose to chief executive officer in 2009.

The plight of Latinas usually is considered part of either the Hispanic or feminist movements, and the distinctive experience of Latinas is ignored. In the past, they have been excluded from decision making in the two social institutions that most affect their daily lives: the family and the Church. The Hispanic family, especially in the lower class, feels the pervasive tradition of male domination. The Catholic Church relegates women to supportive roles while reserving for men the leadership positions (Browne 2001; De Anda 2004).

By considering the matrix of domination, we recognize how much of our discussion has focused on race and ethnicity coupled with data on poverty, low incomes, and meager wealth. Drawing upon this intersection of identities, we consider what Spectrum of Intergroup Relations would look for women and men. We recognize that issues of gender domination must be included to fully understand what women of color experience.

## Conclusion

One hundred years ago, sociologist and activist W. E. B. Du Bois took another famed Black activist, Booker T. Washington, to task for saying that the races could best work together apart, like fingers on a hand. Du Bois felt that Black people had to be a part of all social institutions and not create their own. Now with an African American elected to the presidency, Whites, African Americans, and other groups continue to debate what form society should take. Should we seek to bring everyone together into an integrated whole? Or do we strive to maintain as much of our group identities as possible while working cooperatively as necessary?

In this chapter, we have attempted to organize our approach to subordinate–dominant relations in the United States. We observed that subordinate groups do not necessarily contain fewer members than the dominant group. Subordinate groups are classified into racial, ethnic, religious, and gender groups. Racial classification has been of interest, but scientific findings do not explain contemporary race relations. Biological differences of race are not supported by scientific data. Yet as the continuing debate over standardized tests demonstrates, attempts to establish a biological meaning of race have not been swept entirely into the dustbin of history. However, the social meaning given to physical differences is very significant. People have defined racial differences in such a way as to encourage or discourage the progress of certain groups.

Subordinate-group members' reactions include the seeking of an alternative avenue to acceptance and success: "Why should we forsake what we are, to be accepted by them?" In response to this question, there continues to be strong ethnicity identification. Pluralism describes a society in which several different groups coexist, with no dominant or subordinate groups. People individually chose what cultural patterns to keep and which to let go.

Subordinate groups have not and do not always accept their second-class status passively. They may protest, organize, revolt, and resist society as defined by the dominant group. Patterns of race and ethnic relations are changing, not stagnant. Indicative of the changing landscape, biracial and multiracial children present us with new definitions of identity emerging through a process of racial formation, reminding us that race is socially constructed.

The two significant forces that are absent in a truly pluralistic society are prejudice and discrimination. In an assimilation society, prejudice disparages outgroup differences, and discrimination financially rewards those who shed their past. In the next two chapters, we explore the nature of prejudice and discrimination in the United States.

## Summary

1. When sociologists define a minority group, they are concerned primarily with the economic and political power, or powerlessness, of the group.

2. A racial group is set apart from others primarily by physical characteristics; an ethnic group is set apart primarily by national origin or cultural patterns.

3. People cannot be sorted into distinct racial groups, so race is best viewed as a social construct subject to different interpretations over time.

4. A small but still significant number of people in the United States—more than 7 million—readily see themselves as having a biracial or multiracial identity.

5. Functionalists point out that discrimination is both functional and dysfunctional for a society. Conflict theorists see racial subordination through the presence of tension between competing groups. Labeling theory directs our attention to the role that negative stereotypes play in race and ethnicity.

6. Subordinate-group status has emerged through migration, annexation, and colonialism.

The social consequences of subordinate-group status include extermination, expulsion, secession, segregation, fusion, assimilation, and pluralism.

7. Despite highly public women politicians, the vast majority of elected officials in the United States, especially at the national level, are men. Gender is only one basis for the unequal treatment that women experience; this leads to a formulation called the *matrix of domination* that considers a variety of social dimensions.

8. Racial, ethnic, and other minorities maintain a long history of resisting efforts to restrict their rights.

## Key Terms

| | | |
|---|---|---|
| Afrocentric perspective 35 | functionalist perspective 19 | panethnicity 17 |
| amalgamation 31 | fusion 30 | pluralism 33 |
| assimilation 31 | genocide 27 | racial formation 14 |
| biological race 11 | globalization 25 | racial group 7 |
| blaming the victim 21 | immigration 24 | racism 14 |
| class 18 | intelligence quotient (IQ) 12 | resegregation 30 |
| colonialism 25 | labeling theory 22 | segregation 29 |
| conflict perspective 20 | marginality 17 | self-fulfilling prophecy 23 |
| dysfunction 20 | matrix of domination 36 | sociology 18 |
| emigration 24 | melting pot 31 | stereotypes 22 |
| ethnic cleansing 27 | migration 24 | stratification 18 |
| ethnic group 8 | minority group 5 | world systems theory 27 |

## Review Questions

1. In what different ways is race viewed?
2. How do the concepts of "biracial" and "multiracial" relate to W. E. B. Du Bois's notion of a "color line"?
3. How do the conflict, functionalist, and labeling approach apply to the social construction or race?

## Critical Thinking

1. How diverse is your city? Can you see evidence that some group is being subordinated? What social construction of categories do you see that may be different in your community as compared to elsewhere?
2. Select a racial or ethnic group and apply the Spectrum of Intergroup Relations on page 27. Can you provide an example today or in the past where each relationship occurs?
3. Identify some protest and resistance efforts by subordinated groups in your area. Have they been successful? Why are some people who say they favor equality uncomfortable with such efforts? How can people unconnected with such efforts either help or hinder such protests?

# 2 Prejudice

## CHAPTER OUTLINE

⟨ HIGHLIGHTS ⟩

P rejudice is a negative attitude that rejects an entire group; discrimination is behavior that deprives a group of certain rights or opportunities. Prejudice does not necessarily coincide with discrimination, as is made apparent by a typology developed by sociologist Robert Merton. Several theories have been advanced to explain prejudice: scapegoating, authoritarian personality, exploitation, and the normative approach. Although widespread expression of prejudice has declined, color-blind racism allows the status quo of racial and ethnic inequality to persist.

Prejudice is not limited to the dominant group; members of subordinate groups often dislike one another. The mass media seem to be of limited value in reducing prejudice and may even intensify ill feeling. Equal-status contact and the shared-coping approach may reduce hostility between groups, but data show few friendships cross racial lines. In response to increasing diversity in the workplace, corporations and organizations have mounted diversity-training programs to increase organizational effectiveness and combat prejudice. There are also ten identifiable steps that we as individuals can take to stop prejudice and hatred.

Catherine Donnelly's mother, a single White science teacher from New Orleans, was understandably proud when she dropped her daughter off to start college at Princeton University. Having dinner with Catherine that first night, the mother was shocked to learn of her daughter's first visitor— Craig Robinson, a junior and a Princeton basketball player, had dropped by looking for his sister whom Catherine had yet to see. Craig was Black. The next day, in order to get Catherine a new room assignment, her mother headed to the housing office and telephoned influential Princeton alums in New Orleans. University officials said no room change was possible until the second semester. Catherine got along with her roommate Michelle for a term but barely acknowledged her on campus. Michelle majored in sociology and wrote her senior thesis, "Princeton-Educated Blacks and the Black Community." While not specifically mentioning the slighting by her first-semester roommate, Michelle did write how experiences at Princeton made her far more aware of her "Blackness." Today, Catherine now admits that she gave up a chance of a lifetime by not taking the opportunity to get to know Michelle Robinson, now known as Michelle Obama, wife of the President of the United States (Felsenthal 2009; Robinson 1985).

Many heralded the cable channel TLC's 2011 launch of the *All-American Muslim* series to counter negative images of Muslims by its depiction of the ordinary lives of five families in Dearborn, Michigan. The early episodes showed a Muslim deputy sheriff and the challenges faced by high school football players trying to fast during the month of Ramadan. Conservative religious groups countered that the show failed to show a balanced perspective because of the lack of depiction of terrorists among the people portrayed. So successful were the groups in their opposition that they succeeded in getting one of the major sponsors, Lowe's, to pull all its advertising. It is difficult to determine if ill-will has been strengthened or lessened by this experience.

Prejudice is so prevalent that it is tempting to consider it inevitable or, even more broadly, just part of human nature. Such a view ignores its variability from individual to individual and from society to society. People must learn prejudice as children before they exhibit it as adults. Therefore, prejudice is a social phenomenon, an acquired characteristic. A truly pluralistic society would lack unfavorable distinctions made through prejudicial attitudes among racial and ethnic groups.

What makes the issue of holding ill feelings based on a person's race or ethnicity is that the nation is so increasingly diverse. In Figure 2.1 we look at the increase in minority presence in the first decade of the twenty-first century. Many counties far removed from the urban centers or historic areas with Black and Latino populations saw increases during the period from 2000 to 2010. The likelihood that prejudices will either be expressed or dealt with or hidden is beginning a truly nationwide phenomenon.

Ill feeling between groups may result from **ethnocentrism**, or the tendency to assume that one's culture and way of life are superior to all others'. The ethnocentric person judges other groups and other cultures by the standards of his or her own group. This attitude leads people quite easily to view other cultures as inferior. We see a woman with a veil and may regard it as strange and backward yet find it baffling when other societies see U.S. women in short skirts and view the dress as inappropriate. Ethnocentrism and other expressions of prejudice are voiced very often, but unfortunately they also become the motivation for criminal acts.

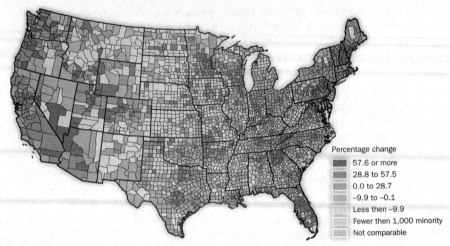

Percentage change

- 57.6 or more
- 28.8 to 57.5
- 0.0 to 28.7
- –9.9 to –0.1
- Less then –9.9
- Fewer then 1,000 minority
- Not comparable

**Figure 2.1**  Change in Minority Population by County, 2000–2010
Growth in the minority population has occurred in the last decade across the country, including in many areas that previously had relatively few members of racial and ethnic minorities.
*Source*: Humes et al. 2011:21.

## Prejudice and Discrimination

Prejudice and discrimination are related concepts but are not the same. **Prejudice** is a negative attitude toward an entire category of people. The two important components in this definition are *attitude* and *entire category*. Prejudice involves attitudes, thoughts, and beliefs, not actions. Prejudice often is expressed through the use of **ethnophaulisms**, or ethnic slurs, which include derisive nicknames such as *honky*, *gook*, and *wetback*. Ethnophaulisms also include speaking to or about members of a particular group in a condescending way, such as saying "José does well in school for a Mexican American" or referring to a middle-aged woman as "one of the girls."

A prejudiced belief leads to categorical rejection. Prejudice is not disliking someone you meet because you find his or her behavior objectionable; it is disliking an entire racial or ethnic group, even if you have had little or no contact with that group. A college student who requests a room change after three weeks of enduring his roommate's sleeping all day, playing loud music all night, and piling garbage on his desk is not prejudiced. However, he is displaying prejudice if he requests a change upon arriving at school and learning that his new roommate is of a different nationality.

Prejudice is a belief or attitude; discrimination is action. **Discrimination** is the denial of opportunities and equal rights to individuals and groups because of prejudice or for other arbitrary reasons. Unlike prejudice, discrimination involves *behavior* that excludes members of a group from certain rights, opportunities, or privileges. Like prejudice, it is categorical, perhaps making for a few rare exceptions. If an employer refuses to hire as a computer analyst an Italian American who is illiterate, it is not discrimination. If an employer refuses to hire any Italian American because he or she thinks they are incompetent and does not make the effort to see whether an applicant is qualified, it is discrimination.

## Merton's Typology

Prejudice does not necessarily coincide with discriminatory behavior. In exploring the relationship between negative attitudes and negative behavior, sociologist Robert Merton (1949, 1976) identified four major categories (Figure 2.2).

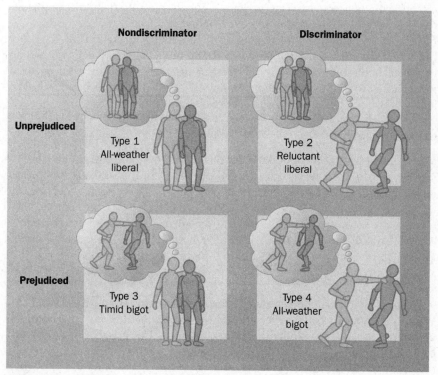

**Figure 2.2**   Prejudice and Discrimination
As sociologist Robert Merton's formulation shows, prejudice and discrimination are related to each other but are not the same.

The label added to each of Merton's categories may more readily identify the type of person being described. These are:

1. The unprejudiced nondiscriminator—or all-weather liberal
2. The unprejudiced discriminator—or reluctant liberal
3. The prejudiced nondiscriminator—or timid bigot
4. The prejudiced discriminator—or all-weather bigot

As the term is used in types 1 and 2, liberals are committed to equality among people. The all-weather liberal believes in equality and practices it. Merton was quick to observe that all-weather liberals may be far removed from any real competition with subordinate groups such as African Americans or women. Furthermore, such people may be content with their own behavior and may do little to change themselves. The reluctant liberal is not that committed to equality between groups. Social pressure may cause such a person to discriminate. Fear of losing employees may lead a manager to avoid promoting women to supervisory capacities. Equal-opportunity legislation may be the best way to influence the reluctant liberal.

Types 3 and 4 do not believe in equal treatment for racial and ethnic groups, but they vary in their willingness to act. The timid bigot, type 3, will not discriminate if discrimination costs money or reduces profits or if he or she is pressured not to by peers or the government. The all-weather bigot unhesitatingly acts on the prejudiced beliefs he or she holds.

## LaPiere's Study

Merton's typology points out that attitudes should not be confused with behavior. People do not always act as they believe. More than a half-century ago, Richard LaPiere (1934, 1969) exposed the relationship between racial attitudes and social conduct. From 1930 to 1932, LaPiere traveled throughout the United States with a Chinese couple. Despite an alleged climate of intolerance of Asians, LaPiere observed that the couple was treated courteously at hotels, motels, and restaurants. He was puzzled by the good reception they received; all the conventional attitude surveys showed extreme prejudice by Whites toward the Chinese.

Was it possible that LaPiere had been fortunate during his travels and consistently stopped at places operated by the tolerant members of the dominant group? To test this possibility, he sent questionnaires asking the very establishments at which they had been served whether the owner would "accept members of the Chinese race as guests in your establishment." More than 90 percent responded no, even though LaPiere's Chinese couple had been treated politely at all of these establishments. How can this inconsistency be explained? People who returned questionnaires reflecting prejudice were unwilling to act based on those asserted beliefs; they were timid bigots.

The LaPiere study is not without flaws. First, he had no way of knowing whether the respondent to the questionnaire was the same person who had served him and the Chinese couple. Second, he accompanied the couple, but the questionnaire suggested that the arrival would be unescorted (and, in the minds of some, uncontrolled) and perhaps would consist of many Chinese people. Third, personnel may have changed between the time of the visit and the mailing of the questionnaire (Deutscher, Pestello, and Pestello 1993).

The LaPiere technique has been replicated with similar results. This technique raises the question of whether attitudes are important if they are not completely reflected in behavior. But if attitudes are not important in small matters, then they are important in other ways: Lawmakers legislate and courts may reach decisions based on what the public thinks.

This is not just a hypothetical possibility. Legislators in the United States often are persuaded to vote in a certain way by what they perceive to be changed attitudes toward immigration, affirmative action, and prayer in public schools. Sociologists have enumerated some of prejudice's functions. For the majority group, it serves to maintain privileged occupations and more power for its members.

What might a contemporary version of the Lapiere study look like? One could imagine that instead of using a Chinese couple, one might look at the treatment of a Muslim man accompanied by his veiled wife. While such a study has yet to be conducted, we can already turn to a lot of existing information about attitudes toward Muslim Americans as indicated in the research focus box Islamaphobia.

## RESEARCH FOCUS

### Islamophobia

In what ways do prejudice and discrimination manifest themselves with respect to Muslim and Arab Americans? In form and magnitude, they are much like what is shown toward other subordinate groups. Regrettably, the situation appears to have gone beyond orientalism, in which one sees people as "the other" and somewhat frightening. **Islamophobia** refers to a range of negative feelings toward Muslims and their religion that ranges from generalized intolerance to hatred. What makes current expressions of hostility strikingly different is that the events of the twenty-first century have been given a decidedly patriotic fervor; that is, for many who overtly express their anti-Muslim or anti-Arab feeling, they also believe themselves to be pro-American.

*(continued)*

There are very few normalizing or positive images. Rarely are Arab and Muslim Americans exhibiting "normal" behavior such as shopping, attending a sporting event, or even just eating without a subtext of terrorism lurking literally in the shadows. Furthermore, the interests of the United States are depicted either as leaning against the Arabs and Muslims, as in the Israeli–Palestinian violence, or presented as hopelessly dependent on them, in the case of our reliance on foreign oil production.

Evidence of hate crimes and harassment toward Arab and Muslim Americans rose sharply after 9/11, compared to studies done in the mid-1990s. It continued to remain high through 2008, according to more recent studies. Incidents have ranged from beatings to vandalism of mosques to organized resistance to opening of Arabic schools. Evidence of a backlash also includes Muslim Americans getting unwarranted eviction notices. Surveys show a complex view in the United States of Arab and Muslim Americans. Surveys since 2001 show one in four people believe a number of anti-Muslim stereotypes such as the idea that Islam teaches violence and hatred. Curiously, while harboring these views, people do not recognize that Arab Americans are poorly treated. Still by 2010, only 30 percent of people had a favorable image of Islam compared to 38 percent who thought of it unfavorably, while 55 percent overall said they knew nothing or not very much about the Muslim religion.

A major flashpoint has been the proposed "Ground Zero Mosque." A mosque operating since 1985, twelve blocks from the World Trade Center (WTC) site, planned to move into some empty retail area to accommodate its growing congregation and out of a desire to create an interfaith outreach center. However, the new site, initially approved by the local community, brought it to within two blocks of the WTC site. By 2009 the plan became a national controversy with many people seeing Muslims, in general, as insensitive to the meaning of Ground Zero. National surveys showed 61 percent opposed to a mosque near Ground Zero with barely a quarter favoring such a location. Plans were set aside as advocates tried to explain they had intended to be reaching out to the nation and not trying to divide it.

Arab Americans and Muslim Americans, like other subordinate groups, have not responded passively to their treatment. Organizations have been created in their communities to counter negative stereotypes and to offer schools material responding to the labeling that has occurred. Even before 2001, Arab Americans and Muslim Americans were beginning to become active in both major political parties in the United States. However, during the 2000 campaign, candidates already were distancing themselves from campaign contributions from Muslim and Arab organizations.

Given the presence of Islamophobia, the position of being Arab or Muslim in the United States grew more complex and contentious in the wake of the events of September 11, 2001, despite the public efforts of many Arabs and Muslims to proclaim their loyalty to the United States.

*Sources:* Bosman 2007; Ghosh 2010; Halstead 2008; Lugo et al. 2011; Mohamed and O'Brien 2011; Pew Forum on Religion and Public Life 2011.

Being White carries with it distinct advantages, which has been called *White privilege*. For example, one can seek assistance and assume your race will not work against you.

The following sections examine the theories of why prejudice exists and discuss the content and extent of prejudice today.

## White Privilege

White travelers unlike LaPiere's Chinese couple rarely, if ever, would have to be concerned about second-class treatment because of race. Being White in the United States may not assure success and wealth but it does avoid encountering a lot of intolerance.

**White privilege** refers to the rights or immunities granted as a particular benefit or favor for being White. This advantage exists unconsciously and is often invisible to the very White people who enjoy it (Ferber 2008).

Scholar Peggy McIntosh of the Wellesley College Center for Research on Women looked at the privilege that comes from being White and the added privilege of being male. The other side of racial oppression is the privilege enjoyed by dominant groups. Being White or being successful in establishing a White identity carries with it distinct advantages. Among those that McIntosh (1988) identified were the following:

- Being considered financially reliable when using checks, credit cards, or cash.
- Taking a job without having coworkers suspect it came about because of race.

- Never having to speak for all the people of your race.
- Watching television or reading a newspaper and seeing people of your own race widely represented.
- Speaking effectively in a large group without being called a credit to your race.
- Assuming that if legal or medical help is needed, your race will not work against you.

Whiteness does carry privileges, but most White people do not consciously think of them except on the rare occasions when they are questioned. We return to the concepts of Whiteness and White privilege, but let us also consider the rich diversity of religion in the United States, which parallels the ethnic diversity of this nation.

Typically, White people do not see themselves as privileged in the way many African Americans and Latinos see themselves as disadvantaged. When asked to comment on their "Whiteness," White people are most likely to see themselves devoid of ethnicity ("no longer Irish," for example), stigmatized as racist, and victims of reverse discrimination. Privilege for many White people may be easy to exercise in one's life, but it is exceedingly difficult to acknowledge (McKinney 2008).

## Theories of Prejudice

Prejudice is learned. Friends, relatives, newspapers, books, movies, television, and the Internet all teach it. Awareness of the differences between people that society judges to be important begins at an early age. Several theories have been advanced to explain the rejection of certain groups in a society. We examine four theoretical explanations. The first two (scapegoating and authoritarian personality) tend to be psychological, emphasizing why a particular person harbors ill feelings. The second two are more sociological (exploitation and normative), viewing prejudice in the context of our interaction in a larger society.

### Scapegoating Theory

Some expressions of prejudice are so that people can blame others and refuse to accept responsibility. **Scapegoating theory** says that prejudiced people believe they are society's victims.

The term *scapegoat* comes from a biblical injunction telling the Hebrews to send a goat into the wilderness to symbolically carry away the people's sins. Similarly, the theory of scapegoating suggests that, rather than accepting guilt for some failure, a person transfers the responsibility for failure to some vulnerable group.

In the major tragic twentieth-century example, Adolf Hitler used the Jews as the scapegoat for all German social and economic ills in the 1930s. This premise led to the passage of laws restricting Jewish life in pre–World War II Germany and eventually escalated into the mass extermination of Europe's Jews. Scapegoating of Jews persists. A national survey in 2009 showed that one out of four people in the United States blame "the Jews" for the financial crisis (Malhotra and Margalit 2009).

Today in the United States, both legal and illegal immigrants often are blamed by "real Americans" for their failure to secure jobs or desirable housing. The immigrant becomes the scapegoat for one's own lack of skills, planning, or motivation. It is so much easier to blame someone else.

## Authoritarian Personality Theory

Prejudice may be influenced by one's upbringing and the lessons taught early in life. Several efforts have been made to detail the prejudiced personality, but the most comprehensive effort culminated in a volume titled *The Authoritarian Personality* (Adorno et al. 1950). Using a variety of tests and relying on more than 2,000 respondents, ranging from middle-class Whites to inmates of San Quentin State Prison (California), the authors claimed they had isolated the characteristics of the authoritarian personality.

In Adorno and colleagues' (1950) view, the basic characteristics of the **authoritarian personality** construct a personality type that is likely to be prejudiced. It encompasses adherence to conventional values, uncritical acceptance of authority, and concern with power and toughness. With obvious relevance to the development of intolerance, the authoritarian personality was also characterized by aggressiveness toward people who did not conform to conventional norms or obey authority. According to the researchers, this personality type developed from an early childhood of harsh discipline. A child with an authoritarian upbringing obeyed and then later treated others as he or she had been raised.

This study has been widely criticized, but the very existence of such wide criticism indicates the influence of the study. Critics have attacked the study's equation of authoritarianism with right-wing politics (although liberals can also be rigid); its failure to see that prejudice is more closely related to other individual traits, such as social class, than to authoritarianism as it was defined; the research methods used; and the emphasis on extreme racial prejudice rather than on more-common expressions of hostility.

Despite these concerns about specifics in the study completed 60 years ago, annual conferences continue to draw attention to how authoritarian attitudes contribute to racism, sexism, and even torture (Kinloch 1974; O'Neill 2008).

## Exploitation Theory

Racial prejudice is often used to justify keeping a group in a subordinate economic position. Conflict theorists, in particular, stress the role of racial and ethnic hostility as a way for the dominant group to keep its position of status and power intact. Indeed, this approach maintains that even the less-affluent White working class uses prejudice to minimize competition from upwardly mobile minorities.

This **exploitation theory** is clearly part of the Marxist tradition in sociological thought. Karl Marx emphasized exploitation of the lower class as an integral part of capitalism. Similarly, the exploitation or conflict approach explains how racism can stigmatize a group as inferior so that the exploitation of that group can be justified. As developed by Oliver Cox (1942), exploitation theory saw prejudice against Blacks as an extension of the inequality faced by the entire lower class.

The exploitation theory of prejudice is persuasive. Japanese Americans were the object of little prejudice until they began to enter occupations that brought them into competition with Whites. The movement to keep Chinese out of the country became strongest during the late nineteenth century, when Chinese immigrants and Whites fought over dwindling numbers of jobs. Both the enslavement of African Americans and the removal westward of Native Americans were to a significant degree economically motivated.

## Normative Approach

Although personality factors are important contributors to prejudice, normative or situational factors must also be given serious consideration. The **normative approach** takes the view that prejudice is influenced by societal norms and situations that encourage or discourage the tolerance of minorities.

Analysis reveals how societal influences shape a climate for tolerance or intolerance. Societies develop social norms that dictate not only what foods are desirable (or forbidden) but also what racial and ethnic groups are to be favored (or despised). Social forces operate in a society to encourage or discourage tolerance. The force may be widespread, such as the pressure on White Southerners to oppose racial equality even though there was slavery or segregation. The influence of social norms may be limited, as when one man finds himself becoming more sexist as he competes with three women for a position in a prestigious law firm.

We should not view the four approaches to prejudice summarized in Table 2.1 as mutually exclusive. Social circumstances provide cues for a person's attitudes; personality determines the extent to which people follow social cues and the likelihood that they will encourage others to do the same. Societal norms may promote or deter tolerance; personality traits suggest the degree to which a person will conform to norms of intolerance. To understand prejudice, we need to use all four approaches together.

**Table 2.1 Theories of Prejudice**

There is no one satisfactory explanation of why prejudice exists, but several approaches taken together offer insight.

| Theory | Explanation | Example |
|--------|-------------|---------|
| Scapegoating | People blame others for their own failures. | An unsuccessful applicant assumes that a minority member or a woman got "his" job. |
| Authoritarian | Childrearing leads one to develop intolerance as an adult. | The rigid personality type dislikes people who are different. |
| Exploitation | People use others unfairly for economic advantage. | A minority member is hired at a lower wage level. |
| Normative | Peer and social influences encourage tolerance or intolerance. | A person from an intolerant household is more likely to be openly prejudiced. |

# Stereotypes

On Christmas Day 2001, Arab American Walied Shater boarded an American Airlines flight from Baltimore to Dallas carrying a gun. Immediately, the cockpit crew refused to let him fly, fearing that Shater would take over the plane and use it as a weapon of mass destruction. Yet Walied Shater carried documentation that he was a Secret Service agent, and calls to Washington, D.C., confirmed that he was flying to join a presidential protection force at President George W. Bush's ranch in Texas. Nevertheless, the crew could not get past the stereotype of Arab American men posing a lethal threat (Leavitt 2002).

## What Are Stereotypes?

In Chapter 1, we saw that stereotypes play a powerful role in how people come to view dominant and subordinate groups. **Stereotypes** are unreliable generalizations about all members of a group that do not take individual differences into account. Numerous scientific studies have been made of these exaggerated images. This research has shown the willingness of people to assign positive and negative traits to entire groups of people, which are then applied to particular individuals. Stereotyping causes people to view Blacks as superstitious, Whites as uncaring, and Jews as shrewd. Over the last 80 years of such research, social scientists have found that people have become less willing to express such views openly, but prejudice persists, as we will see later (Quillian 2006).

If stereotypes are exaggerated generalizations, then why are they so widely held, and why are some traits more often assigned than others? Evidence for traits may arise out of real conditions. For example, more Puerto Ricans live in poverty than Whites, and so the prejudiced mind associates Puerto Ricans with laziness. According to the New Testament, some Jews were responsible for the crucifixion of Jesus, and so, to the prejudiced mind, all Jews are Christ killers. Some activists in the women's movement are lesbians, and so all feminists are seen as lesbians. From a kernel of fact, faulty generalization creates a stereotype.

In "Listen to Our Voices," journalist Tim Giago, born a member of the Oglala Sioux tribe on the Pine Ridge Reservation, comments on the use by college and professional teams of mascots patterned after American Indians. He finds the use neither harmless nor providing honor to the tribal people of the United States.

## LISTEN TO OUR VOICES

### National Media Should Stop Using Obscene Words

*Tim Giago*

I am just sick and tired of hearing students and faculty from schools using Indians as mascots say they are doing it to "honor us. . . ."

Who or what is a redskin? It is a derogatory name for a race of people. It's as simple as that. It is akin to the racist names "nigger" or "gook" or "kike" or "wop." It is not, I repeat NOT, an honor to be called a racist name nor is it an honor to see football fans dressed in supposed Indian attire nor to hear them trumpeting some ludicrous war chant nor to see them mimic or ape our dress, culture, or person.

When I saw the Florida State fans doing the ridiculous "tomahawk chop" and heard their Johnny-one-note band play that asinine version of an Indian song over and over, I was heartsick. I was also highly embarrassed for the people of the Seminole Nation of Florida for allowing their good name to be taken in vain.

I am also sick and tired of fanatical sports fans telling Indians who object to this kind of treatment to "lighten up." You know, I didn't hear those same White folks saying this to African Americans in the 1960s when they were objecting to the hideous Black caricature at Sambo's Restaurants or to the Step-in-Fetch-It character used so often in the early movie days to portray Blacks as dimwitted, shiftless people. I didn't hear anybody tell them to "lighten up."

However, 2000 did give us (Indians) a little reprieve. The Cleveland Indians and their hideous mascot were clobbered and didn't make the playoffs. The Washington Redskins turned into the Washington "Deadskins." The Kansas City Chiefs were real losers. And almost best of all, the Florida State Seminoles were steamrolled by an Oklahoma team with real Indians serving as bodyguards to the Oklahoma coach Bob Stoops. My thrill at watching the Seminoles lose was topped only by watching Ted Turner's Atlanta Braves get "tomahawked" this year. Now that was truly an "honor." . . .

*Webster's Ninth New Collegiate Dictionary*, note the word "collegiate" here, reads the word *redskin* quite simply as "American Indian usually taken to be offensive."

"Usually taken to be offensive." Now what is so hard to understand about this literal translation of the word "redskin"?

Attention major newspapers, CNN, Fox, ABC, CBS and NBC: the word "redskin" is an obscenity to Indians and to people who are sensitive to racism. It is translated by *Webster's* to be offensive. Now what other proof do you need to discontinue its usage?

*Source*: "National Media Should Stop Using Obscene Words" by Tim Giago, as reprinted in *The Denver Post*, January 21, 2001. Copyright © 2001 by Tim Giago. Reprinted by permission of Tim Giago.

The labeling of individuals through negative stereotypes has strong implications for the self-fulfilling prophecy. Studies show that people are all too aware of the negative images other people have of them. When asked to estimate the prevalence of hard-core racism among Whites, one in four Blacks agrees that more than half "personally share the attitudes of groups like the Ku Klux Klan toward Blacks"; only one Black in ten says "only a few" share such views. Stereotypes not only influence how people feel about themselves but also, and perhaps equally important, affect how people interact with others. If people feel that others hold incorrect, disparaging attitudes toward them, then it undoubtedly makes it difficult to have harmonious relations (Sigelman and Tuch 1997).

Although explicit expressions of stereotypes are less common, it is much too soon to write the obituary of racial and ethnic stereotypes. We next consider the use of stereotypes in the contemporary practice of racial profiling.

## Stereotyping in Action: Racial Profiling

A Black dentist, Elmo Randolph, testified before a state commission that he was stopped dozens of times in the 1980s and 1990s while traveling the New Jersey Turnpike to work. Invariably state troopers asked, "Do you have guns or drugs?" "My parents always told me, be careful when you're driving on the turnpike," said Dr. Randolph, age 44. "White people don't have that conversation" (Purdy 2001:37; see also Fernandez and Fahim 2006).

Little wonder that Dr. Randolph was pulled over. Although African Americans accounted for only 17 percent of the motorists on that turnpike, they were 80 percent of the motorists pulled over. Such occurrences gave rise to the charge that a new traffic offense was added to the books: DWB, or "driving while Black" (Bowles 2000).

In recent years, government attention has been given to a social phenomenon with a long history: racial profiling. According to the Department of Justice, **racial profiling** is any police-initiated action based on race, ethnicity, or national origin rather than the person's behavior. Generally, profiling occurs when law enforcement officers, including customs officials, airport security, and police, assume that people fitting certain descriptions are likely to be engaged in something illegal. In 2009, national attention was drawn to the issue as a Cambridge, Massachusetts, police officer was called to the home of renowned Harvard University professor Henry Louis Gates, Jr., to investigate an alleged break-in. The White police officer, James Crowley, a trainer at the police department in diversity issues, asked the African American scholar for proof he lived in the house. Gates's alleged lack of cooperation led to his arrest for disorderly conduct, but the charges were subsequently dropped. For many people this was yet another case of profiling, most of which go unnoticed by the public. To others this alleged profiling was an officer doing his job.

The reliance on racial profiling persists despite overwhelming evidence that it is misleading. Whites are more likely to be found with drugs in the areas in which minority group members are disproportionately targeted. A federal study made public in 2005 found little difference nationwide in the likelihood of being stopped by officers, but African Americans were twice as likely to have their vehicles searched, and Latinos were five times more likely. A similar pattern emerged in the likelihood of force being used

Reflecting racial profiling, the majority of people polled in the United States think that ethnicity and religion should be taken into account to maintain security.

against drivers: it was three times more likely with Latinos and Blacks than with White drivers. A study of New York City police officers released in 2011 found that racial minorities accounted for 87 percent of those police stop and frisk, but the officers were 50 percent more likely to find Whites carrying weapons (Center for Constitutional Rights 2011; Herbert 2010; Tomaskovic-Devey and Warren 2009).

Back in the 1990s, increased attention to racial profiling led not only to special reports and commissions but also to talk of legislating against it. This proved difficult. The U.S. Supreme Court in *Whren v. United States* (1996) upheld the constitutionality of using a minor traffic infraction as an excuse to stop and search a vehicle and its passengers. Nonetheless, states and other government units are discussing policies and training that would discourage racial profiling. At the same time, most law enforcement agencies reject the idea of compiling racial data on traffic stops, arguing that it would be a waste of money and staff time.

The effort to stop racial profiling came to an abrupt end after the September 11, 2001, terrorist attacks on the United States. Suspicions about Muslims and Arabs in the United States became widespread. Foreign students from Arab countries were summoned for special questioning. Legal immigrants identified as Arab or Muslim were scrutinized for any illegal activity and were prosecuted for routine immigration violations that were ignored for people of other ethnic backgrounds and religious faiths (Withrow 2006).

National surveys have found little change since 2001 in support for profiling Arab Americans at airports. In 2010, 53 percent of Americans favored requiring "ethnic and religious profiling," including those who are U.S. citizens, to undergo special and more-intensive security checks before boarding planes in the United States (Zogby 2010).

## Color-Blind Racism

Over the last three generations, nationwide surveys have consistently shown growing support by Whites for integration, interracial dating, and having members of minority groups attain political office, including even becoming president of the United States. Yet how can this be true when the type of hatred described at the beginning of the chapter persists and thousands of hate crimes occur annually?

**Color-blind racism** refers to the use of race-neutral principles to defend the racially unequal status quo. Yes, there should be "no discrimination for college admission," yet the disparity in educational experiences means that the use of formal admissions criteria will privilege White high school graduates. "Healthcare is for all," but if you fail to have workplace insurance, you are unlikely to afford it.

Asian Americans are rarely featured as central characters except where martial arts are a central focus. Exceptions to that are Kalpen Modi (also known as Kal Penn), born of Asian Indian immigrants, shown on the right and Korean-born John Cho in their latest *Harold and Kumar* movie, *A Very Harold & Kumar 3D Christmas*, released in 2011.

Color-blind racism has also been referred to as "laissez-faire" or "postracialism" or "aversive racism," but the common theme is that notions of racial inferiority are rarely expressed and that proceeding color-blind into the future will serve to perpetuate inequality. In the post–civil rights era and with the election of President Barack Obama, people are more likely to assume discrimination is long past and express views that are more proper—that is, lacking the overt expressions of racism of the past.

An important aspect of color-blind racism is the recognition that race is rarely invoked in public debates on social issues. Instead, people emphasize lower social class or the lack of citizenship or illegal aliens; these descriptions serve, in effect, as proxies for race. Furthermore, the emphasis is on individuals failing rather than recognizing patterns of groups being disadvantaged. This leads many White people to declare they are not racist and that they really do not know anyone who is racist. It leads to the mistaken conclusion that more progress has been made toward racial and ethnic equality and even tolerance than has really taken place.

When we survey White attitudes toward African Americans, three conclusions are inescapable. First, attitudes are subject to change; during periods of dramatic social upheaval, dramatic shifts can occur within one generation. Second, less progress was made in the late twentieth and the beginning of the twentieth-first centuries than was made in the relatively brief period of the 1950s and 1960s. Third, the pursuit of a color-blind agenda has created lower levels of support for politics that could reduce racial inequality if implemented.

Economically less-successful groups such as African Americans and Latinos have been associated with negative traits to the point that issues such as urban decay, homelessness, welfare, and crime are now viewed as race issues even though race is rarely spoken of explicitly. Besides making the resolution of very difficult social issues even harder, this is another instance of blaming the victim. These perceptions come at a time when the willingness of the government to address domestic ills is limited by increasing opposition to new taxes and continuing commitments to fight terrorism here and abroad. The color line remains even if more and more people are unwilling to accept its divisive impact on everyone's lives (Ansell 2008; Bonilla-Silva 2006, 2008; Kang and Lane 2010; Mazzocco et al. 2006; Quillian 2006; Winant 2004:106–108).

## The Mood of the Oppressed

Sociologist W. E. B. Du Bois relates an experience from his youth in a largely White community in Massachusetts. He tells how, on one occasion, the boys and girls were exchanging cards, and everyone was having a lot of fun. One girl, a newcomer, refused his card as soon as she saw that Du Bois was Black. He wrote:

> *Then it dawned upon me with a certain suddenness that I was different from others . . . shut out from their world by a vast veil. I had therefore no desire to tear down that veil, to creep through; I held all beyond it in common contempt and lived above it in a region of blue sky and great wandering shadows. (1903:2)*

In using the image of a veil, Du Bois describes how members of subordinate groups learn that they are being treated differently. In his case and that of many others, this leads to feelings of contempt toward all Whites that continue for a lifetime.

Opinion pollsters have been interested in White attitudes on racial issues longer than they have measured the views of subordinate groups. This neglect of minority attitudes reflects, in part, the bias of the White researchers. It also stems from the contention that the dominant group is more important to study because it is in a better position to act on its beliefs. The results of a nationwide survey conducted in the United States offer insight into sharply different views on the state of race relations today (Figure 2.3). Latinos, African Americans, and Asian Americans all have strong reservations about the state of race relations

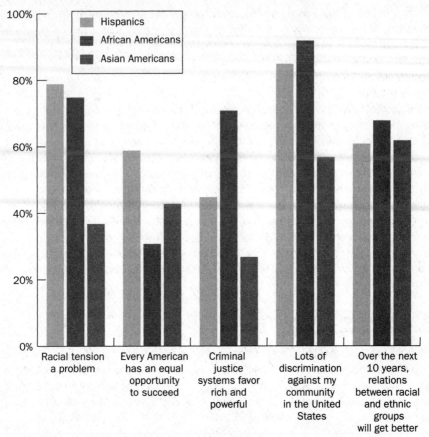

**Figure 2.3**   What Is the State of Race Relations?: Three Views

*Note:* Answers of "very important problem" or "strongly agree" with statements listed. Based on 1,105 interviews in August–September 2007, with bilingual questioners used as necessary.

*Source:* New America Media 2007:6, 12, 14, 24, 26.

in the United States. They are skeptical about the level of equal opportunity and perceive a lot of discrimination. It is interesting to note that Hispanics and Asian Americans, overwhelmingly immigrants, are more likely to feel they will succeed if they work hard. Yet the majority of all three groups have a positive outlook for the next ten years (New America Media 2007; Preston 2007).

National surveys showed that the 2008 successful presidential bid of Senator Barack Obama led to a sense of optimism and national pride among African Americans even though political observers saw Obama running a race-neutral campaign and rarely addressing issues specifically of concern to African Americans. Unlike Whites or Hispanics, Black voters still saw his campaign as addressing issues important to the Black community. Survey researchers closely followed these perceptions in the aftermath of the 2008 election.

Optimism about the present and future increased significantly among African Americans during the Obama campaign and first year of his presidency. Ironically White optimism about positive racial change was even more optimistic during the early period of the Obama administration. Yet other data show little evidence of a new nationwide perspective on race following the election. For example, only 33.9 percent of first-year students in September 2010 indicated a goal of "helping to promote racial understanding" compared to over 37 percent just the year before and 46 percent in 1992 (Pew Research Center 2010; Pryor, Hurtado, DeAngelo, Blake, and Tran 2010).

We have focused so far on what usually comes to mind when we think about prejudice: one group hating another group. But there is another form of prejudice: a group may come to hate itself. Members of groups held in low esteem by society may, as a result, either hate themselves or have low self-esteem themselves, as many social scientists once believed. Research literature of the 1940s through the 1960s emphasized the low self-esteem of minorities. Usually, the subject was African American, but the argument has also been generalized to include any subordinate racial, ethnic, or nationality group.

This view is no longer accepted. We should not assume that minority status influences personality traits in either a good or a bad way. First, such assumptions may create a stereotype. We cannot describe a Black personality any more accurately than we can a White personality. Second, characteristics of minority-group members are not entirely the result of subordinate

How do children come to develop an image about themselves? Toys and playthings play an important role, and for many children of racial and ethnic minorities, it is unusual to find toys that look like them. In 2005, a new doll was released called Fulla—an Arab who reflects modesty, piety, and respect, yet underneath she wears chic clothes that might be typically worn by a Muslim woman in private.

racial status; they are also influenced by low incomes, poor neighborhoods, and so forth. Third, many studies of personality imply that certain values are normal or preferable, but the values chosen are those of dominant groups.

If assessments of a subordinate group's personality are so prone to mis-judgments, then why has the belief in low self-esteem been so widely held? Much of the research rests on studies with preschool-age Black children when asked to express their preferences for dolls with different facial colors. Indeed, one such study by psychologists Kenneth and Mamie Clark (1947) was cited in the arguments before the U.S. Supreme Court in the landmark 1954 case *Brown v. Board of Education*. The Clarks' study showed that Black children preferred White dolls, a finding suggesting that the children had developed a negative self-image. Although subsequent doll studies have sometimes shown Black children's preference for white-faced dolls, other social scientists contend that this shows a realization of what most commercially sold dolls look like rather than documenting low self-esteem (Bloom 1971; Powell-Hopson and Hopson 1988).

Because African American children, as well as other subordinate groups' children, can realistically see that Whites have more power and resources and, therefore, rate them higher does not mean that they personally feel inferior. Children who actually experience overt discrimination are more likely to continue to display feelings of distress and anxiety later in life. However, studies, even those with children, show that when the self-images of middle-class or affluent African Americans are measured, their feelings of self-esteem are more positive than those of comparable Whites (Coker et al. 2009; Gray-Little and Hafdahl 2000).

## Intergroup Hostility

Prejudice is as diverse as the nation's population. It exists not only between dominant and subordinate peoples but also between specific subordinate groups. Unfortunately, until recently little research existed on this subject except for a few social distance scales administered to racial and ethnic minorities.

A national survey revealed that, like Whites, many African Americans, Hispanic Americans, and Asian Americans held prejudiced and stereotypical views of other racial and ethnic minority groups:

- Majorities of Black, Hispanic, and Asian American respondents agreed that Whites are "bigoted, bossy, and unwilling to share power." Majorities of these non-White groups also believed that they had less opportunity than Whites to obtain a good education, a skilled job, or decent housing.
- Forty-six percent of Hispanic Americans and 42 percent of African Americans agreed that Asian Americans are "unscrupulous, crafty, and devious in business."

- Sixty-eight percent of Asian Americans and 49 percent of African Americans believed that Hispanic Americans "tend to have bigger families than they are able to support."
- Thirty-one percent of Asian Americans and 26 percent of Hispanic Americans agreed that African Americans "want to live on welfare."

Members of oppressed groups obviously have adopted the widely held beliefs of the dominant culture concerning oppressed groups. At the same time, the survey also revealed positive views of major racial and ethnic minorities:

- More than 80 percent of respondents admired Asian Americans for "placing a high value on intellectual and professional achievement" and "having strong family ties."
- A majority of all groups surveyed agreed that Hispanic Americans "take deep pride in their culture and work hard to achieve a better life."
- Large majorities from all groups stated that African Americans "have made a valuable contribution to American society and will work hard when given a chance." (National Conference of Christians and Jews 1994)

Do we get along? Although this question often is framed in terms of the relationships between White Americans and other racial and ethnic groups, we should recognize the prejudice between groups. In a national survey conducted in 2000, people were asked whether they felt they could generally get along with members of other groups. In Figure 2.4, we can see that Whites felt they had the most difficulty getting along with Blacks. We also see the different views that Blacks, Latinos, Asian Americans, and American Indians hold toward other groups.

It is curious that we find that some groups feel they get along better with Whites than with other minority groups. Why would that be? Often, low-income people are competing daily with other low-income people and do not readily see the larger societal forces that contribute to their low status. As we can see from the survey results, many Hispanics are more likely to see Asian Americans as getting in their way than White Americans who are actually the real decision makers in their community.

Most troubling is when intergroup hostility becomes violent. Ethnic and racial tension among African Americans, Latinos, and immigrants may become manifest in hate crimes. Violence can surface in neighborhoods where there is competition for scarce resources such as jobs and housing. Gangs become organized along racial lines, much like private clubs "downtown." In recent years, Los Angeles has been particularly concerned about rival Black and Hispanic gangs. Conflict theorists see this violence as resulting from larger structural forces, but for the average person in such areas, life itself becomes more of a challenge (Archibold 2007).

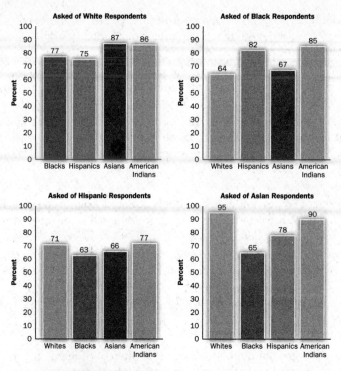

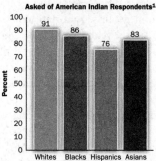

**Figure 2.4** Do We Get Along?

Percentage saying groups get along with each other ("Don't Knows" excluded).

[1]Sample size for American Indians is very small and subject to large sample variance.

*Note*: The wording of the question was, "We hear a lot these days about how various groups in society get along with each other. I'm going to mention several groups and ask whether you think they generally get along with each other or generally do not get along with each other." So, in the "Asked of White Respondents" graph, Whites are asked how Whites get along with each ethnic group; in the "Asked of Black Respondents" graph, Blacks are asked how Blacks get along with each ethnic group, and so on.

*Source*: Smith 2006:65. Reprinted by permission of the author.

# Reducing Prejudice

Focusing on how to eliminate prejudice involves an explicit value judgment: Prejudice is wrong and causes problems for those who are prejudiced and for their victims. The obvious way to eliminate prejudice is to eliminate its causes: the desire to exploit, the fear of being threatened, and the need to blame others for one's own failure. These might be eliminated by personal therapy, but therapy, even if it works for every individual, is no solution for an entire society in which prejudice is a part of everyday life.

The answer appears to rest with programs directed at society as a whole. Prejudice is attacked indirectly when discrimination is attacked. Despite prevailing beliefs to the contrary, we *can* legislate against prejudice: statutes and decisions do affect attitudes. In the past, people firmly believed that laws could not overcome norms, especially racist ones. Recent history, especially after the civil rights movement began in 1954, has challenged that common wisdom. Laws and court rulings that have equalized the treatment of Blacks and Whites have led people to reevaluate their beliefs about what is right and wrong. The increasing tolerance by Whites during the civil rights era from 1954 to 1965 seems to support this conclusion.

Much research has been done to determine how to change negative attitudes toward groups of people. The most encouraging findings point to education, mass media, intergroup contact, and workplace training programs.

Members of racial and ethnic minorities do not often appear on a regular basis in starring roles on television drama and comedy shows; when they do, it is often in roles that reflect negative stereotypes.

*Source*: LALO ALCARAZ ©2001 Dist. by UNIVERSAL UCLICK. Reprinted with permission. All rights reserved.

## Education

Research on education and prejudice considers special programs aimed at promoting mutual respect as well as what effect more formal schooling generally has on expressions of bigotry.

Most research studies show that well-constructed programs do have some positive effect in reducing prejudice, at least temporarily. The reduction is rarely as much as one might wish, however. The difficulty is that a single program is insufficient to change lifelong habits, especially if little is done to reinforce the program's message once it ends. Persuasion to respect other groups does not operate in a clear field because, in their ordinary environments, people are still subjected to situations that promote prejudicial feelings. Children and adults are encouraged to laugh at Polish jokes and cheer for a team named "Redskins." Black adolescents may be discouraged by peers from befriending a White youth. All this undermines the effectiveness of prejudice-reduction programs (Allport 1979).

Studies document that increased formal education, regardless of content, is associated with racial tolerance. Research data show that highly educated people are more likely to indicate respect and liking for groups different from themselves. Why should more years of schooling have this effect? It could be that more education gives a broader outlook and makes a person less likely to endorse myths that sustain racial prejudice. Formal education teaches the importance of qualifying statements and the need to question rigid categorizations, if not reject them altogether. Colleges increasingly include a graduation requirement that students complete a course that explores diversity or multiculturalism. Another explanation is that education does not actually reduce intolerance but simply makes people more careful about revealing it. Formal education may simply instruct people in the appropriate responses. Despite the lack of a clear-cut explanation, either theory suggests that the continued trend toward a better-educated population will contribute to a reduction in overt prejudice.

However, college education may not reduce prejudice uniformly. For example, some White students will come to believe that minority students did not earn their admission into college. Students may feel threatened to see large groups of people of different racial and cultural backgrounds congregating together and forming their own groups. Racist confrontations do occur outside the classroom and, even if they do involve only a few individuals, the events themselves will be followed by hundreds more. Therefore, some aspects of the college experience may only foster "we" and "they" attitudes (Schaefer 1986, 1996).

## Mass Media

Mass media, like schools, may reduce prejudice without requiring specially designed programs. Television, radio, motion pictures, newspapers, magazines, and the Internet present only a portion of real life, but what effect do they have on prejudice if the content is racist or antiracist, sexist or antisexist? As with measuring the influence of programs designed to reduce prejudice, coming to strong conclusions on mass media's effect is hazardous, but the evidence points to a measurable effect.

Today, 40 percent of all youths in the nation are children of color, yet few of the faces they see on television reflect their race or cultural heritage. As of spring 2007, only five of the nearly 60 primetime series carried on the four major networks featured performers of color in leading roles, and only two— *Ugly Betty* and *George Lopez*—focused on minority performers. What is more, the programs shown earlier in the evening, when young people are most likely to watch television, are the least diverse of all.

Why the underrepresentation? Incredibly, network executives seemed surprised by the research demonstrating an all-White season. Producers, writers, executives, and advertisers blamed each other for the alleged oversight. In recent years, the rise of both cable television and the Internet has fragmented the broadcast entertainment market, siphoning viewers away from the general-audience sitcoms and dramas of the past. With the proliferation of cable channels such as Black Entertainment Television (BET) and the Spanish-language Univision and Web sites that cater to every imaginable taste, there no longer seems to be a need for broadly popular series such as *The Cosby Show*, whose

Unlike much of television, unscripted or reality programming, such as *"Project Runway"* pictured here, tends to show a diversity more in align with the general population.

tone and content appealed to Whites as well as Blacks in a way that newer series do not. The result of these sweeping technological changes has been a sharp divergence in viewer preferences.

The absence of racial and ethnic minorities in television is well documented. They are less likely to play recurring roles and are well underrepresented in key decision-making positions such as directors, producers, and casting agents. Television series are only part of the picture. News broadcasting is done predominantly by Whites, and local news emphasizes crime, often featuring Black or Hispanic perpetrators; print journalism is nearly the same. This is especially troubling given another finding in the study discussed at the beginning of the chapter. Research showed that people were quicker to "shoot" an armed Black person than a White man in a video simulation. In another variation of that same study, the researchers showed subjects fake newspaper articles describing a string of armed robberies that showed either Black or White suspects. The subjects were quicker to "shoot" the armed suspect if he was Black but had no impact on their willingness to "shoot" the armed White criminal. This is a troubling aspect of the potential impact that media content may have (Correll et al. 2007a, 2007b; Park, Judd, Wittenbrink, Sadler, and Keesee 2007a, 2007b).

It is not surprising that young people quickly develop expectations of the roles that various racial and ethnic group members are depicted to play in the mass media such as television and motion pictures. A national survey of teens (ages 12–18) asked what characters members of racial and ethnic groups would be likely to play. The respondents' perception of media, as shown in Table 2.2, shows a significant amount of stereotyping occurring in their minds, in the media, or both.

### Table 2.2 Stereotyping in the Twenty-First Century

When asked to identify the role a person of a particular ethnic or racial background would be most likely to play in a movie or on television, teenagers cited familiar stereotypes.

| Group | Media Roles Identified |
|---|---|
| African American | Athlete, gang member, police officer |
| Arab American | Terrorist, convenience store clerk |
| Asian American | Physician, lawyer, CEO, factory worker |
| Hispanic | Gang member, factory worker |
| Irish American | Drunkard, police officer, factory worker |
| Italian American | Crime boss, gang member, restaurant worker |
| Jewish American | Physician, lawyer, CEO, teacher |
| Polish American | Factory worker |

*Note:* Based on national survey of 1,264 people between ages 13 and 18.

*Source:* Zogby 2001.

## Avoidance versus Friendship

Is prejudice reduced or intensified when people cross racial and ethnic boundaries? Two parallel paths have been taken to look at this social distance and equal-status contact.

**The Social Distance Scale Robert**   Park and Ernest Burgess (1921:440) first defined **social distance** as the tendency to approach or withdraw from a racial group. Emory Bogardus (1968) conceptualized a scale that could measure social distance empirically. His social distance scale is so widely used that it is often called the **Bogardus scale**.

The scale asks people how willing they would be to interact with various racial and ethnic groups in specified social situations. The situations describe different degrees of social contact or social distance. The items used, with their corresponding distance scores, follow. People are asked whether they would be willing to work alongside someone or be a neighbor to someone of a different group, and, showing the least amount of social distance, be related through marriage. Over the 70-year period in which the tests were administered, certain patterns emerged. In the top third of the hierarchy are White Americans and northern Europeans. Held at greater social distance are eastern and southern Europeans, and generally near the bottom are racial minorities (Bogardus 1968; Song 1991; Wark and Galliher 2007).

Generally, the researchers also found that among the respondents who had friends of different racial and ethnic origins, they were more likely to show greater social distance—that is, they were less likely to have been in each other's homes, shared in fewer activities, and were less likely to talk about their problems with each other. This is unlikely to promote mutual understanding.

**Equal Status Contact**   An impressive number of research studies have confirmed the **contact hypothesis**, which states that intergroup contact between people of equal status in harmonious circumstances will cause them to become less prejudiced and to abandon previously held stereotypes. The importance of equal status in interaction cannot be stressed enough. If a Puerto Rican is abused by his employer, little interracial harmony is promoted. Similarly, the situation in which contact occurs must be pleasant, making a positive evaluation likely for both individuals. Contact between two nurses, one Black and the other White, who are competing for one vacancy as a supervisor may lead to greater racial hostility. On the other hand, employed together in a harmonious workplace or living in the same neighborhood would work against harboring stereotypes or prejudices (Krysan, Farley, and Couper 2008; Schaefer 1976).

The key factor in reducing hostility, in addition to equal-status contact, is the presence of a common goal. If people are in competition, as already noted, contact may heighten tension. However, bringing people together to share a common task has been shown to reduce ill feelings when these people belong to different racial, ethnic, or religious groups. A study released in 2004 traced the transformations that occurred over the generations in the composition of the Social Service Employees Union in New York City. Always a mixed membership, the union was founded by Jews and Italian Americans, only to experience an influx of Black Americans. More recently, it comprises Latin Americans, Africans, West Indians, and South Asians. At each point, the common goals of representing the workers effectively overcame the very real cultural differences among the rank and file of Mexican and El Salvadoran immigrants in Houston. The researchers found that when the new arrivals had contact with African Americans, intergroup relations generally improved, and the absence of contact tended to foster ambivalent, even negative, attitudes (Fine 2008; Foerstrer 2004; Paluck and Green 2009).

The limited amount of intergroup contact is of concern given the power of the contact hypothesis. If there is no positive contact, then how can we expect there to be less prejudice? National surveys show prejudice directed toward Muslim Americans, but social contact bridges that hatred. In a 2006 survey, 50 percent of people who were not acquainted with a Muslim favor special identification for Muslim Americans, but only 24 percent of those who know a Muslim embrace that same view. Similarly, people personally familiar with Muslims are more than one-third less likely to endorse special security checks just for Muslims and are less nervous to see a Muslim man on the same flight with themselves. Although negative views are common toward Muslim Americans today, they are much less likely to be endorsed by people who have had intergroup contact (Saad 2006).

We often are unaware of all the social situations that allow us to meet people of different ethnic and racial backgrounds. Such opportunities may increase understanding.

*Source*: Mike Lester

As African Americans and other subordinate groups slowly gain access to better-paying and more-responsible jobs, the contact hypothesis takes on greater significance. Usually, the availability of equal-status interaction is taken for granted, yet in everyday life intergroup contact does not conform to the equal-status idea of the contact hypothesis. Furthermore, as we have seen, in a highly segregated society such as the United States, contact tends to be brief and superficial, especially between Whites and minorities. The apartheid-like friendship patterns prevent us from learning firsthand not just how to get along but also how to revel in interracial experiences (Bonilla-Silva and Embrick 2007; Miller 2002).

**Avoidance Via the Internet**   The emergence of the Internet, smart phones, and social media are all often heralded as transforming social behavior. While this may often be the case, avoiding people racially, ethnically, and religiously different is just another means of doing what one's parents and grandparents did.

Take dating for example. While in the past, one avoided people who looked different at social occasions, Internet daters have a new tool to use. Studies document that people who use Internet dating services typically use filters or respond to background questions to exclude people different from themselves. While many daters use such means, Whites are least open to dating racial and ethnic groups different from themselves, African Americans are most open, and Latinos and Asian Americans are somewhere in between the two extremes (Robnett and Feliciano 2011).

Sometimes the avoidance is not necessarily initiated by people but by the "helpful" technology. Search engines are becoming increasingly sophisticated and give the user the best match for their desired destination on the Internet based on past searches. This means that if a person in the past has selected certain Web sites, that stored information is used by a search engine like Google to offer the best match in future searches. Consequently, when a person enters the digital world searching for everything from a vacation destination to a restaurant to a politically oriented Web site, past usage is a guide. Any given person who, in the past, has clicked on a site that is say more White-oriented or Asian American–oriented, even in a relatively harmless way, is more likely to stay within the digital bubble. True, people can opt out of these "helpful" features, but most do not and end up navigating the cyber world much like they do the real world (Parsier 2011a, 2011b).

## Corporate Response: Diversity Training

Prejudice carries a cost. This cost is not only to the victim but also to any organization that allows prejudice to interfere with its functioning. Workplace hostility can lead to lost productivity and even staff attrition. Furthermore, if left unchecked, an organization—whether a corporation, government agency, or nonprofit enterprise—can develop a reputation for having a "chilly climate."

This reputation of a business unfriendly to people of color or to women discourages both qualified people from applying for jobs and potential clients from seeking products or services.

In an effort to improve workplace relations, most organizations have initiated some form of diversity training. These programs are aimed at eliminating circumstances and relationships that cause groups to receive fewer rewards, resources, or opportunities. Typically, programs aim to reduce ill treatment based on race, gender, and ethnicity. In addition, diversity training may deal with (in descending order of frequency) age, disability, religion, and language, as well as other aspects, including citizenship status, marital status, and parental status (Society for Human Resource Management 2008).

It is difficult to make any broad generalization about the effectiveness of diversity-training programs because they vary so much in structure between organizations. At one extreme are short presentations that seem to have little support from management. People file into the room feeling that this is something they need to get through quickly. Such training is unlikely to be effective and may actually be counterproductive by heightening social tensions. At the other end of the continuum is a diversity training program that is integrated into initial job training, reinforced periodically, and presented as part of the overall mission of the organization, with full support from all levels of management. In these businesses, diversity is a core value, and management demands a high degree of commitment from all employees (Dobbin, Kalev, and Kelly 2007).

As shown in Figure 2.5, the workforce is becoming more diverse, and management is taking notice. An increasing proportion of the workforce is foreign-born, and the numbers of U.S.-born African Americans, Latinos,

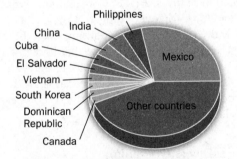

**Figure 2.5**   Foreign-Born Workers in the United States, by Country
About 15 percent of the civilian labor force is foreign-born, with Mexico the largest source.

*Source*: Data for 2004 from the Bureau of Labor Statistics, in Mosisa 2006:48.

and Asian Americans are also growing. Growing research in business and the social sciences is documenting that diversity is an asset in bringing about creative changes. The benefits of workplace diversity are especially true at management levels where leadership teams can develop innovative solutions and creative ideas. However, it is troubling to note that organizations that have the least diverse leadership are much less likely to adopt any kind of diversity program whatever its effectiveness (DiTomaso, Post, and Parks-Yancy 2007; Dobbin, Kim, and Kalev 2011; Leung et al. 2008; Page 2007).

It is not in an organization's best interests if employees start to create barriers based on, for example, racial lines. We saw in the previous section that equal-status contact can reduce hostility. However, in the workplace, people compete for promotions, desirable work assignments, and better office space, to name a few sources of friction. When done well, an organization undertakes diversity training to remove ill feelings among workers, which often reflect the prejudices present in larger society.

If it is to have a lasting impact on an organization, diversity training should not be separated from other aspects of the organization. For example, even the most inspired program will have little effect on prejudice if the organization promotes a sexist or ethnically offensive image in its advertising. The University of North Dakota launched an initiative in 2001 to become one of the top institutions for Native Americans in the nation. Yet at almost the same time, the administration reaffirmed its commitment, despite tribal objections, to having as its mascot for athletic teams the "Fighting Sioux." It does little to do diversity training if overt actions by an organization propel it in the opposite direction. In 2005, the National Collegiate Athletic Association began a review of logos and mascots that could be considered insulting to Native Americans. Some colleges have resisted suggestions to change or alter their publicity images, although others have abandoned the practice (University of North Dakota 2008).

Despite the problems inherent in confronting prejudice, an organization with a comprehensive, management-supported program of diversity training can go a long way toward reducing prejudice in the workplace. The one major qualifier is that the rest of the organization must also support mutual respect.

## Ways to Fight Hate

What can schools do? Television and movie producers? Corporate big shots? It is easy to shift the responsibility for confronting prejudice to the movers and shakers, and certainly they do play a critical role. Yet there definitely are actions one can take in the course of everyday life to challenge intergroup hostility.

The Southern Poverty Law Center (SPLC), founded in 1971 and based in Montgomery, Alabama, organized committed activists all over the country to mount legal cases and challenges against hate groups such as the Ku Klux Klan. The center's courtroom challenges led to the end of many discriminatory practices. Its cases have now gone beyond conventional race-based cases, with the center winning equal benefits for women in the armed forces, helping to end involuntary sterilization of women on welfare, and working to reform prison and mental health institution conditions.

Recognizing that social change can also begin at the individual level, the SPLC has identified ten ways to fight hate on the basis of its experience working at the community level:

1. *Act.* Do something. In the face of hatred, apathy will be taken as acceptance even by the victims of prejudice themselves. The SPLC tells of a time when a cross was burned in the yard of a single mother of Portuguese descent in Missouri; one person acted and set in motion a community uprising against hatred.

2. *Unite.* Call a friend or coworker. Organize a group of like-thinking friends from school or your place of worship or club. Create a coalition that is diverse and includes the young, the old, law enforcement representatives, and the media. Frustrated when a neo-Nazi group got permission to march in Illinois, a Jewish couple formed Project Lemonade. Money raised helps to create education projects or monuments in communities that witness such decisive events.

3. *Support the victims.* Victims of hate crimes are especially vulnerable. Let them know you care by words, in person, or by e-mail. If you or your friend is a victim, report it. When a church in Manchester, New Hampshire, was vandalized with racist and hateful graffiti, other houses of worship showed solidarity by leaving their lights on all night, all across town.

4. *Do your homework.* If you suspect a hate crime has been committed, do your research to document it. A mother walked out of her Montgomery, Alabama, home to find hate at her door-step: an anonymous flyer from a known hate group. The leaflets, placed in plastic bags and weighted down with everything from pennies to cat litter, were filled with racist and anti-immigrant propaganda. She used the incident to educate her two preteen sons about hate groups but also brought it to the attention of her neighborhood association and the police.

5. *Create an alternative.* Never attend a rally where hate is a part of the agenda. Find another outlet for your frustration, whatever the cause. When the Ku Klux Klan held a rally in Wisconsin, a coalition of ministers organized citizens to spend the day in minority neighborhoods.

6. *Speak up.* You, too, have First Amendment rights. Denounce the hatred, the cruel jokes. If you see a news organization misrepresenting a group, speak up. When a newspaper exposed the 20-year-old national leader of the Aryan Nation, he resigned and closed his Web site.

7. *Lobby leaders.* Persuade policymakers, business heads, community leaders, and executives of media outlets to take a stand against hate. Levi Strauss contributed $5 million to an anti-prejudice project and a program that helps people of color to get loans in communities where it has plants.

8. *Look long term.* Participate or organize events such as annual parades or cultural fairs to celebrate diversity and harmony. Supplement it with a Web site that can be a 24/7 resource. The Cornbread Club in Lubbock, Texas, brings together people of different ethnicities and income levels. The group has no agenda, no speakers, and only one rule at its monthly dinners at a local cafeteria: Sit next to someone you don't know.

9. *Teach tolerance.* Prejudice is learned, and parents and teachers can influence the content of curriculum. In a first-grade class in Seattle, children paint self-portraits, mixing colors to match their skin tone. They then name their colors, which have included "gingerbread," "melon," and "terra cotta." They learn that everyone has a color, that no one is actually "White."

10. *Dig deeper.* Look into the issues that divide us—social inequality, immigration, and sexual orientation. Work against prejudice. Dig deep inside yourself for prejudices and stereotypes you may embrace. Find out what is happening and act!

Expressing prejudice and expressing tolerance are fundamentally personal decisions. These steps recognize that we have the ability to change our attitudes, resist ethnocentrism and prejudice, and avoid the use of ethnophaulisms and stereotypes (Southern Poverty Law Center 2010; Willoughby 2004).

## Conclusion

This chapter has examined theories of prejudice and measurements of its extent. Clearly prejudice has a long history in the United States. Whispering campaigns suggested that presidents Martin Van Buren and William McKinley were secretly working with the Pope. This whispering emerged into the national debate when John F. Kennedy became the first Roman Catholic to become president. Much more recently, in 2010, 18 percent of Americans believed President Obama to be a Muslim and only 34 percent a Christian (Kristof 2010; Pew Forum on Religion and Public Life 2010).

So are some minority groups now finally being respected? People cheered on May 1, 2011, on hearing that Osama bin Laden had been found and killed. However, the always patriotic American

Indian people were very troubled to learn that the military had assigned the code name "Geronimo" to the operation to capture the terrorist. The Chiricahua Apache of New Mexico were particularly disturbed to learn that the name of their freedom fighter was being associated with a global terrorist. In response, the U.S. Defense Department said no disrespect was meant to Native Americans. But, of course, one can imagine that it would have never named the operation "Operation Lafayette" or "Operation Jefferson" (Daly 2011).

Several theories try to explain why prejudice exists. Theories for prejudice include two that tend to be psychological (scapegoating and authoritarian personality) and emphasize why a particular person harbors ill feelings. Others are more sociological (exploitation and normative), viewing prejudice in the context of our interaction in a larger society.

Surveys conducted in the United States over the past 60 years point to a reduction of prejudice as measured by the willingness to express stereotypes or maintain social distance. Survey data also show that African Americans, Latinos, Asian Americans, and American Indians do not necessarily feel comfortable with each other. They have adopted attitudes toward other oppressed groups similar to those held by many White Americans.

The absence of widespread public expression of prejudice does not mean prejudice itself is absent by any means. Recent prejudice aimed at Hispanics, Asian Americans, and large recent immigrant groups such as Arab Americans and Muslim Americans is well documented.

Issues such as immigration and affirmative action reemerge and cause bitter resentment. Furthermore, ill feelings exist between subordinate groups in schools, on the streets, and in the workplace. Color-blind racism allows one to appear to be tolerant while allowing racial and ethnic inequality to persist.

Equal-status contact may reduce hostility between groups. However, in a highly segregated society defined by inequality, such opportunities are not typical. The mass media can be of value in reducing discrimination, but they have not done enough and may even intensify ill feelings by promoting stereotypical images.

Even though we can be encouraged by the techniques available to reduce intergroup hostility, there are still sizable segments of the population that do not want to live in integrated neighborhoods, do not want to work for or be led by someone of a different race, and certainly object to the idea of their relatives marrying outside their own group. People still harbor stereotypes toward one another, and this tendency includes racial and ethnic minorities having stereotypes about one another.

Reducing prejudice is important because it can lead to support for policy change. There are steps we can take as individuals to confront prejudice and overcome hatred. Another real challenge and the ultimate objective is to improve the social condition of oppressed groups in the United States. To consider this challenge, we turn to discrimination in Chapter 3. Discrimination's costs are high to both dominant and subordinate groups. With this fact in mind, we examine some techniques for reducing discrimination.

## Summary

1. Prejudice consists of negative attitudes, and discrimination consists of negative behavior toward a group.

2. Typically unconsciously, White people accept privilege automatically extended to them in everyday life.

**3.** Robert Merton's formulation clarifies how individuals may be prejudiced and not necessarily discriminatory and find themselves acting in discriminatory ways while not harboring prejudices.

**4.** Although evidence indicates that the public expression of prejudice has declined, there is ample evidence that people are expressing race-neutral principles or color-blind racism that still serves to perpetuate inequality in society.

**5.** Typically, members of minority groups have a significantly more negative view of social inequality and are more pessimistic about the future compared to Whites.

**6.** Not only is prejudice directed at racial and ethnic minorities by people in dominant positions but also intergroup hostility among the minorities themselves persists and may become violent.

**7.** Various techniques are utilized by the corporate sector to reduce prejudice, including educational programs, mass media, friendly intergroup contact, and diversity-training programs.

## Key Terms

authoritarian personality  51
Bogardus scale  69
color-blind racism  57
contact hypothesis  69
discrimination  44
ethnocentrism  43

ethnophaulisms  44
exploitation theory  52
Islamophobia  47
normative approach  52
prejudice  44
racial profiling  56

scapegoating theory  50
social distance  69
stereotypes  53
White privilege  49

## Review Questions

**1.** How are prejudice and discrimination both related and unrelated to each other?

**2.** How do theories of prejudice relate to different expressions of prejudice?

**3.** How is color-blind racism expressed?

**4.** Are there steps that you can identify that have been taken against prejudice in your community?

## Critical Thinking

1. What privileges do you have that you do not give much thought to? Are they in any way related to race, ethnicity, religion, or social class?

2. Identify stereotypes associated with a group of people such as older adults or people with physical disabilities.

3. Consider the television programs you watch the most. In terms of race and ethnicity, how well do the programs you watch reflect the diversity of the population in the United States?

# 3 Discrimination

## CHAPTER OUTLINE

⟨ HIGHLIGHTS ⟩

Just as social scientists have advanced theories to explain why prejudice exists, they have also presented explanations of why discrimination occurs. Social scientists look more and more at the manner in which institutions, not individuals, discriminate. Hate crimes are a particularly violent and personal way by which people are denied their rights. Institutional discrimination is a pattern in social institutions that produces or perpetuates inequalities, even if individuals in the society do not intend to be racist or sexist.

Income data document that gaps exist between racial and ethnic groups. Historically, attempts have been made to reduce discrimination, usually through strong lobbying efforts by minorities themselves. Patterns of total discrimination make solutions particularly difficult for people in the informal economy or the underclass. Affirmative action was designed to equalize opportunity but has encountered significant resentment by those who charge that it constitutes reverse discrimination. Despite many efforts to end discrimination, glass ceilings and glass walls remain in the workplace.

All they wanted to do was go for a swim. The 65 children of the Creative Steps Camp of Philadelphia were to swim each summer Monday afternoon at the Valley Club in suburban Huntingdon Village. Upon their arrival at the pool that first Monday in July 2009, some parents called their children out of the pool, fearing it was dangerous. The Creative Step swimmers were almost all either Black or Latino while the Valley Club's were overwhelmingly White. The next day the Valley Club said the campers were not permitted to return and refunded the camp's $1,950 without explanation except the club president expressed concern "that a lot of kids would change the complexion . . . and the atmosphere of the club." Fortunately, another private organization offered its pool, while a U.S. senator called for an investigation into whether the incident violated the civil rights of the children (Lattanzio 2009).

Discrimination has no age restrictions. Here women protest the Valley Club outside of Philadelphia when the club took back a contract they had made to allow a day camp to pay to use their facilities. Unlike the Valley Club, most of the camp's swimmers were African American and Latino children.

The human casualties from natural disasters are well documented. This has been especially true with the impact of Hurricane Katrina on the Gulf Coast in 2005. Also well known now are the ill-planned evacuation plan in New Orleans, the subsequent high death toll, the ineffectiveness of levee construction and maintenance, and the initial slow response and the subsequent prolonged recovery, especially for low-income residents.

The persistent role of discrimination in the aftermath has been less a part of the national consciousness. Although Hurricane Katrina made victims of everyone, poor minority people have been especially victimized. Rural tribal Native American groups and Vietnamese American Gulf residents fell through the cracks of recovery plans. Latino workers who came to the area in the aftermath have been disadvantaged.

The storms destroyed more than 200,000 homes and apartments in Louisiana. Therefore, housing for those who wish to remain or move back is at a premium. But if you are Black and especially of modest means, the ability to reestablish a homestead is much more difficult in metropolitan New Orleans. Courts have had to intervene to restrain St. Bernard Parish, a county just outside New Orleans that is 93 percent White, from limiting rentals to only blood relatives and limiting new residential construction to single-family homes.

On March 8, 2007, an African American responded to a housing advertisement in another area but was told that the owner was out of state and would send information when he or she was back in town and could show the property. Nothing ever happened. A White person responded to the same advertisement the next day and learned from the same person that he or she would be in town that weekend and could arrange to show the property. The absentee landlord told the person that he or she could apply immediately and stated, "We don't want any loud rap music," and "We are looking for people who are more settled."

This is just one example from a study that sent well-trained Black and White testers presenting similar financial circumstances and family types out to attempt to rent housing throughout metropolitan New Orleans. When discrimination appeared to be present, follow-up testing occurred. In the final analysis, in six of every ten cases, African American testers faced differential treatment. Whites were granted appointments when Blacks were not. Whites were told about available apartments, Blacks were told nothing was available. Blacks were frequently quoted a higher monthly rental charge. White testers' voice mail requests for information were returned whereas many Black testers did not receive callbacks. Recovery is a much harder road if you are a person of color (Greater New Orleans Fair Housing Action Center 2007, 2011).

Discrimination has a long history, right up to the present, of taking its toll on people. We examine the many faces of discrimination, its many victims, and the many ways scholars have documented its presence today in the United States. We not only return to more examples of discrimination in housing but also look at differential treatment in employment opportunities, wages, voting, vulnerability to environmental hazards, and even access to membership in private clubs.

## Understanding Discrimination

**Discrimination** is the denial of opportunities and equal rights to individuals and groups because of prejudice or for other arbitrary reasons. People in the United States find it difficult to see discrimination as a widespread phenomenon. "After all," it is often said, "these minorities drive cars, hold jobs, own their homes, and even go to college." An understanding of discrimination in modern industrialized societies such as the United States must begin by distinguishing between relative and absolute deprivation.

### Relative versus Absolute Deprivation

Conflict theorists have said correctly that it is not absolute, unchanging standards that determine deprivation and oppression. Although minority groups may be viewed as having adequate or even good incomes, housing, healthcare, and educational opportunities, it is their position relative to some other group that offers evidence of discrimination.

**Relative deprivation** is defined as the conscious experience of a negative discrepancy between legitimate expectations and present actualities. After settling in the United States, immigrants often enjoy better material comforts and more political freedom than were possible in their old countries. If they compare themselves with most other people in the United States, however, they will feel deprived because, although their standards have improved, the immigrants still perceive relative deprivation.

**Absolute deprivation**, on the other hand, implies a fixed standard based on a minimum level of subsistence below which families should not be expected to exist. Discrimination does not necessarily mean absolute deprivation. A Japanese American who is promoted to a management position may still be a victim of discrimination if he or she had been passed over for years because of corporate reluctance to place an Asian American in a highly visible position.

Dissatisfaction is also likely to arise from feelings of relative deprivation. The members of a society who feel most frustrated and disgruntled by the social and economic conditions of their lives are not necessarily worse off in an objective sense. Social scientists have long recognized that what is most significant is how people perceive their situations. Karl Marx pointed out that although the misery of the workers was important in reflecting their oppressed state, so was their position relative to the ruling class. In 1847, Marx wrote, "Although the enjoyment of the workers has risen, the social satisfaction that they have has fallen in comparison with the increased enjoyment of the capitalist" (Marx and Engels 1955:94).

This statement explains why the groups or individuals who are most vocal and best organized against discrimination are not necessarily in the worst economic and social situation. However, they are likely to be those who most strongly perceive that, relative to others, they are not receiving their fair share. Resistance to perceived discrimination, rather than the actual amount of absolute discrimination, is the key.

## Total Discrimination

Social scientists—and increasingly policymakers—have begun to use the concept of **total discrimination**, which, as shown in Figure 3.1, refers to current discrimination operating in the labor market and past discrimination. Past discrimination experienced by an individual includes the poorer education and job experiences of racial and ethnic minorities compared with those of many White Americans. When considering discrimination, therefore, it is not enough to focus only on what is being done to people now. Discrimination is cumulative in its impact over what occurs in one's own lifetime. Sometimes a person may be dealt with fairly but may still be at a disadvantage because he or she suffered from poorer healthcare, inferior counseling in the school system, less access to books and other educational materials, or a poor job record resulting from absences to take care of brothers and sisters (Pager and Shepherd 2008).

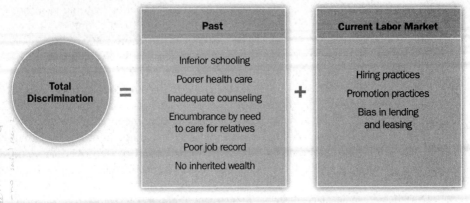

**Figure 3.1**  Total Discrimination

Discrimination is not an isolated occurrence today. A study released by the National Fair Housing Alliance and the federal Department of Housing and Urban Development found that discriminatory housing practices were routine. Consider the sobering results of a two-year study conducted in 12 metropolitan areas with 73 real estate firms: White real estate shoppers are steered away from houses in mixed neighborhoods even when they express interest in integrated areas. Latinos and African Americans looking for housing are steered toward minority neighborhoods even when their incomes justify seeing more-affluent neighborhoods. The challenge to being a minority homebuyer does not stop there. Studies document that Black and Hispanic homebuyers tend to pay higher interest rates than Whites with similar credit ratings. All things are hardly equal in home buying (Bocian, Ernst, and Li 2006).

Past experiences carry a heavier burden for racial minorities as is documented in the Research Focus box considering the barriers to job seeking.

---

## RESEARCH FOCUS

### Discrimination in Job Seeking

A dramatic confirmation of discrimination came with research begun by sociologist Devah Pager in 2003. She sent four men out as trained "testers" to look for entry-level jobs in Milwaukee, Wisconsin, that required no experience or special training. Each tester was a 23-year-old college student, but each one presented himself as having a high school diploma and similar job history.

The job-seeking experiences with 350 different employers were vastly different among the four men. Why was that? Two of the testers were Black and two were White. Furthermore, one tester of each pair indicated in the job application that he had served 18 months of jail time for a felony

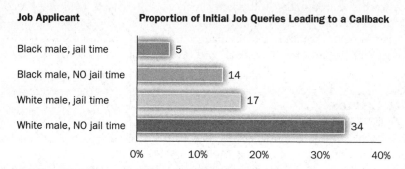

**Figure 3.2**   Discrimination in Job Seeking

Source: Pager 2003:958. Reprinted by permission of the University of Chicago.

conviction (possession of cocaine with intent to distribute). As you can see in Figure 3.2, applicants with a prison record received significantly fewer callbacks. But as dramatic a difference as a criminal record made, race was clearly more important.

The differences were to the point that a White job applicant with a jail record actually received more callbacks for further consideration than a Black man with no criminal record. Whiteness has a privilege even when it comes to jail time; race, it seems, was more of a concern to potential employers than a criminal background. Little wonder that analysis of labor patterns after release finds that wages grow at a 21 percent slower rate for Black compared to White ex-inmates.

"I expected there to be an effect of race, but I did not expect it to swamp the results as it did," Pager told an interviewer. Her finding was especially significant because the majority of convicts who are released from prison each year (52 percent) are, in fact, Black men. Pager's research, which was widely publicized, eventually contributed to a change in public policy. In his 2004 State of the Union address, and specifically referring to Pager's work, President George W. Bush announced a $300 million monitoring program for ex-convicts who are attempting to reintegrate into society.

These findings, however, are not isolated to this one study or to one city. Similar studies sending out job applicants have confirmed discrimination in action in Chicago, New York City, San Diego, and Washington, D.C.

Sources: Bordt 2005; Bureau of Justice Statistics 2004; Favreault 2008; Kroeger 2004; Lyons and Pettit 2011; Pager 2003, 2007a, 2007b; Pager and Quillian 2005; Pager and Western 2006; Pager, Western, and Bonikowski 2009.

We find another variation of this past-in-present discrimination when apparently nondiscriminatory current practices have negative effects because of prior intentionally biased practices. Although unions that purposely discriminated against minority members in the past may no longer do so, some people are still prevented from achieving higher levels of seniority because of those past practices. Upward social mobility is blocked and the likelihood of downward social mobility in the labor market is increased. Personnel records include a cumulative record that is vital in promotion and selection for desirable assignments. Blatantly discriminatory judgments and recommendations in the past remain part of a person's record (Mong and Roscigno 2010).

## Hate Crimes

Although prejudice certainly is not new in the United States, it is receiving increased attention as it manifests itself in neighborhoods, at meetings, and on college campuses. The Hate Crime Statistics Act, which became law in 1990, directs the Department of Justice to gather data on hate or bias crimes.

### What are Hate Crimes?

The government defines an ordinary crime as a **hate crime** when offenders are motivated to choose a victim because of some characteristic—for example, race, ethnicity, religion, sexual orientation, or disability—and provide evidence that hatred prompted them to commit the crime. Hate crimes are also sometimes referred to as *bias crimes* (Department of Justice 2011).

This law created a national mandate to identify such crimes, whereas previously only 12 states had monitored hate crimes. The act has since been amended to include disabilities, both physical and mental, as well as sexual orientation as factors that could be considered as a basis for hate crimes.

In 2009, law enforcement agencies released hate crime data submitted by police agencies covering 89 percent of the United States. Even though many, many hate crimes are not reported (less than one in seven participating agencies reported an incident), a staggering number of offenses that come to law agencies' attention were motivated by hate. While most incidents receive relatively little attention, some become the attention of headlines and online sites for days. Such was the case in 2009 when a Maryland man with a long history of ties to neo-Nazi groups walked in to the U.S. Holocaust Memorial Museum in Washington, D.C., and opened fire, killing a security guard.

There were official reports of more than 6,600 hate crimes and bias-motivated incidents in 2010. As indicated in Figure 3.3, race was the apparent motivation for the bias in approximately 47 percent of the reports, and religion, sexual orientation, and ethnicity accounted for 12–20 percent each. Vandalism against property and intimidation were the most common crimes, but among the more than 4,800 crimes directed against people, 53 percent of the incidents involved assault, rape, or murder.

The vast majority of hate crimes are directed by members of the dominant group toward those who are, relatively speaking, powerless. One in five bias incidents based on race are anti-White. Hate crimes, except for those that are most horrific, receive little media attention, and anti-White incidents probably

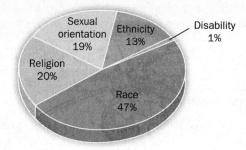

**Figure 3.3**  Distribution of Reported Hate Crimes
*Source*: Department of Justice 2011.

receive even less. Hostility based on race knows no boundaries (Department of Justice 2011; Witt 2007).

The official reports of hate or bias crimes appear to be only the tip of the iceberg. Government-commissioned surveys conducted over a national cross section indicate that 192,000 people annually report they have been victims of hate crimes, but only half of these are reported to police. Of these, only one out of ten, according to the victims, are confirmed as hate crimes. Although definitions vary, considerable racial hostility in this country becomes violent (Harlow 2005; Perry 2003).

National legislation and publicity have made hate crime a meaningful term, and we are beginning to recognize the victimization associated with such incidents. A current proposal would make a violent crime a federal crime if it were motivated by racial or religious bias. Although passage is uncertain, the serious consideration of the proposal indicates a willingness to consider a major expansion of federal jurisdiction. Currently, federal law prohibits crimes motivated by race, color, religion, or national origin only if they involve violation of a federally guaranteed right such as voting.

Victimized groups are not merely observing hate crimes and other acts of prejudice. Watchdog organizations play an important role in documenting bias-motivated violence; among such groups are the Anti-Defamation League, the National Institute Against Prejudice and Violence, the Southern Poverty Law Center, and the National Gay and Lesbian Task Force.

Established hate groups have even set up propaganda sites on the World Wide Web. This also creates opportunities for previously unknown haters and hate groups to promote themselves. However, hate crime legislation does not affect such outlets because of legal questions involving freedom of speech. An even more recent technique has been to use instant messaging software, which enables Internet users to create a private chat room with another individual. Enterprising bigots use directories to target their attacks through instant messaging, much as harassing telephone calls were placed in the past. Even more creative and subtle are people who have constructed Web sites to attract people who are surfing for information on Martin Luther King, Jr., only to find a site that looks educational but savagely discredits the civil rights activist. A close inspection will reveal that the site is hosted by a White-supremacist organization (Davis 2008; Simon Wiesenthal Center 2008; Working 2007).

## Why Do Hate Crimes Carry Harsher Penalties?

Frequently one hears the identification of hate crimes questioned. After all, is not every assault or act of vandalism involving hate? While many non-hate crimes may include a motivation of hatred toward an individual or organization, the use of hate or bias crimes toward minorities recognizes that they are intended to carry a message well beyond the actual victim. When a person assaults an individual because they are gay or lesbian, the act is meant to terrorize all gay and lesbians. Vandalizing a mosque or synagogue is meant to warn all Muslims or Jews that they are not wanted and their religious faith is felt to be inferior.

In many respects today's hate crimes are like the terrorist efforts of the Ku Klux Klan of generations ago. Targets may be randomly selected but the group being terrorized is carefully chosen. In many jurisdictions having a crime being classified as a hate crime can increase the punishment. So, for example, a misdemeanor, like vandalism, can be increased to a felony. A felony that is a hate crime can carry a greater prison sentence, These sanctions were upheld by the Supreme Court in the 1993 decision *Mitchell v. Wisconsin* which recognized that greater harm may be done by hate motivated crimes (Blazak 2011).

## Institutional Discrimination

Individuals practice discrimination in one-on-one encounters, and institutions practice discrimination through their daily operations. Indeed, a consensus is growing today that this institutional discrimination is more significant than acts committed by prejudiced individuals.

Social scientists are particularly concerned with the ways in which patterns of employment, education, criminal justice, housing, healthcare, and government operations maintain the social significance of race and ethnicity. **Institutional discrimination** is the denial of opportunities and equal rights to individuals and groups that results from the normal operations of a society.

Civil rights activist Stokely Carmichael and political scientist Charles Hamilton are credited with introducing the concept of institutional racism. *Individual discrimination* refers to overt acts of individual Whites against individual Blacks; Carmichael and Hamilton reserved the term *institutional racism* for covert acts committed collectively against an entire group. From this perspective, discrimination can take place without an individual intending to deprive others of privileges and even without the individual being aware that others are being deprived (Ture and Hamilton 1992).

How can discrimination be widespread and unconscious at the same time? The following are a few documented examples of institutional discrimination:

1. Standards for assessing credit risks work against African Americans and Hispanics who seek to establish businesses because many lack conventional credit references. Businesses in low-income areas where these groups often reside also have much higher insurance costs.
2. IQ testing favors middle-class children, especially the White middle class, because of the types of questions included.
3. The entire criminal justice system, from the patrol officer to the judge and jury, is dominated by Whites who find it difficult to understand life in poverty areas.
4. Hiring practices often require several years' experience at jobs only recently opened to members of subordinate groups.
5. Many jobs automatically eliminate people with felony records or past drug offenses, which disproportionately reduces employment opportunities for people of color.

Institutional discrimination is so systemic that it takes on the pattern of what has been termed "woodwork racism" in that racist outcomes become so widespread that African Americans, Latinos, Asian Americans, and others endure them as a part of everyday life (Feagin and McKinney 2003).

In some cases, even apparently neutral institutional standards can turn out to have discriminatory effects. African American students at a midwestern state university protested a policy under which fraternities and sororities that wanted to use campus facilities for a dance were required to post a $150 security deposit to cover possible damage. The Black students complained that this policy had a discriminatory impact on minority student organizations. Campus police countered that the university's policy applied to all student groups interested in using these facilities. However, because almost all White fraternities and sororities at the school had their own houses, which they used for dances, the policy affected only African American and other subordinate groups' organizations.

The 2000 presidential election created headlines because it took weeks to resolve who won—Bush or Gore. Yet for 1.4 million African Americans who were denied the right to vote, this seemed like a national issue that had left them on the sidelines. The prohibition was not because they were Black, which would have been clearly racist and legally discriminatory, but because they were convicted felons. In 11 states, a felony conviction can result in a ban from voting for life, even after a prison sentence is served. Because many of these states are in the South and have large Black populations, the voting prohibition

Despite numerous laws and steep penalties, discrimination
continues in the housing market.

disproportionately covers African American men. Currently, 13 percent of the
nation's Black male population is precluded from voting by such laws. Florida
was the deciding state in the close 2000 elections, and more than 200,000
potential Black voters were excluded. This case of institutional discrimination
may have changed the outcome of a presidential election (Cooper 2004; Sentencing Project 2008).

Institutional discrimination continuously imposes more hindrances on and
awards fewer benefits to certain racial and ethnic groups than it does to others.
This is the underlying and painful context of American intergroup relations.

## Discrimination Today

Discrimination is widespread in the United States. It sometimes results from
prejudices held by individuals. More significantly, it is found in institutional
discrimination and the presence of the informal economy. The presence of an

underclass is symptomatic of many social forces, and total discrimination—past and present discrimination taken together—is one of them.

## Discrimination Hits the Wallet

How much discrimination is there? As in measuring prejudice, problems arise in quantifying discrimination. Measuring prejudice is hampered by the difficulties in assessing attitudes and by the need to take many factors into account. It is further limited by the initial challenge of identifying different treatment. A second difficulty of measuring discrimination is assigning a cost to the discrimination.

Some tentative conclusions about discrimination can be made, however. Figure 3.4 uses income data to show vividly the disparity in income between African Americans and Whites and also between men and women. This encompasses all full-time workers. White men, with a median income of $52,273, earn one-third more than Black men and more than twice what Hispanic women earn in wages.

Yet we see Asian American men are at the top edging out White males by a little less than $200 a year. Why do Asian American men earn so much if race serves as a barrier? The economic picture is not entirely positive. Some Asian American groups such as Laotians and Vietnamese have high levels of

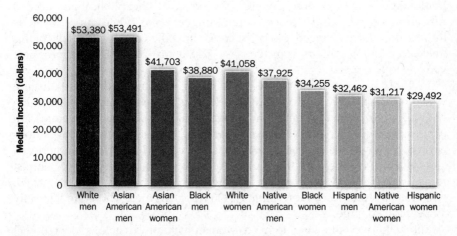

**Figure 3.4** Median Income by Race, Ethnicity, and Gender

Even at the very highest levels of schooling, the income gap remains between Whites and Blacks. Education also has little apparent effect on the income gap between male and female workers. Even a brief analysis reveals striking differences in earning power between White men and other groups in the United States. Furthermore, the greater inequality is apparent for African American and Hispanic women.

Note: Data released in 2011 for income earned in 2010. Median income is from all sources and is limited to year-round, full-time workers at least 25 years old. Data for White men and women are for non-Hispanics.

Source: DeNavas-Walt, Proctor, and Smith 2011:PINC-03. For Native Americans, author's estimate based on American Community Survey 2011: Tables B20017c, B20017H, and B20017I.

poverty. However, a significant number of Asian Americans with advanced educations have high-earning jobs, which brings up the median income. However, as we will see, given their high levels of schooling, their incomes should be even higher.

Clearly, regardless of race or ethnicity, men outpace women in annual income. This disparity between the incomes of Black women and White men has remained unchanged over the more than 50 years during which such data have been tabulated. It illustrates yet another instance of the greater inequality experienced by minority women. Also, Figure 3.4 includes only data for full-time, year-round workers; it excludes homemakers and the unemployed. Even in this comparison, the deprivation of Blacks, Hispanics, and women is confirmed again.

We might be drawn to the fact that Asian American income appears to slightly overtake that of Whites. However, as we will see shortly, this is totally due to Asian Americans collectively having much more formal schooling than Whites as a group and deriving some benefits from that achievement.

Are these differences entirely the result of discrimination in employment? No, individuals within the four groups are not equally prepared to compete for high-paying jobs. Past discrimination is a significant factor in a person's current social position. As discussed previously and illustrated in Figure 3.3, past discrimination continues to take its toll on modern victims. Taxpayers, predominantly White, were unwilling to subsidize the public education of African Americans and Hispanics at the same levels as White pupils. Even as these actions have changed, today's schools show the continuing results of this uneven spending pattern from the past. Education clearly is an appropriate variable to control.

In Table 3.1, median income is compared, holding education constant, which means that we can compare Blacks and Whites and men and women with approximately the same amount of formal schooling. More education means more money, but the disparity remains. The gap between races does narrow somewhat as education increases. However, both African Americans and women lag behind their more affluent counterparts. The contrast remains dramatic: Women with a master's degree typically receive $59,099, which means they earn more than $4,000 less than men who complete only a bachelor's degree.

Thinking over the long term, a woman with a bachelor's degree will work full time three years to earn $142,000. The typical male can work just 28 months, take the 8 months off without pay, and still exceed the woman's earnings. Women, regardless of race, pay at every point. They are often hired at lower starting salaries in jobs comparable to those held by men. Salary increases come slower. And by their 30s, they rarely recover from even short maternity leaves (Dey and Hill 2007; Gittell and McKinney 2007; Jacobs 2008).

Note what happens to Asian American households. Although highly educated Asian Americans earn a lot of money, they trail well behind their White

**Table 3.1 Median Income by Race and Sex, Holding Education Constant**

Even at the very highest levels of schooling, the income gap remains between Whites and Blacks. Education also has little apparent effect on the income gap between male and female workers (income values in dollars).

| | Race | | | | Sex | |
|---|---|---|---|---|---|---|
| | White Families | Black Families | Asian Families | Hispanic Families | Male | Female |
| Total | 70,328 | 40,439 | 77,201 | 41,053 | 50,361 | 38,294 |
| High school | | | | | | |
|   Nongraduate | 28,947 | 22,944 | 35,971 | 29,394 | 29,435 | 20,883 |
|   Graduate | 52,312 | 32,838 | 50,330 | 40,502 | 40,282 | 29,857 |
| College | | | | | | |
|   Associate degree | 72,581 | 47,079 | 75,840 | 57,337 | 50,282 | 37,773 |
|   Bachelor's degree | 95,388 | 71,952 | 94,302 | 69,144 | 63,737 | 47,405 |
|   Master's degree | 110,246 | 91,351 | 113,511 | 95,294 | 80,958 | 59,099 |
|   Professional degree | 140,120 | 124,616 | 130,927 | 147,248 | 115,298 | 76,737 |

Note: Data released in 2011 for income earned in 2010. Figures are median income from all sources except capital gains. Included are public assistance payments, dividends, pensions, unemployment compensation, and so on. Incomes are for all workers 25 years of age and older. High school graduates include those with GEDs. Data for Whites are for White non-Hispanics. "Some college" excludes associate degree holders. Family data above bachelor's degree are derived from median incomes, and data for doctorate-holders' families are author's estimate.

Source: DeNavas-Walt, Proctor, and Smith 2011:FINC-01, PINC-01.

counterparts. With a professional degree holder in the family, the typical Asian American household earns an estimated $130,927, compared to $140,120 in a White household.

This is the picture today, but is it getting better? According to a Census Bureau report released in 2011, the answer is no. During the early years of the twenty-first century, Blacks were more likely to stay poor than Whites and those African Americans in the top rung of income were more likely to fall than their White counterparts among the wealthy. The inequality is dramatic and the trend is not toward it diminishing (Hisnanick and Giefer 2011).

Now that education has been held constant, is the remaining gap caused by discrimination? No, not necessarily. Table 3.1 uses only the amount of schooling, not its quality. Racial minorities are more likely to attend inadequately financed schools. Some efforts have been made to eliminate disparities between school districts in the amount of wealth available to tax for school support, but they have met with little success.

The inequality of educational opportunity may seem less important in explaining sex discrimination. Although women usually are not segregated from men, educational institutions encourage talented women to enter fields that pay less (nursing or elementary education) than other occupations that require similar amounts of training. Even when they do enter the same occupation, the earnings disparity persists. Even controlling for age, a study of census data showed that female physicians and surgeons earned 69 percent of what their male counterparts did (Weinberg 2007).

## Eliminating Discrimination

Two main agents of social change work to reduce discrimination: voluntary associations organized to solve racial and ethnic problems and the federal government, including the courts. The two are closely related: Most efforts initiated by the government were urged by associations or organizations that represent minority groups, following vigorous protests by African Americans against racism. Resistance to social inequality by subordinate groups has been the key to change. Rarely has any government of its own initiative sought to end discrimination based on such criteria as race, ethnicity, and gender.

All racial and ethnic groups of any size are represented by private organizations that are, to some degree, trying to end discrimination. Some groups originated in the first half of the twentieth century, but most have been founded since World War II or have become significant forces in bringing about change only since then. These include church organizations, fraternal social groups, minor political parties, and legal defense funds, as well as more militant organizations operating under the scrutiny of law enforcement agencies. The purposes, membership, successes, and failures of these resistance organizations dedicated to eliminating discrimination are discussed throughout this book.

The judiciary, charged with interpreting laws and the U.S. Constitution, has a much longer history of involvement in the rights of racial, ethnic, and religious minorities. However, its early decisions protected the rights of the dominant group, as in the 1857 U.S. Supreme Court's *Dred Scott* decision, which ruled that slaves remained slaves even when living or traveling in states where slavery was illegal. Not until the 1940s did the Supreme Court revise earlier decisions and begin to grant African Americans the same rights as those held by Whites. The 1954 *Brown v. Board of Education* decision, which stated that "separate but equal" facilities—including education—were unconstitutional, heralded a new series of rulings, arguing that distinguishing between races in order to segregate was inherently unconstitutional.

The most important legislative effort to eradicate discrimination was the Civil Rights Act of 1964. This act led to the establishment of the Equal Employment Opportunity Commission (EEOC), which had the power to investigate complaints against employers and to recommend action to the Department of Justice. If the justice department sued and discrimination was found, then the court could order appropriate compensation. The act covered employment practices of all businesses with more than 25 employees and nearly all employment agencies and labor unions. A 1972 amendment broadened the coverage to employers with as few as 15 employees.

The Civil Rights Act of 1964 prohibited discrimination in public accommodations—that is, hotels, motels, restaurants, gasoline stations, and amusement parks. Publicly owned facilities such as parks, stadiums, and swimming pools were also prohibited from discriminating. Another important provision forbade discrimination in all federally supported programs and institutions such as hospitals, colleges, and road construction projects.

The Civil Rights Act of 1964 was not perfect. Since 1964, several acts and amendments to the original act have been added to cover the many areas of discrimination it left untouched, such as criminal justice and housing. Even in areas singled out for enforcement in the act, discrimination still occurs. Federal agencies charged with enforcement complain that they are underfunded or are denied wholehearted support by the White House. Also, regardless of how much the EEOC may want to act in a particular case, the person who alleges discrimination has to pursue the complaint over a long time that is marked by lengthy periods of inaction. Despite these efforts, devastating forms of discrimination persist. African Americans, Latinos, and others fall victim to **redlining**, or the pattern of discrimination against people trying to buy homes in minority and racially changing neighborhoods.

People living in predominantly minority neighborhoods have found that service deliverers refuse to go to their area. In one case that attracted national attention in 1997, a Pizza Hut in Kansas City refused to deliver 40 pizzas to an honor program at a high school in an all-Black neighborhood. A Pizza Hut spokesperson called the neighborhood unsafe and said that almost every city has "restricted areas" to which the company will not deliver. This admission was particularly embarrassing because the high school already had a $170,000-a-year contract with Pizza Hut to deliver pizzas as a part of its school lunch program. Service redlining covers everything from parcel deliveries to repair people as well as food deliveries. The red pencil appears not to have been set aside in cities throughout the United States (Fuller 1998; Rusk 2001; Schwartz 2001; Turner et al. 2002; Yinger 1995).

Although civil rights laws often have established rights for other minorities, the Supreme Court made them explicit in two 1987 decisions involving groups other than African Americans. In the first of the two cases, an Iraqi American professor asserted that he had been denied tenure because of his Arab origins; in the second, a Jewish congregation brought suit for damages in response to the defacement of its synagogue with derogatory symbols. The Supreme Court ruled unanimously that, in effect, any member of an ethnic minority may sue under federal prohibitions against discrimination. These decisions paved the way for almost all racial and ethnic groups to invoke the Civil Rights Act of 1964 (Taylor 1987).

A particularly insulting form of discrimination seemed finally to be on its way out in the late 1980s. Many social clubs had limitations that forbid membership to minorities, Jews, and women. For years, exclusive clubs argued that they were merely selecting friends, but, in fact, a principal function of these clubs is as a forum to transact business. Denial of membership meant more than the inability to attend a luncheon; it also seemed to exclude certain groups from part of the marketplace. In 1988, the Supreme Court ruled unanimously in *New York State Clubs Association v. City of New York* that states and cities may ban sex discrimination by large private clubs where business lunches and similar activities take place. Although the ruling does not apply to all clubs and leaves the issue of racial and ethnic barriers unresolved, it did chip away at the arbitrary exclusiveness of private groups (Steinhauer 2006; Taylor 1988).

Memberships and restrictive organizations remain perfectly legal. The rise to national attention of professional golfer Tiger Woods, of mixed Native American, African, and Asian ancestry, made the public aware that there were at least 23 golf courses where he would be prohibited from playing by virtue of race. In 2002, women's groups tried unsuccessfully to have the golf champion speak out as the Master's and British Open were played on courses closed to women as members. The issue does go away as an African American joined an Atlanta Freemason lodge only to have the Georgia head call for a Masonic trial that could have resulted in the man's expulsion after other lodges objected to his presence. While the threat of a lawsuit put off the trial, the ill will hardly seems fitting of any social group (Dewan and Brown 2009; Scott 2003; Sherwood 2010).

A setback in anti-discrimination lawsuits came when the Supreme Court told Lilly Ledbetter, in effect, she was "too late." Ledbetter had been a supervisor for many years at the Godsden, Alabama, Goodyear Tire Rubber plant when she realized that she was being paid $6,500 less per year than the lowest-paid male supervisor. The Court ruled that she must sue within 180 days of the initial discriminatory paycheck even though it had taken years before she even knew of the differential payment. Congress later enacted legislation eliminating the 180-day restriction.

Proving discrimination even as outlined for generations in legislation continues to be difficult. In the 2007 *Ledbetter v. Goodyear Tire and Rubber Co.* ruling, the Supreme Court affirmed that victims had to file a formal complaint within 180 days of the alleged discrimination. This set aside thousands of cases where employees learned their initial pay was lower to comparably employed White or male workers only after they had been in a job for years. Given the usual secrecy in workplaces around salaries, it would have made it difficult for potential cases of pay disparity to be effectively advanced. Two years later, Congress enacted the Lilly Ledbetter Fair Pay Act, which gives victims more time to file a lawsuit.

The inability of the Civil Rights Act, similar legislation, and court decisions to end discrimination does not result entirely from poor financial and political support, although it does play a role. The number of federal employees assigned to investigate and prosecute bias cases is insufficient. Many discriminatory practices, such as those described as institutional discrimination, are seldom subject to legal action.

# Wealth Inequality: Discrimination's Legacy

Discrimination that has occurred in the past carries into the present and future. As noted in Figure 3.1, a lack of inherited wealth is one element of the past. African American and other minority groups have had less opportunity to accumulate assets such as homes, land, and savings that can insulate them and later their children from economic setbacks.

**Income** refers to salaries and wages, and **wealth** is a more inclusive term that encompasses all of a person's material assets, including land, stocks, and other types of property. Wealth allows one to live better; even modest assets provide insurance against the effects of job layoffs, natural disasters, and long-term illness, and they afford individuals much better interest rates when they need to borrow money. It allows children to graduate from college relatively debt free or perhaps without any college loans to pay back. This reminds us that for many people it is not a question of wealth in the sense of assets but wealth as measured by indebtedness.

Studies document that the kinds of disparities in income we have seen are even greater when wealth is considered. In 2010, only 6 percent of home-buyers were African Americans and another 6 percent Latino. This is, unfortunately, to be expected, because if individuals experience lower incomes throughout their lives, they are less likely to be able to put anything aside for a down payment. They are more likely to have to pay for today's expenses rather than save for their future or their children's future.

A 2009 study among the affluent shows the wealth gap will continue. For people earning more than $120,000, Whites typically had set aside $223,000 in retirement accounts—Asian Americans $62,000 less, African Americans $69,000 less, and Latinos $73,000 less.

Little wonder then that White children are more likely to surpass parents' income than Black children are. Furthermore, White children are more likely to move up the economic social class ladder than are Black children, who are also more likely to actually fall back in absolute terms. As adults, well-off Black Americans are less likely to have acquired from their parents knowledge about how to invest wisely and are more likely to make "safe" economic decisions for the future of themselves and their children.

A close analysis of wealth shows that typically African American families have $95,000 less in wealth than their White counterparts, even when comparing members of comparably educated and employed households. The median wealth of White households is 20 times that of Black households and 18 times that of Latino households.

Evidence indicates that this inequality in wealth has been growing with the wealth gap between White and African American families having more than quadrupled over the course of a generation (Ariel/Hewitt 2009; Bowman 2011; Economic Mobility Project 2007; Kochhar, Fry, and Taylor 2011; Lautz 2011; Oliver and Shapiro 2006; Shapiro 2004, 2010; Shapiro, Meschede, and Sullivan 2010).

## Environmental Justice

Discrimination takes many forms and is not necessarily apparent, even when its impact can be far reaching. Take the example of Kennedy Heights, a well-kept working-class neighborhood nestled in southeastern Houston. This community faces a real threat, and it is not from crime or drugs. The threat that community residents fear is right under their feet in the form of three oil pits abandoned by Gulf Oil in 1927. The residents, mostly African American, argue that they have suffered high rates of cancer, lupus, and other illnesses because the chemicals from the oil fields poison their water supply. The residents first sued Chevron USA in 1985, and the case is still making its way through the courtrooms of no fewer than six states and the federal judiciary.

Lawyers and other representatives for the residents say that the oil company is guilty of environmental racism because it knowingly allowed a predominantly Black housing development to be built on the contaminated land. They are able to support this charge with documents, including a 1954 memorandum from an appraiser who suggested that the oil pits be drained of any toxic substances and the land filled for "low-cost houses for White occupancy." When the land did not sell right away, an oil company official in a 1967 memorandum suggested a tax-free land exchange with a developer who intended to use the land for "Negro residents and commercial development." For this latter intended use by African Americans, there was no mention of any required environmental cleanup of the land. The oil company counters that it just assumed the developer would do the necessary cleanup of the pits (Maning 1997; Sze and London 2008).

The conflict perspective sees the case of the Houston suburb as one in which pollution harms minority groups disproportionately. **Environmental justice** refers to the efforts to ensure that hazardous substances are controlled so that all communities receive protection regardless of race or socioeconomic circumstance. After the Environmental Protection Agency and other organizations documented discrimination in the location of hazardous waste sites, an executive order was issued in 1994 that requires all federal agencies to ensure that low-income and minority communities have access to better information about their environment and have an opportunity to participate in shaping government policies that affect their communities' health. Initial efforts to implement the policy have met widespread opposition, including criticism from some proponents of economic development who argue that the guidelines unnecessarily delay or altogether block locating new industrial sites.

Low-income communities and areas with significant minority populations are more likely to be adjacent to waste sites than are affluent White communities. Studies in California show the higher probability that people of color live closer to sources of air pollution. Another study concluded that grade schools in Florida nearer to environmental hazards are disproportionately Black or Latino. People of color jeopardized by environmental problems also lack the resources and political muscle to do something about it (Pastor, Morello-Frosch, and Saad 2005; Pellow and Brulle 2007; Stretesky and Lynch 2002).

Issues of environmental justice are not limited to metropolitan areas. Another continuing problem is abuse of Native American reservation land. Many American Indian leaders are concerned that tribal lands are too often regarded as dumping grounds for toxic waste that go to the highest bidder. On the other hand, the economic devastation faced by some tribes in isolated areas has led one tribe in Utah to actually seek out becoming a depot for discarded nuclear waste (Jefferies 2007).

As with other aspects of discrimination, experts disagree. There is controversy within the scientific community over the potential hazards of some of the problems, and there is even some opposition within the subordinate communities being affected. This complexity of the issues in terms of social class and race is apparent, as some observers question the wisdom of an executive order that slows economic development coming to areas in dire need of employment

So desperate are the economic conditions of isolated Indian tribes that they often seek out questionable forms of economic development. The Skull Valley Goshute Indian Reservation in Utah is trying to attract a nuclear waste dump, and local and state officials are trying to block this possibility.

opportunities. On the other hand, some observers counter that such businesses typically employ few less-skilled workers and only make the environment less livable for those left behind. Despite such varying viewpoints, environmental justice is an excellent example of resistance and change in the 1990s that could not have been foreseen by the civil rights workers of the 1950s.

## Affirmative Action

Affirmative action is the positive effort to recruit subordinate-group members, including women, for jobs, promotions, and educational opportunities. The phrase *affirmative action* first appeared in an executive order issued by President John F. Kennedy in 1961. The order called for contractors to "take affirmative action to ensure that applicants are employed, and that employees are treated during employment, without regard to their race, creed, color, or national origin." However, at that time, no enforcement procedures were specified. Six years later, the order was amended to prohibit discrimination on the basis of sex, but affirmative action was still defined vaguely.

Today, affirmative action has become a catchall term for racial preference programs and goals. It has also become a lightning rod for opposition to any programs that suggest special consideration of women or racial minorities.

### Affirmative Action Explained

Affirmative action has been viewed as an important tool for reducing institutional discrimination. Whereas previous efforts were aimed at eliminating individual acts of discrimination, federal measures under the heading of affirmative action have been aimed at procedures that deny equal opportunities, even if they are not intended to be overtly discriminatory. This policy has been implemented to deal with both current discrimination and past discrimination, outlined earlier in this chapter.

Affirmative action has been aimed at institutional discrimination in such areas as the following:

- Height and weight requirements that are unnecessarily geared to the physical proportions of White men without regard to the actual characteristics needed to perform the job and that therefore exclude women and some minorities.
- Seniority rules, when applied to jobs historically held only by White men, that make more recently hired minorities and females more subject to layoff—the "last hired, first fired" employee—and less eligible for advancement.
- Nepotism-based membership policies of some unions that exclude those who are not relatives of members who, because of past employment practices, are usually White.

- Restrictive employment leave policies, coupled with prohibitions on part-time work or denials of fringe benefits to part-time workers, that make it difficult for the heads of single-parent families, most of whom are women, to get and keep jobs and also meet the needs of their families.
- Rules requiring that only English be spoken at the workplace, even when not a business necessity, which result in discriminatory employment practices toward people whose primary language is not English.
- Standardized academic tests or criteria geared to the cultural and educational norms of middle-class or White men when these are not relevant predictors of successful job performance.
- Preferences shown by law and medical schools in admitting children of wealthy and influential alumni, nearly all of whom are White.
- Credit policies of banks and lending institutions that prevent the granting of mortgages and loans in minority neighborhoods or that prevent the granting of credit to married women and others who have previously been denied the opportunity to build good credit histories in their own names.

Employers have also been cautioned against asking leading questions in interviews such as "Did you know you would be the first Black to supervise all Whites in that factory?" or "Does your husband mind your working on weekends?" Furthermore, the lack of minority-group or female employees may in itself represent evidence for a case of unlawful exclusion (Commission on Civil Rights 1981; see also Bohmer and Oka 2007).

## The Legal Debate

How far can an employer go in encouraging women and minorities to apply for a job before it becomes unlawful discrimination against White men? Since the late 1970s, a number of bitterly debated cases on this difficult aspect of affirmative action have reached the U.S. Supreme Court. The most significant cases are summarized in Table 3.2.

In the 1978 *Bakke* case (*Regents of the University of California v. Bakke*), by a narrow 5–4 vote, the Court ordered the medical school of the University of California at Davis to admit Allan Bakke, a qualified White engineer who had originally been denied admission solely on the basis of his race. The justices ruled that the school had violated Bakke's constitutional rights by establishing a fixed quota system for minority students. However, the Court added that it was constitutional for universities to adopt flexible admission programs that use race as one factor in making decisions.

Colleges and universities responded with new policies designed to meet the *Bakke* ruling while broadening opportunities for traditionally underrepresented minority students. However, in 1996, the Supreme Court allowed a lower court decision to stand: that affirmative action programs for African

## Table 3.2 Key Decisions on Affirmative Action

In a series of split and often very close decisions, the Supreme Court has expressed a variety of reservations in specific situations.

| Year | Favorable (+) or Unfavorable (–) to Policy | Case | Vote | Ruling |
|---|---|---|---|---|
| 1971 | + | *Griggs v. Duke Power Co.* | 9–0 | Private employers must provide a remedy where minorities were denied opportunities, even if unintentional. |
| 1978 | – | *Regents of the University of California v. Bakke* | 5–4 | Prohibited holding specific number of places for minorities in college admissions. |
| 1979 | + | *United Steelworkers of America v. Weber* | 5–2 | Okay for union to favor minorities in special training programs. |
| 1984 | – | *Firefighters Local Union No. 1784 (Memphis, TN) v. Stotts* | 6–1 | Seniority means recently hired minorities may be laid off first in staff reductions. |
| 1986 | + | *International Association of Firefighters v. City of Cleveland* | 6–3 | May promote minorities over more-senior Whites. |
| 1986 | + | *New York City v. Sheet Metal* | 5–4 | Approved specific quota of minority workers for union. |
| 1987 | + | *United States v. Paradise* | 5–4 | Endorsed quotas for promotions of state troopers. |
| 1987 | + | *Johnson v. Transportation Agency, Santa Clara, CA* | 6–3 | Approved preference in hiring for minorities and women over better-qualified men and Whites. |
| 1989 | – | *Richmond v. Croson Company* | 6–3 | Ruled a 30 percent set-aside program for minority contractors unconstitutional. |
| 1989 | – | *Martin v. Wilks* | 5–4 | Ruled Whites may bring reverse discrimination claims against Court-approved affirmative action plans. |

**Table 3.2** *continued*

| Year | Favorable (+) or Unfavorable (−) to Policy | Case | Vote | Ruling |
|------|------|------|------|--------|
| 1990 | + | *Metro Broadcasting v. FCC* | 5–4 | Supported federal programs aimed at increasing minority ownership of broadcast licenses. |
| 1995 | − | *Adarand Constructors Inc. v. Peña* | 5–4 | Benefits based on race are constitutional only if narrowly defined to accomplish a compelling interest. |
| 1996 | − | *Texas v. Hopwood* | * | Let stand a lower court decision covering Louisiana, Mississippi, and Texas that race could not be used in college admissions. |
| 2003 | + | *Grutter v. Bollinger* | 5–4 | Race can be a limited factor in admissions at the University of Michigan Law School. |
| 2003 | − | *Gratz v. Bollinger* | 6–3 | Cannot use a strict formula awarding advantage based on race for admissions to the University of Michigan. |
| 2009 | − | *Ricci v. DeStefano* | 5–4 | May not disregard a promotion test because Blacks failed to qualify for advancement. |

*U.S. Court of Appeals Fifth Circuit decision.

American and Mexican American students at the University of Texas law school were unconstitutional. The ruling effectively prohibited schools in the lower court's jurisdiction of Louisiana, Mississippi, and Texas from taking race into account in admissions. In 2003, the Supreme Court made two rulings concerning the admissions policies at the University of Michigan. In one case involving the law school, the Court upheld the right of the school to use applicants' race as criteria for admission decisions but ruled against a strict admissions formula awarding points to minority applicants who applied to the university's undergraduate school. Given the various legal actions, further challenges to affirmative action can be expected (Colburn et al. 2008).

Has affirmative action actually helped alleviate employment inequality on the basis of race and gender? This is a difficult question to answer, given the complexity of the labor market and the fact that there are other anti-discrimination measures, but it does appear that affirmative action has had a significant impact in the sectors where it has been applied. Sociologist Barbara Reskin (1998) reviewed available studies looking at workforce composition in terms of race and gender in light of affirmative action policies. She found that gains in minority employment can be attributed to affirmative action policies. This includes both firms mandated to follow affirmative action guidelines and those that took them on voluntarily. There is also evidence that some earnings gains can be attributed to affirmative action. Economists M. V. Lee Badgett and Heidi Hartmann (1995), reviewing 26 other research studies, came to similar conclusions: affirmative action and other federal compliance programs have had a modest impact, but it is difficult to assess, given larger economic changes such as recessions or the rapid increase in women in the paid labor force.

Scholars of labor force patterns still make a case for affirmative action even if few, if any, political leaders are likely to publicly endorse the policy. Harvard law professor Randall Kennedy makes the case for there still being an aggressive program of affirmative action.

## LISTEN TO OUR VOICES

### The Enduring Relevance of Affirmative Action
#### By Randall Kennedy

*Randall Kennedy*

One of the most notable accomplishments of liberalism over the past 20 years is something that didn't happen: the demise of affirmative action. Contrary to all predictions, affirmative action has survived. This is a triumph not only for race relations but also for the liberal vision of an inclusive society with full opportunity for all. . . .

Conservatives charged that affirmative action amounts to "reverse racism"; discriminates against "innocent whites"; stigmatizes its putative beneficiaries; erodes the incentives that prompt individuals to put forth their best efforts; lowers standards; produces inefficiencies; goes to those racial minorities who need it least; and generates racial resentments. This indictment and the backlash it rationalized resonated not only with Republicans but also with Democrats, some of whom [sic] shared the conservatives' philosophical objections to the policy, while others worried that supporting it meant electoral suicide.

Writing . . . in 1990, sociologist William Julius Wilson asserted that "the movement for racial equality needs a new political strategy . . . that appeals to a broader coalition." Eschewing affirmative action (though he has subsequently changed his mind), Wilson championed redistributive reforms through "race-neutral policies," contending that they could help the Democratic Party regain lost political support while simultaneously benefiting those further down within minority groups. . . .

One key Democrat attracted to this critique is Barack Obama. Writing in *The Audacity of Hope*, he did not expressly condemn affirmative action, but he did consign it to a category of exhausted programs that "dissect[s] Americans into 'us' and 'them' " and that "can't serve as the basis for the kinds of sustained, broad-based political coalitions needed to transform America." As president, Obama has repeatedly eschewed race targeting (with respect most notably to employment policy) in favor of "universal" reforms that allegedly lift all boats.

Over the years, affirmative action has been truncated by judicial rulings and banned by voters in some states. In one guise or another, however, special efforts to assist marginalized racial minorities remain a major force in many schools and firms, foundations, and governments. Affirmative action survived principally because many rightly believe what President Bill Clinton declared on July 19, 1995, in what is (thus far) the only presidential address wholly devoted to the subject: "Affirmative action has been good for America." Clinton argued that ongoing injuries of past racial wrongs require redress; that affirmative action can usefully serve to prevent new invidious discrimination that is difficult, if not impossible, to reach through litigation; that the adverse consequences of affirmative action on whites are often grossly exaggerated and can easily be minimized; and that better learning and decision making arise in environments that are racially diverse.

The amorphous and malleable idea of "diversity" provided much needed buoyancy to affirmative action, especially in the 2003 University of Michigan affirmative-action cases when 65 major companies, including American Express, Coca Cola, and Microsoft, asserted that maintaining racial diversity in institutions of higher education is vital to their efforts to hire and maintain a diverse workforce. A group of former high-ranking officers and civilian leaders of the military concurred, declaring that "a highly qualified, racially diverse officer corps . . . is essential to the military's ability to fulfil its principal mission to provide national security." Even Theodore Olson, the Bush administration's solicitor general, took pains to defer to "diversity" in a brief on the case. . . .

Liberals have been key supporters of the modern struggle for racial equality. Affirmative action is both a major strategy and central accomplishment of that struggle. Its status is paradoxical. The election of the first African American president represents a coming of age of the "affirmative-action babies," but the right has so successfully vilified the policy that Obama is embarrassed by it. He has yet to say forthrightly what Bill Clinton aptly declared: Affirmative action is good for America.

This observation is not necessarily a criticism of Obama. The president should be pragmatic. If quietude about affirmative action serves its purposes or is essential to him retaining office, then by all means he should remain quiet. Fortunately, though, Obama's acts and omissions, justifiable or not, will not prove decisive. The true measure of affirmative action's staying power is that its absence now is virtually inconceivable.

*Source*: Kennedy 2010:31–33.

During her confirmation hearings in 2009 to become a Justice of the U.S. Supreme Court, Sonia Sotomayor, born in New York City of Puerto Rican parents, did not hide the fact that she benefited from scholarship programs. She eventually graduated *summa cum laude* from Princeton at a time when the university had not a single full-time Latino professor or any classes on Latin America.

Sonia Sotomayor, who joined the Supreme Court in 2009, is only the third woman and the first Latino to ever serve on the high court. She created quite a stir with her past self-descriptions as "an affirmative action baby." While she acknowledged that her Puerto Rican heritage played a role in college admissions, she did eventually graduate *summa cum laude* from Princeton University and was a top student at Yale Law School (Gomez 2010).

## Reverse Discrimination

Although researchers debated the merit of affirmative action, the public—particularly Whites but also some affluent African Americans and Hispanics—questioned the wisdom of the program. Particularly strident were the charges of reverse discrimination: that government actions cause better-qualified White men to be bypassed in favor of women and minority men. **Reverse discrimination** is an emotional term, because it conjures up the notion that somehow women and minorities will subject White men in the United States to the same treatment received by minorities during the last three centuries. Such cases are not unknown, but they are uncommon—fewer than ten of the race-related

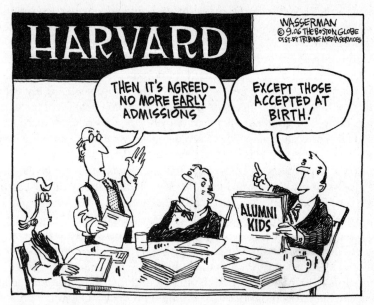

Affirmative action is criticized for giving preferential treatment, but colleges have a long history of giving admissions preferences to relatives of past graduates who are much more likely to be White rather than Black or Latino.

complaints to the federal government were filed by Whites, and only 18 percent of gender-related complaints and 4 percent of the court cases were filed by men.

Increasingly, critics of affirmative action call for color-blind policies that would end affirmative action and, they argue, allow all people to be judged fairly. However, will that mean an end to the institutional practices that favored Whites? For example, according to the latest data, 40 percent of applicants who are children of Harvard's alumni, who are almost all White, are admitted to the university, compared to 11 percent of nonalumni children.

By contrast, at the competitive California Institute of Technology, which specifically does not use legacy preferences, only 1.5 percent of students are children of alumni. Ironically, studies show that these children of alumni typically are far more likely than either minority students or athletes to run into academic trouble (Kahlenberg 2010; Massey and Mooney 2007; Pincus 2003, 2008).

Is it possible to have color-blind policies prevail in the United States in the twenty-first century? Supporters of affirmative action contend that as long as businesses rely on informal social networks, personal recommendations, and family ties, White men will have a distinct advantage built on generations of being in positions of power. Furthermore, an end to affirmative action should also mean an end to the many programs that give advantages to certain businesses, homeowners, veterans, farmers, and others. Most of these preference holders are White.

Consequently, by the 1990s and into the twenty-first century, affirmative action had emerged as an increasingly important issue in state and national political campaigns. As noted earlier, in 2003, the Supreme Court reviewed the admission policies at the University of Michigan, which may favor racial minorities (see Table 3.2). In 2006, Michigan citizens, by a 58 percent margin, voted to restrict all their state universities from using affirmative action in their admissions policies. Generally, discussions have focused on the use of quotas in hiring practices. Supporters of affirmative action argue that hiring goals establish "floors" for minority inclusion but do not exclude truly qualified candidates from any group. Opponents insist that these "targets" are, in fact, quotas that lead to reverse discrimination (Lewin 2006; Mack 1996).

The State of California, in particular, was a battleground for this controversial issue. The California Civil Rights Initiative (Proposition 209) was placed on the ballot in 1996 as a referendum to amend the state constitution and prohibit any programs that give preference to women and minorities for college admission, employment, promotion, or government contracts. Overall, 54 percent of the voters backed the state proposition.

In 2009, the Supreme Court ruled 5–4 in the *Ricci v. DeStefano* case in favor of White firefighters that many observers saw as recognizing reverse racism. Back in 2003, in New Haven, Connecticut, firefighters took an examination to identify possible promotions but no African Americans taking the test qualified to be eligible for advancement. Rather than select all White (including one Hispanic) firefighters, the city threw out the results. The qualifying firefighters sued that they were victims of discrimination and the Court eventually concurred. The decision was limited in its applications since the justices seem to say that possible test bias could be considered in the design stage of a test, but others saw it as "impending" the use of race in hiring even advantaged minorities.

## The Glass Ceiling

We have been talking primarily about racial and ethnic groups as if they have uniformly failed to keep pace with Whites. Although this notion is accurate, there are tens of thousands of people of color who have matched and even exceeded Whites in terms of income. For example, in 2009, more than 1.3 million Black households and over 1.5 million Hispanic households earned more than $100,000. What can we say about financially better-off members of subordinate groups in the United States (DeNavas-Walt, Proctor, and Smith 2010:Table HINC-01)?

Prejudice does not necessarily end with wealth. Black newspaper columnist De Wayne Wickham (1993) wrote of the subtle racism he had experienced. He heard a White clerk in a supermarket ask a White customer whether she knew the price of an item the computer would not scan; when the problem occurred while the clerk was ringing up Wickham's groceries, she called for a price check. Affluent subordinate-group members routinely report being blocked as they move toward the first-class section aboard airplanes or seek service in upscale stores. Another journalist, Ellis Cose (1993), has called these insults the soul-destroying slights to affluent minorities that lead to the "rage of a privileged class."

Discrimination persists for even educated and qualified people from the best family backgrounds. As subordinate-group members are able to compete successfully, they sometimes encounter attitudinal or organizational bias that prevents them from reaching their full potential. They have confronted what has come to be called the **glass ceiling**. This refers to the barrier that blocks the promotion of a qualified worker because of gender or minority membership (Figure 3.5). Often, people entering nontraditional areas of employment become

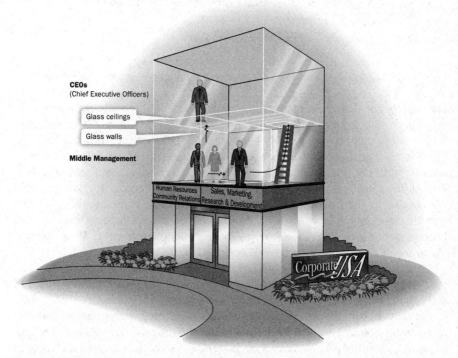

**Figure 3.5** Glass Ceilings and Glass Walls
Women and minority men are moving up in corporations but encounter glass ceilings that block entry to top positions. In addition, they face glass walls that block lateral moves to areas from which executives are promoted. These barriers contribute to women and minority men not moving into the ultimate decision-making positions in the nation's corporate giants.

marginalized and are made to feel uncomfortable, much like the situation of immigrants who feel a part of two cultures, as we discussed in Chapter 1.

The reasons for glass ceilings are as many as the occurrences. It may be that one Black or one woman vice president is regarded as enough, so the second potential candidate faces a block to movement up through management. Decision makers may be concerned that their clientele will not trust them if they have too many people of color or may worry that a talented woman could become overwhelmed with her duties as a mother and wife and thus perform poorly in the workplace.

Concern about women and minorities climbing a broken ladder led to the formation in 1991 of the Glass Ceiling Commission, with the U.S. secretary of labor chairing the 21-member group. Initially, it regarded the following as some of the glass ceiling barriers:

- Lack of management commitment to establishing systems, policies, and practices for achieving workplace diversity and upward mobility
- Pay inequities for work of equal or comparable value
- Sex-, race-, and ethnicity-based stereotyping and harassment
- Unfair recruitment practices
- Lack of family-friendly workplace policies
- "Parent-track" policies that discourage parental leave policies
- Limited opportunities for advancement to decision-making positions

This significant derrepresentation of women and minority males in managerial positions results in large part from the presence of glass ceilings. Sociologist Max Weber wrote more than a century ago that the privileged class monopolizes the purchase of high-priced consumer goods and wields the power to grant or withhold opportunity from others. To grasp just how White and male the membership of this elite group is, consider the following: 71 percent of the 1,219 people who serve on the boards of directors of *Fortune* 100 corporations are White non-Hispanic males. For every 82 White men on these boards, there are two Latinos, two Asian Americans, three African Americans, and 11 White women (Alliance for Board Diversity 2009; Weber [1913–1922] 1947).

Glass ceilings are not the only barrier. There are also glass walls. Catalyst, a nonprofit research organization, conducted interviews in 1992 and again in 2001 with senior and middle managers from larger corporations. The study found that even before glass ceilings are encountered, women and racial and ethnic minorities face **glass walls** that keep them from moving laterally. Specifically, the study found that women tend to be placed in staff or support positions in areas such as public relations and human resources and are often directed away from jobs in core areas such as marketing, production, and sales. Women are assigned to and, therefore, trapped in jobs that reflect their stereotypical helping nature and encounter glass walls that cut off access to jobs that might lead to broader experience and advancement (Bjerk 2008; Catalyst 2001; Lopez 1992).

Researchers have documented a differential impact than the glass ceiling has on White males. It appears that men who enter traditionally female occupations are more likely to rise to the top. Male elementary teachers become principals, and male nurses become supervisors. The **glass escalator** refers to the male advantage experienced in occupations dominated by women. Whereas females may become tokens when they enter traditionally male occupations, men are more likely to be advantaged when they move out of sex-typical jobs. In summary, women and minority men confront a glass ceiling that limits upward mobility and glass walls that reduce their ability to move into fast-track jobs leading to the highest reaches of the corporate executive suite. Meanwhile, men who do choose to enter female-dominated occupations are often rewarded with promotions and positions of responsibility coveted by their fellow female workers (Budig 2002; Cognard-Black 2004).

## Conclusion

The job advertisement read "African Americans and Arabians tend to clash with me so that won't work out." Sounds like it was from your grandfather's era? Actually, it appeared on the popular Craigslist Web site in 2006 and is just one example of how explicit discrimination thrives even in the digital age. Similar charges have been made concerning "no minorities" wording in housing advertisements. Courts have not held Craigslist responsible and accepted the Web site's argument that it cannot screen out all racism in online advertising (Hughlett 2006; U.S. Court of Appeals 2008).

Discrimination takes its toll, whether or not a person who is discriminated against is part of the informal economy or looking for a job on the Internet. Even members of minority groups who are not today being overtly discriminated against continue to fall victim to past discrimination. We have also identified the costs of discrimination to members of the privileged group.

From the conflict perspective, it is not surprising to find the widespread presence of the informal economy proposed by the dual labor market model and even

an underclass. Derrick Bell (1994), an African American law professor, has made the sobering assertion that "racism is permanent." He contends that the attitudes of dominant Whites prevail, and society is willing to advance programs on behalf of subordinate groups only when they coincide with needs as perceived by those Whites.

The surveys presented in Chapter 2 show gradual acceptance of the earliest efforts to eliminate discrimination, but that support is failing as color-blind racism takes hold, especially as it relates to affirmative action. Indeed, concerns about doing something about alleged reverse discrimination are as likely to be voiced as concerns about racial or gender discrimination or glass ceilings and glass walls.

Institutional discrimination remains a formidable challenge in the United States. Attempts to reduce discrimination by attacking institutional discrimination have met with staunch resistance. Partly as a result of this outcry from some of the public, especially White Americans, the federal government gradually deemphasized its affirmative action efforts, beginning in the 1980s and into the twenty-first century. Most of the material in this chapter has been about racial groups, especially Black and White Americans. It would be easy to see intergroup hostility as a racial phenomenon, but that would be incorrect. Throughout the history of the United States, relations between some White groups have been characterized by resentment and violence. The next two chapters examine the ongoing legacy of immigration and the nature and relations of White ethnic groups.

## Summary

1. Discrimination has a cumulative effect so that people today are victims of past and current differential practices.
2. Hate crimes highlight hostility that culminates in a criminal offense.
3. Institutional discrimination results from the normal operations of a society.
4. Discrimination in hiring is documented through job-testing experiments.
5. Inequality continues to be apparent in the analysis of annual incomes, controlling for the amount of education attained and wealth, and even in the absence of environmental justice.
6. Presidential executive orders, legislative acts, and judicial decisions have all played a part in reducing discrimination.
7. For over 50 years, affirmative action as a remedy to inequality has been a hotly contested issue, with its critics contending it amounts to reverse discrimination.
8. Upwardly mobile professional women and minority males may encounter a glass ceiling and be thwarted in their efforts by glass walls to become more attractive candidates for advancement.

## Key Terms

| | | |
|---|---|---|
| absolute deprivation  83 | glass escalator  111 | redlining  95 |
| affirmative action  100 | glass wall  110 | relative deprivation  82 |
| discrimination  82 | hate crime  86 | reverse discrimination  106 |
| environmental justice  98 | income  97 | total discrimination  83 |
| glass ceiling  109 | institutional discrimination  88 | wealth  97 |

## Review Questions

1. Why might people feel disadvantaged even though their incomes are rising and their housing circumstances have improved?
2. Why does institutional discrimination sometimes seem less objectionable than individual discrimination?

3. In what way may national income data point to discrimination?

4. Why are questions raised about affirmative action even though inequality persists?

5. Distinguish among glass ceilings, glass walls, and glass escalators. How do they differ from more obvious forms of discrimination in employment?

## Critical Thinking

1. Discrimination can take many forms. Select a case of discrimination that you think just about everyone would agree is wrong. Then describe another incident in which the alleged discrimination was of a more subtle form. Who is likely to condemn and who is likely to overlook such situations?

2. Resistance is a continuing theme of intergroup race relations. Discrimination implies the oppression of a group, but how can discrimination also unify the oppressed group to resist such unequal treatment? How can acceptance, or integration, for example, weaken the sense of solidarity within a group?

3. Voluntary associations such as the National Association for the Advancement of Colored People (NAACP) and government units such as the courts have been important vehicles for bringing about a measure of social justice. In what ways can the private sector—corporations and businesses—also work to bring about an end to discrimination?

# 4 Immigration

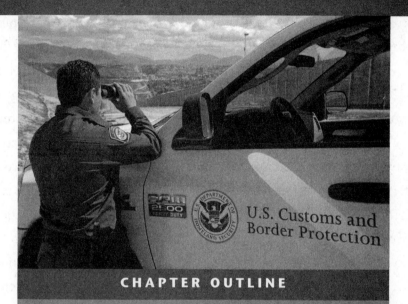

U.S. Customs and Border Protection

## CHAPTER OUTLINE

---

{ HIGHLIGHTS }

---

The diversity of the American people is unmistakable evidence of the variety of places from which immigrants have come. Yet each succeeding generation of immigrants found itself being reluctantly accepted, at best, by the descendants of earlier arrivals. The Chinese were the first immigrant group to be singled out for restriction, with the passage of the 1882 Exclusion Act. The initial Chinese immigrants became scapegoats for America's sagging economy in the last half of the nineteenth century. Growing fears that too many non-American types were immigrating motivated the creation of the national origin system and the quota acts of the 1920s. These acts gave preference to certain nationalities until the passage of the Immigration and Nationality Act in 1965 ended that practice.

Today in the United States many immigrants are transnationals who still maintain close ties to their countries of origin, sending money back, keeping current with political events, and making frequent return trips. Concern about both illegal and legal immigration continues with renewed attention in the aftermath of the September 11, 2001, terrorist attacks. Restrictionist sentiment has grown, and debates rage over whether immigrants, even legal ones, should receive services such as education, government-subsidized healthcare, and welfare. The challenges to an immigrant household upon arrival are not evenly felt, as women play the central role in facilitating the transition. Controversy also continues to surround the policy of the United States toward refugees.

---

The Caribbean immigrant Joseph E. Joseph was just doing what he felt was his civic duty when he registered to vote in Brooklyn back in 1992 when he came across some volunteers signing people up to vote. A legal permanent resident, he worked toward naturalization and it was then that he learned he violated federal law by registering to vote and now faces deportation.

Mohammed Reza Ghaffarpour is willing to adjust and is not against assimilating. The Iranian-born engineering professor aced his citizenship test in 2003 but had to wait until 2008 to gain citizenship. His trips from his Chicago home to Iran for academic meetings and to tend to ailing parents led to scrutiny by the U.S. authorities. The 53-year-old man felt discriminated against but is not bitter; although he waited to become a citizen, he feels the "system is working" (Glascock 2008; Semple 2010).

Lewiston, Maine, a town of 37,000, was dying. A once bustling mill town, jobs and people began leaving in the 1970s. A family of Somali refugees found housing very cheap and after settling there in 2001, shared the good news with immigrant friends and relatives. Initially the greeting was hardly positive as the town's mayor wrote an open letter to the Somali community begging them to stop encouraging their fellow Somalis to come. They kept coming, some 5,000 accompanied by Sudanese, Congolese, and other Africans. The economy has been transformed by the sophisticated trading skills the Somalis brought with them, importing fabric and spices (Sharon 2010).

Faeza Jaber is a 48-year-old single mother in her first months in the United States with her seven-year-old son, Khatab. When she arrived in Phoenix, Arizona, it was 114 degrees, which is hotter than her home in Baghdad. She was granted her refugee status after her husband, who was an office manager and interpreter for *Time* magazine, was murdered in 2004 on his way to work at a time when Iraqi interpreters for foreign companies were being targeted.

Refugee Faeza Jaber and her son, Khatab, pause outside a mall in Phoenix, Arizona, where they relocated after her husband Omar was shot and killed by an unknown assailant in Baghdad in March 2004.

Previously a computer programmer at the Baghdad airport, Jaber has found the transition difficult. She now works as a part-time teacher's assistant at Khatab's elementary school. She is striving to learn English and is encouraged by the knowledge that of the 600 Iraqi refugees who pass annually through Phoenix, 91 percent find a job and are able to support themselves without any state and federal subsidies within five months of arrival (Bennett 2008).

These dramas being played out in Brooklyn, Chicago, Lewiston, and Phoenix among other places, illustrate the themes in immigration today. Immigrant labor is needed, but concerns over illegal immigration persist and, even for those who arrive legally, the transition can be difficult. For the next generation it gets a little easier and, for some, perhaps too easy as they begin to forget their family's heritage. Many come legally, applying for immigrant visas, but others enter illegally. In the United States, we may not like lawbreakers, but we often seek services and low-priced products made by people who come here illegally. How do we control this immigration without violating the principle of free movement within the nation? How do we decide who enters? And how do we treat those who come here either legally or illegally?

The world is now a global network, with the core and periphery countries, described in world systems theory (see page 27 in Chapter 1), linking not only commercial goods but also families and workers across political borders. The social forces that cause people to emigrate are complex. The most important have been economic: financial failure in the old country and expectations of higher incomes and standards of living in the new land. Other factors include dislike of new political regimes in their native lands, the experience of being victims of racial or religious bigotry, and a desire to reunite families. All these factors push people from their homelands and pull them to other nations such as the United States. Immigration into the United States, in particular, has been facilitated by cheap ocean transportation and by other countries' removal of restrictions on emigration.

## Immigration: A Global Phenomenon

Immigration, as we noted in Chapter 1, is a worldwide phenomenon and contributes to globalization as more and more people see the world as their "home" rather than one specific country, as shown in Figure 4.1. Throughout human history, people have moved either out of choice but more often necessity. Today people frequently move to escape violence and poverty in pursuit of better living conditions. Domestic policies are scrutinized as people move across national borders throughout the world. Generally, immigration is from countries with lower standards of living to those that offer better wages. However, wars and famine may precipitate the movement of hundreds of thousands of people into neighboring countries and sometimes permanent resettlement (Goldin, Cameron, and Balarajan 2011).

Scholars of immigration often point to *push* and *pull factors*. For example, economic difficulties, religious or ethnic persecution, and political unrest may push individuals from their homelands. Immigration to a particular nation, the

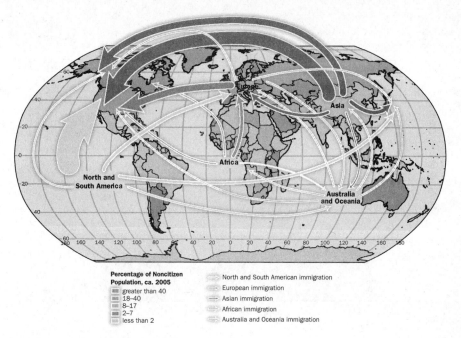

**Percentage of Noncitizen Population, ca. 2005**
- greater than 40
- 18–40
- 8–17
- 2–7
- less than 2

- North and South American immigration
- European immigration
- Asian immigration
- African immigration
- Australia and Oceania immigration

**Figure 4.1**   International Migration
*Source*: Fernandez-Armesto 2007:1006.

pull factors, may be a result of perceptions of a better life ahead or a desire to join a community of their fellow nationals already established abroad.

A potent factor contributing to immigration anywhere in the world is chain immigration. **Chain immigration** refers to an immigrant who sponsors several other immigrants who, on their arrival, may sponsor still more. In time, networks develop to create a self-sustaining flow of immigrants. Laws that favor people who desire to enter a given country who already have relatives there or someone who can vouch for them financially may facilitate this sponsorship. But probably the most important aspect of chain immigration is that immigrants anticipate knowing someone who can help them adjust to their new surroundings and find a new job, place to live, and even the kinds of foods that are familiar to them. Later in this chapter, we revisit the social impact of worldwide immigration (Goldin, Cameron, and Balarajan 2011).

## Patterns of Immigration to the United States

There have been three unmistakable patterns of immigration to the United States: (1) the number of immigrants has fluctuated dramatically over time largely because of government policy changes, (2) settlement has not been uniform

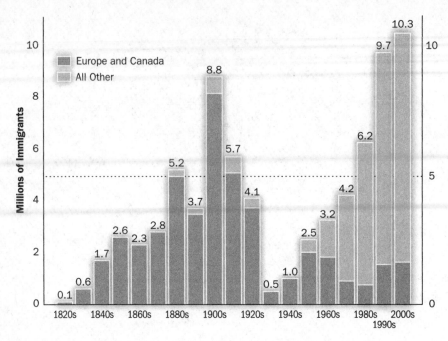

**Figure 4.2** Legal Immigration to the United States, 1820–2010
*Source:* Office of Immigration Statistics 2011.

across the country but centered in certain regions and cities, and (3) the source of immigrants has changed over time. We first look at the historical picture of immigrant numbers.

Vast numbers of immigrants have come to the United States. Figure 4.2 indicates the high but fluctuating number of immigrants who arrived during every decade from the 1820s through the beginning of the twenty-first century. The United States received the largest number of legal immigrants during the first decade of the 1900s, which is likely to be surpassed in the first decade of the twenty-first century, but because the country was much smaller in the period from 1900 through 1910, the numerical impact was even greater then.

The reception given to immigrants in this country has not always been friendly. Open bloodshed, restrictive laws, and the eventual return of almost one-third of immigrants and their children to their home countries attest to some Americans' uneasy feelings toward strangers who want to settle here. Opinion polls in the United States from 1999 through 2011 have never shown more than 18 percent of the public in favor of more immigration, and usually about 43–50 percent want less (Jones 2011).

## Today's Foreign-Born Population

Before considering the sweep of past immigration policies, let us consider today's immigrant population. About 12–13 percent of the nation's people are foreign-born; this proportion is between the high figure of about 15 percent in 1890 and a low of 4.7 percent in 1970. By global comparisons, the foreign-born population in the United States is large but not unusual. Whereas most industrial countries have a foreign population of around 5 percent, Canada's foreign population is 19 percent and Australia's is 25 percent.

As noted earlier, immigrants have not settled evenly across the nation. As shown in the map in Figure 4.3, six states—California, New York, Texas, Florida, New Jersey, and Illinois—account for two-thirds of the nation's total foreign-born population but less than 40 percent of the nation's total population.

Cities in these states are the focus of the foreign-born population. Almost half (43.3 percent) live in the central city of a metropolitan area, compared with about one-quarter (27 percent) of the nation's population. More than one-third of residents in the cities of Miami, Los Angeles, San Francisco, San Jose, and New York City are now foreign-born.

The source of immigrants has changed. The majority of today's 38.5 million foreign-born people are from Latin America rather than Europe, as it was through the 1950s. Primarily, they are from Central America and, more specifically, Mexico. By contrast, Europeans, who dominated the early settlement of the United States, now account for fewer than one in seven of the foreign-born today (Camarota 2007a; Grieco and Trevelyan 2010).

## Early Immigration

European explorers of North America were soon followed by settlers, the first immigrants to the Western Hemisphere. The Spanish founded St. Augustine, Florida, in 1565, and the English founded Jamestown, Virginia, in 1607. Protestants from England emerged from the colonial period as the dominant force numerically, politically, and socially. The English accounted for 60 percent of the 3 million White Americans in 1790. Although exact statistics are lacking for the early years of the United States, the English were soon outnumbered by other nationalities as the numbers of Scotch-Irish and Germans, in particular, swelled. However, the English colonists maintained their dominant position, as Chapter 5 examines.

Throughout American history, immigration policy has been politically controversial. The policies of the English king, George III, were criticized in the U.S. Declaration of Independence for obstructing immigration to the colonies. Toward the end of the nineteenth century, the American republic itself was criticized for enacting immigration restrictions. In the beginning, however,

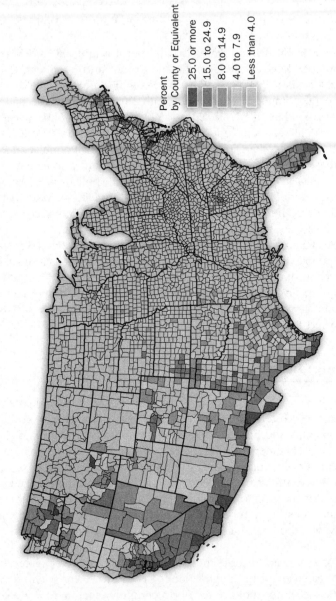

**Figure 4.3** Foreign-Born Population by Counties

*Source:* American Community Survey 2006–2009 at www.census.gov.

Percent
by County or Equivalent

25.0 or more
15.0 to 24.9
8.0 to 14.9
4.0 to 7.9
Less than 4.0

the country encouraged immigration. Legislation initially fixed the residence requirement for naturalization at five years, although briefly, under the Alien Act of 1798, it was 14 years, and so-called dangerous people could be expelled. Despite this brief harshness, immigration was unregulated through most of the 1800s, and naturalization was easily available. Until 1870, naturalization was limited to "free white persons" (Calavita 2007).

Besides holding the mistaken belief that concerns about immigration are something new, we also assume that immigrants to the United States rarely reconsider their decision to come to a new country. Analysis of available records, beginning in the early 1900s, suggests that about 35 percent of all immigrants to the United States eventually emigrated back to their home country. The proportion varies, with the figures for some countries being much higher, but the overall pattern is clear: About one in three immigrants to this nation eventually chooses to return home (Wyman 1993).

The relative absence of federal legislation from 1790 to 1881 does not mean that all new arrivals were welcomed. **Xenophobia** (the fear or hatred of strangers or foreigners) led naturally to **nativism** (beliefs and policies favoring native-born citizens over immigrants). Although the term *nativism* has largely been used to describe nineteenth-century sentiments, anti-immigration views and organized movements have continued into the twenty-first century. Political scientist Samuel P. Huntington (1993, 1996) articulated the continuing immigration as a "clash of civilizations" that could be remedied only by significantly reducing legal immigration, not to mention to close the border to illegal arrivals. His view, which enjoys support, was that the fundamental world conflicts of the new century are cultural in nature rather than ideological or even economic (Citrin, Lerman, Murakami, and Pearson 2007; Schaefer 2008b).

Historically, Roman Catholics in general and the Irish in particular were among the first Europeans to be ill-treated. We look at how organized hostility toward Irish immigrants eventually gave way to their acceptance into the larger society in Chapter 5.

However, the most dramatic outbreak of nativism in the nineteenth century was aimed at the Chinese. If there had been any doubt by the mid-1800s that the United States could harmoniously accommodate all and was some sort of melting pot, debate on the Chinese Exclusion Act would negatively settle the question once and for all.

## The Anti-Chinese Movement

Before 1851, official records show that only 46 Chinese had immigrated to the United States. Over the next 30 years, more than 200,000 came to this country, lured by the discovery of gold and the opening of job opportunities in the West. Overcrowding, drought, and warfare in China also encouraged them to take a chance in the United States. Another important factor was improved oceanic transportation; it was actually cheaper to travel from Hong Kong to

Chinese workers, such as these pictured in 1844, played a major role in building railroads in the West.

San Francisco than from Chicago to San Francisco. The frontier communities of the West, particularly in California, looked on the Chinese as a valuable resource to fill manual jobs. As early as 1854, so many Chinese wanted to emigrate that ships had difficulty handling the volume.

In the 1860s, railroad work provided the greatest demand for Chinese labor until the Union Pacific and Central Pacific railroads were joined at Promontory Summit, Utah, in 1869. The Union Pacific relied primarily on Irish laborers, but 90 percent of the Central Pacific's labor force was Chinese because Whites generally refused to do the back-breaking work over the Western terrain. Despite the contribution of the Chinese, White workers physically prevented them from attending the driving of the golden spike to mark the joining of the two railroads.

With the dangerous railroad work largely completed, people began to rethink the wisdom of encouraging Chinese to immigrate to do the work no one else would do. Reflecting their xenophobia, White settlers found the Chinese immigrants and their customs and religion difficult to understand. Indeed, few people actually tried to understand these immigrants from Asia. Although they had had no firsthand contact with Chinese Americans, Easterners and legislators were soon on the anti-Chinese bandwagon as they read sensationalized accounts of the lifestyle of the new arrivals.

Even before the Chinese immigrated, stereotypes of them and their customs were prevalent. American traders returning from China, European diplomats, and Protestant missionaries consistently emphasized the exotic and sinister aspects of life in China. **Sinophobes,** people with a fear of anything associated with China, appealed to the racist theory developed during the slavery controversy that non-Europeans were subhuman. Similarly, Americans were beginning to be more conscious of biological inheritance and disease, so it was not hard to conjure up fears of alien genes and germs. The only real challenge the anti-Chinese movement had was to convince people that the negative consequences of unrestricted Chinese immigration outweighed any possible economic gain. Perhaps briefly, racial prejudice had earlier been subordinated to industrial dependence on Chinese labor for the work that Whites shunned, but acceptance of the Chinese was short-lived. The fear of the "yellow peril" overwhelmed any desire to know more about Asian peoples and their customs (Takaki 1989).

Employers were glad to pay the Chinese low wages, but laborers came to direct their resentment against the Chinese rather than against their compatriots' willingness to exploit the Chinese. Only a generation earlier, the same concerns had been felt about the Irish, but with the Chinese, the hostility reached new heights because of another factor.

Although many arguments were voiced, racial fears motivated the anti-Chinese movement. Race was the critical issue. The labor market fears were largely unfounded, and most advocates of restrictions at that time knew that. There was no possibility that the Chinese would immigrate in numbers that would match those of Europeans at that time, so it is difficult to find any explanation other than racism for their fears (Winant 1994).

From the sociological perspective of conflict theory, we can explain how the Chinese immigrants were welcomed only when their labor was necessary to fuel growth in the United States. When that labor was no longer necessary, the welcome mat for the immigrants was withdrawn. Furthermore, as conflict theorists would point out, restrictions were not applied evenly: Americans focused on a specific nationality (the Chinese) to reduce the overall number of foreign workers in the nation. Because decision making at that time rested in the hands of the descendants of European immigrants, the steps to be taken were most likely to be directed against the least powerful: immigrants from China who, unlike Europeans seeking entry, had few allies among legislators and other policymakers.

In 1882, Congress enacted the Chinese Exclusion Act, which outlawed Chinese immigration for ten years. It also explicitly denied naturalization rights to the Chinese in the United States; that is, they were not allowed to become citizens. There was little debate in Congress, and discussion concentrated on how suspension of Chinese immigration could best be handled. No allowance was made for spouses and children to be reunited with their husbands and fathers in the United States. Only brief visits of Chinese government officials, teachers, tourists, and merchants were exempted.

The rest of the nineteenth century saw the remaining loopholes allowing Chinese immigration closed. Beginning in 1884, Chinese laborers were not allowed to enter the United States from any foreign place, a ban that also lasted ten years. Two years later, the Statue of Liberty was dedicated, with a poem by Emma Lazarus inscribed on its base. To the Chinese, the poem welcoming the tired, the poor, and the huddled masses must have seemed a hollow mockery.

In 1892, Congress extended the Exclusion Act for another ten years and added that Chinese laborers had to obtain certificates of residence within a year or face deportation. After the turn of the century, the Exclusion Act was extended again. Two decades later, the Chinese were not alone; the list of people restricted by immigration policy had expanded many times.

## Restrictionist Sentiment Increases

As Congress closed the door to Chinese immigration, the debate on restricting immigration turned in new directions. Prodded by growing anti-Japanese feelings, the United States entered into the so-called gentlemen's agreement, which was completed in 1908. Japan agreed to halt further immigration to the United States, and the United States agreed to end discrimination against the Japanese who had already arrived. The immigration ended, but anti-Japanese feelings continued. Americans were growing uneasy that the "new immigrants" would overwhelm the culture established by the "old immigrants." The earlier immigrants, if not Anglo-Saxon, were from similar groups such as

**Ellis Island**
Although it was not opened until 1892, New York harbor's Ellis Island—the country's first federal immigration facility—quickly became the symbol of all the migrant streams to the United States. By the time it was closed in late 1954, it had processed 17 million immigrants. Today their descendants number over 100 million Americans. A major renovation project was launched in 1984 to restore Ellis Island as a national monument and a tourist destination.

the Scandinavians, the Swiss, and the French Huguenots. These people were more experienced in democratic political practices and had a greater affinity with the dominant Anglo-Saxon culture. By the end of the nineteenth century, however, more and more immigrants were neither English speaking nor Protestant and came from dramatically different cultures.

## The National Origin System

Beginning in 1921, a series of measures was enacted that marked a new era in American immigration policy. Whatever the legal language, the measures were drawn up to block the growing immigration from southern Europe (from Italy and Greece, for example) and also were drawn to block all Asian immigrants by establishing a zero quota for them.

To understand the effect of the national origin system on immigration, it is necessary to clarify the quota system. The quotas were deliberately weighted in favor of immigration from northern Europe. Because of the ethnic composition of the country in 1920, the quotas placed severe restrictions on immigration from the rest of Europe and other parts of the world. Immigration from the Western Hemisphere (i.e., Canada, Mexico, Central and South America, and the Caribbean) continued unrestricted. The quota for each nation was set at 3 percent of the number of people descended from each nationality recorded in the 1920 census. Once the statistical manipulations were completed, almost 70 percent of the quota for the Eastern Hemisphere went to just three countries: Great Britain, Ireland, and Germany.

The absurdities of the system soon became obvious, but it was nevertheless continued. British immigration had fallen sharply, so most of its quota of 65,000 went unfilled. However, the openings could not be transferred, even though countries such as Italy, with a quota of only 6,000, had 200,000 people who wanted to enter. However one rationalizes the purpose behind the act, the result was obvious: Any English person, regardless of skill and whether related to anyone already here, could enter the country more easily than, say, a Greek doctor whose children were American citizens. The quota for Greece was 305, with the backlog of people wanting to come reaching 100,000.

By the end of the 1920s, annual immigration had dropped to one-fourth of its pre–World War I level. The worldwide economic depression of the 1930s decreased immigration still further. A brief upsurge in immigration just before World War II reflected the flight of Europeans from the oppression of expanding Nazi Germany. The war virtually ended transatlantic immigration. The era of the great European migration to the United States had been legislated out of existence.

## The 1965 Immigration and Nationality Act

The national origin system was abandoned with the passage of the 1965 Immigration and Nationality Act, signed into law by President Lyndon B. Johnson at the foot of the Statue of Liberty. The primary goals of the act were to reunite families and to protect the American labor market. The act also initiated restrictions on immigration from Latin America. After the act, immigration increased by one-third, but the act's influence was primarily on the composition rather than the size of immigration. The sources of immigrants now included Italy, Greece, Portugal, Mexico, the Philippines, the West Indies, and South America.

The lasting effect is apparent when we compare the changing sources of immigration over the last 190 years, as shown in Figure 4.4. The most recent period shows that Asian and Latin American immigrants combined to account

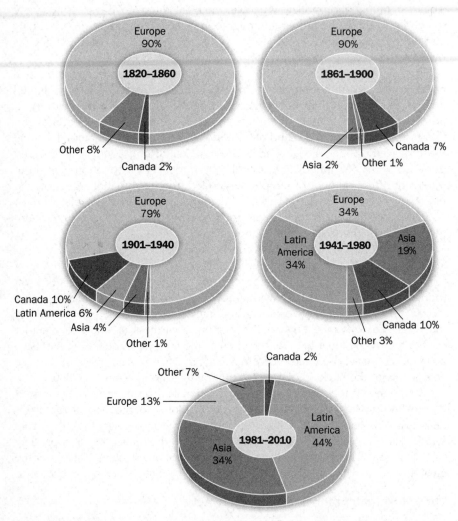

**Figure 4.4** Legal Immigrants Admitted to the United States by Region of Last Residence, 1820–2010

*Source:* Office of Immigration Statistics 2011.

for 81 percent of the people who were permitted entry. This contrasts sharply with early immigration, which was dominated by arrivals from Europe.

The nature of immigration laws is exceedingly complex and is subjected to frequent, often minor, adjustments. In 2000 and 2010, between 840,000 and 1,270,000 people were legally admitted each year. For 2010, people were admitted for the following reasons:

| | |
|---|---|
| Relatives of citizens | 57% |
| Relatives of legal residents | 9% |
| Employment based | 14% |
| Refugees/people seeking political asylum | 13% |
| Diversity (lottery among applications from nations historically sending few immigrants) | 5% |
| Other | 2% |

Overall, two-thirds of the immigrants come to join their families, one-seventh because of skills needed in the United States, and another one-seventh because of special refugee status (Monger and Yankay 2011).

## Contemporary Social Concerns

Although our current immigration policies are less restrictive than other nations', they are the subjects of great debate. Table 4.1 summarizes the benefits and concerns regarding immigration to the United States. Now we consider five continuing criticisms relating to our immigration policy: the brain drain, population growth, mixed status, English language acquisition, and illegal immigration.

### Table 4.1 Immigration Benefits and Concerns

| *Potential Benefits* | *Areas of Concern* |
|---|---|
| Provide needed skills | Drain needed resources from home country |
| Contribute to taxes | Send remittances home |
| May come with substantial capital to start business | Less-skilled immigrants compete with those already disadvantaged |
| Maintain growth of consumer market | Population growth |
| Diversify the population (intangible gain) | Language differences |
| Maintain ties with countries throughout the world | May complicate foreign policy by lobbying the government |
| | Illegal immigration |

All five, but particularly illegal immigration, have provoked heated debates on the national level and continuing efforts to resolve them with new policies. We then consider the economic impact of immigration, followed by the nation's policy toward refugees, a group distinct from immigrants.

## The Brain Drain

How often have you identified your science or mathematics teacher or your physician as someone who was not born in the United States? This nation has clearly benefited from attracting human resources from throughout the world, but this phenomenon has had its price for the nations of origin.

**Brain drain** is the immigration to the United States of skilled workers, professionals, and technicians who are desperately needed by their home countries. In the mid-twentieth century, many scientists and other professionals from industrial nations, principally Germany and Great Britain, came to the United States. More recently, however, the brain drain has pulled emigrants from developing nations, including India, Pakistan, the Philippines, and several African nations. They are eligible for H-1B visas that qualify them for permanent work permits.

One out of four physicians in the United States is foreign-born and plays a critical role in serving areas with too few doctors. Thousands of skilled, educated Indians now seek to enter the United States, pulled by the economic opportunity. The pay differential is so great that, beginning in 2004, when foreign physicians were no longer favored with entry to the United States, physicians in the Philippines were retraining as nurses so that they could immigrate to the United States where, employed as nurses, they would make four times what they would as doctors in the Philippines (Mullen 2005; *New York Times* 2005b).

Many foreign students say they plan to return home. Fortunately for the United States, many do not and make their talents available in the United States. One study showed that the majority of foreign students receiving their doctorates in the sciences and engineering remain here four years later. Critics note, however, that this foreign supply means that this country overlooks its own minority scholars. Currently, for every two minority doctorates, three foreign citizens are receiving this degree. More encouragement needs to be given to African Americans and Latinos to enter high-tech career paths.

Conflict theorists see the current brain drain as yet another symptom of the unequal distribution of world resources. In their view, it is ironic that the United States gives foreign aid to improve the technical resources of African and Asian countries while maintaining an immigration policy that encourages professionals in such nations to migrate to our shores. These are the very countries that have unacceptable public health conditions and need native scientists, educators, technicians, and other professionals. In addition, by relying on foreign talent, the United States is not encouraging native members of subordinate groups to enter these desirable fields of employment (National Center for Education Statistics 2009:Table 319; Pearson 2006; Wessel 2001; West 2010).

## Population Growth

The United States, like a few other industrial nations, continues to accept large numbers of permanent immigrants and refugees. Although such immigration has increased since the passage of the 1965 Immigration and Nationality Act, the nation's birthrate has decreased. Consequently, the contribution of immigration to population growth has become more significant. As citizen "baby boomers" age, the country has increasingly depended on the economically younger population fueled by immigrants (Meyers 2007).

Immigration, legal and illegal, is projected to account for nearly 50 percent of the nation's growth from 2005 to 2050 with the children and grandchildren of immigrants accounting for another 35 percent. To some observers, the United States is already overpopulated. Environmentalists have weighed in the immigration issue questioning immigration's possible negative impact on the nation's natural resources. We consider that aspect of the immigration debate later in this chapter. Thus far, the majority of the club's members have indicated a desire to keep a neutral position rather than enter the politically charged immigration debate (Kotkin 2010).

The patterns of uneven settlement by immigrants in the United States are expected to continue so that future immigrants' impact on population growth will be felt much more in certain areas, say, California and New York rather than Wyoming or West Virginia. Although immigration and population growth may be viewed as national concerns, their impact is localized in certain areas such as Southern California and large urban centers nationwide (Camarota and Jensenius 2009; Passel and Cohn 2009).

## Mixed-Status Families

Very little is simple when it comes to immigration, and this is particularly true to the challenge of "mixed status." **Mixed status** refers to families in which one or more members are citizens and one or more are noncitizens. This especially becomes problematic when the noncitizens are illegal or undocumented immigrants.

The problem of mixed status clearly emerges on two levels. On the macro level, when policy debates are made about issues that seem clear to many people—such as whether illegal immigrants should be allowed to attend state colleges or whether illegal immigrants should be immediately deported—the complicating factor of mixed-status families quickly emerges. On the micro level, the daily toll on members of mixed-status households is very difficult. Often the legal resident or even the U.S. citizen in a household finds daily life limited for fear of revealing the undocumented status of a parent or brother or even a son.

About three-quarters of illegal immigrants' children were born in the United States and thus are citizens. This means that perhaps as many as half of all adult illegal immigrants have a citizen in their immediate family. This proportion has grown in recent years. This means that some of the issues facing illegal immigrants, whom we discuss later, will also affect the citizens in the families because they are reluctant to bring attention to themselves for fear of revealing the illegal status of their mother or father (Gonzalez 2009; Passel and Cohn 2009).

## Language Barriers

For many people in the United States, the most visible aspect of immigration are non–English speakers, businesses with foreign-language storefronts, and even familiar stores assuring potential customers that their employees speak Spanish or Polish or Chinese or some other foreign language.

About 20 percent of the population speaks a language other than English, as shown in Figure 4.5. Indeed, 32 different languages are spoken at home by at least 200,000 residents. As of 2008, about half of the 38 million people born abroad spoke English less than "very well." This rises to 74 percent among those born in Mexico. Nationally, about 64 percent of Latino schoolchildren report speaking Spanish at home (American Community Survey 2009:Tables S0501 and S0506; Shin and Kominski 2010).

The myth of Anglo superiority has rested in part on language differences. (The term *Anglo* in the following text is used to mean all non-Hispanics but primarily Whites.) First, the criteria for economic and social achievement usually include proficiency in English. By such standards, Spanish-speaking pupils are judged less able to compete until they learn English. Second, many Anglos

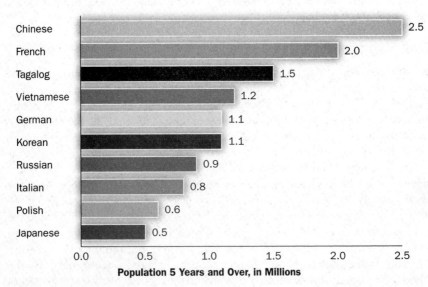

**Figure 4.5** Ten Languages Most Frequently Spoken at Home, Other Than English and Spanish

*Source*: Data for 2007 in Shin and Kominski 2010.

believe that Spanish is not an asset occupationally. Only recently, as government agencies have belatedly begun to serve Latino people and as businesses recognize the growing Latino consumer market, have Anglos recognized that knowing Spanish is not only useful but also necessary to carry out certain tasks.

Until the last 40 years, there was a conscious effort to devalue Spanish and other languages and to discourage the use of foreign languages in schools. In the case of Spanish, this practice was built on a pattern of segregating Hispanic schoolchildren from Anglos. In the recent past in the Southwest, Mexican Americans were assigned to Mexican schools to keep Anglo schools all-White. These Mexican schools, created through de jure school segregation, were substantially underfunded compared with the regular public schools. Legal action against such schools dates back to 1945, but it was not until 1970 that the U.S. Supreme Court ruled, in *Cisneros v. Corpus Christi Independent School District*, that the de jure segregation of Mexican Americans was unconstitutional. Appeals delayed implementation of that decision, and not until September 1975 was the de jure plan forcibly overturned in Corpus Christi, Texas (Commission on Civil Rights 1976).

Is it essential that English be the sole language of instruction in schools in the United States? **Bilingualism** is the use of two or more languages in places of work or educational facilities, according each language equal legitimacy. Thus, a program of **bilingual education** may instruct children in their native language (such as Spanish) while gradually introducing them to the language of the dominant society (English). If such a program is also bicultural, it will teach children about the culture of both linguistic groups. Bilingual education allows students to learn academic material in their own language while they are learning a second language. Proponents believe that, ideally, bilingual education programs should also allow English-speaking pupils to be bilingual, but generally they are directed only at making non–English speakers proficient in more than one language.

In Listen to Our Voices, journalist Galina Espinoza of *Latina* magazine considers the role the English language has played in her own life as well as her chosen profession in the mass media.

## LISTEN TO OUR VOICES

### That Latino "Wave" Is Very Much American

In 1990, I had just started my senior year at an Ivy League college when my political science professor asked me to come see her about the first paper I had turned in. While she complimented me on how much work I had put into it, she went on to explain that writing a college paper must be especially difficult for someone for whom English was not her first language.

*Galina Espinoza*

I don't remember anything else she said after that, so consumed was I with trying to understand how she could have made this assumption. I was, after all an English major. Was it my accent I picked up during my childhood in Queens, N.Y.? Or my last name?

I find myself asking the same question now, with the release of the 2010 U.S. Census figures. Today, Hispanics number more than 50 million strong and account for 1 out of every 6 adults. Some politicians and pundits see our country besieged by a wave of non-English speaking immigrants coming through a porous border.

Here's why they—like my professor—are wrong. What accounts for the dramatic rise in the Latino population are births: fluent in English, a percentage that rises "among later generations of Hispanic adults."

Of course, like many Americans of different cultural backgrounds, Latinos identify strongly with their roots. But even if many of us are bilingual, or want our children to learn Spanish, our true link to Hispanic identity is not through language. It's through culture. We like to know how to cook the foods of our home countries and what our traditional holiday celebrations are. We like to see authentic portrayals of ourselves. Our favorite TV series, according to *Advertising Age*, are *Grey's Anatomy* and *Desperate Housewives*, which prominently feature Latino characters.

And when it comes to politics, we like leaders who understand that Cubans in Miami just might vote differently from Mexicans in Chicago. It is in the ways that our cultural identity begins to reshape the national one that the true social impact of Latinos will be felt. And so if you want to understand who your new Latino neighbors really are, know this: We want to eat our rice and beans. But our apple pie, too.

*Source*: Espinoza 2011:9A.

Do bilingual programs help children learn English? It is difficult to reach firm conclusions on the effectiveness of the bilingual programs in general because they vary so widely in their approach to non-English-speaking children. The programs differ in the length of the transition to English and how long they allow students to remain in bilingual classrooms. A major study analyzed more than three decades of research, combining 17 different studies, and found that bilingual education programs produce higher levels of student achievement in reading. The most successful are paired bilingual programs—those offering ongoing instruction in a native language and English at different times of the day (Slavin and Cheung 2003; Soltero 2008).

Attacks on bilingualism in both voting and education have taken several forms and have even broadened to question the appropriateness of U.S.

residents using any language other than English. Federal policy has become more restrictive. Local schools have been given more authority to determine appropriate methods of instruction; they have also been forced to provide more of their own funding for bilingual education. In the United States, as of 2011, 30 states have made English their official language. Repeated efforts have been made to introduce a constitutional amendment declaring English as the nation's official language. Even such an action would not completely outlaw bilingual or multilingual government services. It would, however, require that such services be called for specifically as in the Voting Rights Act of 1965, which requires voting information to be available in multiple languages (U.S. English 2010).

Non–English speakers cluster in certain states, but bilingualism attracts nationwide passions. The release in 2006 of "Nuestro Himno," the Spanish-language version of "The Star-Spangled Banner," led to a strong reaction, with 69 percent of people saying it was appropriate to be sung only in English. Yet at least one congressman who decried the Spanish version sang the anthem himself in English with incorrect lyrics. Similarly, a locally famous restaurant owner in Philadelphia posted signs at his Philly steak sandwich diner announcing he would accept orders only in English. Passions remain strong as policymakers debate how much support should be given to people who speak other languages (Carroll 2006; Koch 2006b).

*Source*: Permission of Harley Schwadron.

# Illegal Immigration

The most bitterly debated aspect of U.S. immigration policy has been the control of illegal or undocumented immigrants. These immigrants and their families come to the United States in search of higher-paying jobs than their home countries can provide.

Because by definition illegal immigrants are in the country illegally, the exact number of these undocumented or unauthorized workers is subject to estimates and disputes. Based on the best available information in 2011, there are more than 11.2 million illegal or unauthorized immigrants in the United States. This compares with about 3.5 million in 1990. With employment opportunities drying up during the economic downturn beginning in 2008, significantly fewer people tried to enter illegally and many unauthorized immigrants returned to their countries (Passel and Cohn 2011).

Illegal immigrants, and even legal immigrants, have become tied by the public to almost every social problem in the nation. They become the scapegoats for unemployment; they are labeled as "drug runners" and, especially since September 11, 2001, "terrorists." Their vital economic and cultural contribution to the United States is generally overlooked, as it has been for more than a hundred years.

The cost of the federal government's attempt to police the nation's borders and locate illegal immigrants is sizable. There are significant costs for aliens—that is, foreign-born noncitizens—and for other citizens as well. Civil rights advocates have expressed concern that the procedures used to apprehend and deport people are discriminatory and deprive many aliens of their legal rights. American citizens of Hispanic or Asian origin, some of whom were born in the United States, may be greeted with prejudice and distrust, as if their names automatically imply that they are illegal immigrants. Furthermore, these citizens and legal residents of the United States may be unable to find work because employers wrongly believe that their documents are forged.

In the context of this illegal immigration, Congress approved the Immigration Reform and Control Act of 1986 (IRCA) after debating it for nearly a decade. The act marked a historic change in immigration policy compared with earlier laws, as summarized in Table 4.2. Amnesty was granted to 1.7 million illegal immigrants who could document that they had established long-term residency in the United States. Under the IRCA, hiring illegal aliens became illegal, subjecting employers to fines and even prison sentences. Little workplace enforcement occurred for years, but beginning in 2009 federal agents concentrated on auditing large employers rather than raiding workplaces (Simpson 2009).

Many illegal immigrants continue to live in fear and hiding, subject to even more severe harassment and discrimination than before. From

## Table 4.2 Major Immigration Policies

| Policy | Target Group | Impact |
| --- | --- | --- |
| Chinese Exclusion Act, 1882 | Chinese | Effectively ended all Chinese immigration for more than 60 years |
| National origin system, 1921 | Southern Europeans | Reduced overall immigration and significantly reduced likely immigration from Greece and Italy |
| Immigration and Nationality Act, 1965 | Western Hemisphere and the less skilled | Facilitated entry of skilled workers and relatives of U.S. residents |
| Immigration Reform and Control Act of 1986 | Illegal immigrants | Modest reduction of illegal immigration |
| Illegal Immigration Reform and Immigrant Responsibility Act of 1996 | Illegal immigrants | Greater border surveillance and increased scrutiny of legal immigrants seeking benefits |

a conflict perspective, these immigrants, primarily poor and Hispanic or Asian, are being firmly lodged at the bottom of the nation's social and economic hierarchies. However, from a functionalist perspective, employers, by paying low wages, are able to produce goods and services that are profitable for industry and more affordable to consumers. Despite the poor working conditions often experienced by illegal immigrants here, they continue to come because it is still in their best economic interest to work here in disadvantaged positions rather than seek wage labor unsuccessfully in their home countries.

Amidst heated debate, Congress reached a compromise and passed the Illegal Immigration Reform and Immigrant Responsibility Act of 1996, which emphasized making more of an effort to keep immigrants from entering the country illegally. The act prevented illegal immigrants from having access to such programs as Social Security and welfare. Legal immigrants would still be entitled to such benefits, although social service agencies were now required to verify their legal status. Another significant element was to increase border control and surveillance.

Illegal aliens or undocumented workers are not necessarily transient. One estimate indicates 60 percent had been here for at least five years. Many have established homes, families, and networks with relatives and friends in the United States whose legal status might differ. These are the mixed-status households noted earlier. For the most part, their lives are not much different from legal residents, except when they seek services that require citizenship status to be documented (Passel 2005).

Policymakers continue to avoid the only real way to stop illegal immigration: discourage employment opportunities. This has certainly been the approach taken in recent years. The Immigration and Customs Enforcement (ICE) notifies major companies that it will soon audit its employment records looking for illegal immigrants who, if found, can lead to both civil and criminal penalties against the business. This has led corporations such as American Apparel and Chipotle Mexican Grill to look closer and fire hundreds of employees lacking sufficient documentation. Just in the period from October 2010 through March 2011 over 260,000 people have been deported (Jordan 2011).

The public often thinks in terms of controlling illegal immigration through greater surveillance at the border. After the terrorist attacks of September 11, 2001, greater control of border traffic took on a new sense of urgency, even though almost all the men who took over the planes had entered the United States legally. It is very difficult to secure the vast boundaries that mark the United States on land and sea.

Numerous civil rights groups and migrant advocacy organizations expressed alarm over people crossing into the United States illegally who perish in their

Perhaps the grimmest aspect of illegal immigration is the death of those who perish trying to cross the border. Here pictured are bodies stored in a refrigerated area of Pima County morgue of those found dead in the deserts around Tucson.

attempt. Some die in deserts, in isolated canyons, and while concealed in containers or locked in trucks during smuggling attempts. Several hundred die annually in the Southwest, seeking more and more dangerous crossing points, as border control has increased. However, this death toll has received little attention, causing one journalist to liken it to a jumbo jet crashing between Los Angeles and Phoenix every year without anyone giving it much notice (Del Olmo 2003; Sullivan 2005).

The immigration policy debate was largely absent from both the 2008 presidential race and 2010 midterm elections, having been replaced by concerns over the economy and the war in Afghanistan. Locally, concerns continued. Erecting a 700-mile-long double concrete wall hardened the Mexico–United States border. This action, which was heavily supported by the general public, still brought concerns that desperate immigrants would take even more chances with their lives in order to work in the United States. Legal measures to make unauthorized crossings more difficult are being augmented by self-appointed border guards such as the Minuteman movement. Sometimes these armed volunteers engage in surveillance that leads to more violence and an atmosphere of suspicion and incidents of racial profiling along the United States–Mexican border.

An immigration-related issue that began to be raised in 2010 has been concern over the children of illegal immigrants born here who then are regarded as citizens at birth. These concerns, supported in public opinion polls by about half of the population, seek to alter the Fourteenth Amendment to revise the "birthright citizenship" that was intended for children of slaves but has since been long interpreted to cover anyone born in the United States regardless of their partners' legal status. While such a movement is unlikely to succeed it is yet another example of a relatively minor issue that sidetracks any substantive discussion of immigration reform (Gomez 2010).

## Path to Citizenship: Naturalization

In **naturalization**, citizenship is conferred on a person after birth, a process that has been outlined by Congress and extends to foreigners the same benefits given to native-born U.S. citizens. Naturalized citizens, however, cannot serve as president.

Until the 1970s, most people who were naturalized had been born in Europe. Reflecting changing patterns of immigration, Asia and Latin America are now the largest sources of new citizens. In fact, the number of naturalized citizens from Mexico has come close to matching those from all of Europe. In recent years, the number of new citizens going through the naturalization process has been between 600,000 and one million a year (Lee 2011).

To become a naturalized U.S. citizen, a person must meet the following general conditions:

- be 18 years of age;
- have continually resided in the United States for at least five years (three years for the spouses of U.S. citizens);
- have good moral character as determined by the absence of conviction of selected criminal offenses;
- be able to read, write, speak, and understand words of ordinary usage in the English language; and
- pass a test in U.S. government and history.

Table 4.3 offers a sample of the types of questions immigrants face on the citizenship test. As of 2011, the fee for applying for citizenship is $680, compared with $95 in 1998.

Although we often picture the United States as having a very insular, nativistic attitude toward foreigners living here, the country has a rather liberal policy toward people maintaining the citizenship of their old countries. Although most countries do not allow people to maintain dual (or even multiple) citizenships, the United States does not forbid it. Dual citizenship is most common when a person goes through naturalization after already being a citizen of another country or is a U.S.-born citizen and goes through the process of becoming a citizen of another country—for example, after marrying a foreigner (Department of State 2008a).

**Table 4.3  So You Want to Be a Citizen?**

Try these sample questions from the naturalization test (answers below).

1. What do the stripes on the flag represent?

2. How many amendments are there to the Constitution?

3. Who is the chief justice of the Supreme Court?

4. Who was president during World War I?

5. What do we call the first ten amendments to the Constitution?

6. What are two rights in the Declaration of Independence?

7. Name one right or freedom from the First Amendment.

8. When was the Constitution written?

*Source*: Department of Homeland Security 2009.

*Answers:*
(1) The first 13 states; (2) 27; (3) John Roberts; (4) Woodrow Wilson; (5) The Bill of Rights; (6) Life, liberty, and the pursuit of happiness; (7) The rights are freedom of speech, religion, assembly, and press and freedom to petition the government; (8) 1787.

# The Economic Impact of Immigration

There is much public and scholarly debate about the economic effects of immigration, both legal and illegal. Varied, conflicting conclusions have resulted from research ranging from case studies of Korean immigrants' dominance among New York City greengrocers to mobility studies charting the progress of all immigrants and their children. The confusion results in part from the different methods of analysis. For example, the studies do not always include political refugees, who generally are less prepared than other refugees to become assimilated. Sometimes, the research focuses only on economic effects, such as whether people are employed or are on welfare; in other cases, it also considers cultural factors such as knowledge of English.

Perhaps the most significant factor in determining the economic impact of immigration is whether a study examines the national impact of immigration or only its effects on a local area. Overall, we can conclude from the research that immigrants adapt well and are an asset to the local economy. In some areas, heavy immigration may drain a community's resources. However, it can also revitalize a local economy. Marginally employed workers, most of whom are either immigrants or African Americans themselves, often experience a negative impact by new arrivals. With or without immigration, competition for low-paying jobs in the United States is high, and those who gain the most from this competition are the employers and the consumers who want to keep prices down (Steinberg 2005; Zimmerman 2008).

The impact of immigration on African Americans deserves special attention. Given that African Americans are a large minority and many continue to be in the underclass, many people, including some Blacks themselves, perceive immigrants as advancing at the expense of the African American community. There is evidence that in the very lowest paid jobs—for example, workers in chicken-processing plants—wages have dropped with the availability of unskilled immigrants to perform them, and Blacks have left these jobs for good. Many of these African Americans do not necessarily move to better or even equivalent jobs. This pattern is repeated in other relatively low-paying, undesirable employment sectors, so Blacks are not alone in being impacted; but given other job opportunities, the impact is longer lasting (Borjas, Grogger, and Hanson 2006; Holzer 2008).

About 75 percent of illegal immigrant workers pay taxes of one type or another. Many of them do not file to receive entitled refunds, tax credits, or other benefits. For example, in 2006, the Social Security Administration identified thousands of unauthorized workers contributing about $9 billion to the fund but that could not be credited properly (Lipman 2008).

Social science studies generally contradict many of the negative stereotypes about the economic impact of immigration. A variety of recent studies found that immigrants are a net economic gain for the population in times of economic boom as well as in periods of recession. But despite national gains, in some areas and for some groups, immigration may be an economic burden or create unwanted competition for jobs (Kochhar 2006).

What about the immigrants themselves? Considering contemporary immigrants as a group, we can make the following conclusions that show a mix of successes and challenges to adaptation.

### Less Encouraging

- Although immigrants have lower divorce rates and are less likely to form single-parent households than natives, their rates equal or exceed these rates by the second generation.
- Children in immigrant families tend to be healthier than U.S.-born children, but the advantage declines. We consider this in greater detail later in this chapter.
- Immigrant children attend schools that are disproportionately attended by other poor children and students with limited English proficiency, so they are ethnically, economically, and linguistically isolated.

### Positive Signs

- Immigrant families and, more broadly, noncitizen households are more likely to be on public assistance, but their time on public assistance is less and they receive fewer benefits. This is even true when considering special restrictions that may apply to noncitizens.
- Second-generation immigrants (i.e., children of immigrants) are overall doing as well as or better than White non-Hispanic natives in educational attainment, labor force participation, wages, and household income.
- Immigrants overwhelmingly (65 percent) continue to see learning English as an ethical obligation of all immigrants.

These positive trends diverge among specific immigrant groups, with Asian immigrants doing better than European immigrants, who do better than Latino immigrants (Capps, Leighton, and Fix 2002; Farkas 2003; Fix and Passel 2001; Myers, Pitkin, and Park 2004; Zimmerman 2008).

One economic aspect of immigration that has received increasing attention is the role of **remittances**, or the monies that immigrants return to their countries of origin. The amounts are significant and measure in the hundreds of millions of dollars flowing from the United States to a number of countries where they provide substantial support for families and even venture capital for new businesses. Although some observers express concern over this outflow of money, others counter that it probably represents a small price to pay for the human capital that the United States is able to use in the form of the immigrants themselves. Immigrants in the United States send billions to their home countries and worldwide remittances bring about $325 billion to all the world's developing countries, easily surpassing all other forms of foreign aid. While this cash inflow is integral to the economies of many nations, it also means that during the global economic recession that occurred recently, this resource drops off significantly (Migration News 2011).

The concern about immigration today is both understandable and perplexing. The nation has always been uneasy about new arrivals, especially those who are different from the more affluent and the policymakers. In most of the 1990s, we had paradoxical concerns about immigrants hurting the economy despite strong economic growth. With the economic downturn beginning in 2008, it was clear that low-skilled immigrants (legal or illegal) took the hardest hit and, as a result, remittances immediately declined.

## Women and Immigration

Immigration is presented as if all immigrants are similar, with the only distinctions being made concerning point of origin, education, and employment prospects. Another significant distinction is whether immigrants travel with or without their families. We often think that historical immigrants to the United States were males in search of work. Men dominate much of the labor migration worldwide, but because of the diversified labor force in the United States and some policies that facilitate relatives coming, immigration to the United States generally has been fairly balanced. Actually, most immigration historically appears to be families. For example, from 1870 through 1940, men entering the United States exceeded women by only about 10–20 percent. Since 1950, women immigrants have actually exceeded men by a modest amount. This pattern is being repeated globally (Gibson and Jung 2006; Jones 2008).

The second-class status women normally experience in society is reflected in immigration. Most dramatically, women citizens who married immigrants who were not citizens actually lost their U.S. citizenship from 1907 through 1922 with few exceptions. However, this policy did not apply to men (Johnson 2004).

Immigrant women face not only all the challenges faced by immigrant men but also additional ones. Typically, they have the responsibility of navigating the new society when it comes to services for their family and, in particular, their children. Many new immigrants view the United States as a dangerous place to raise a family and therefore remain particularly vigilant of what happens in their children's lives.

Male immigrants are more likely to be consumed with work, leaving the women to navigate the bureaucratic morass of city services, schools, medical

Immigration is a challenge to all family members, but immigrant women must navigate a new culture and a new country not only for themselves but also for their children, such as in this household in Colorado.

facilities, and even everyday concerns such as stores and markets. Immigrant women are often reluctant to seek outside help, whether they are in need of special services for medical purposes or they are victims of domestic violence. Yet immigrant women are more likely to be the liaison for the household, including adult men, to community associations and religious organizations (Hondagneu-Sotelo 2003; Jones 2008).

Women play a critical role in overseeing the household; for immigrant women, the added pressures of being in a new country and trying to move ahead in a different culture heighten this social role.

## The Global Economy and Immigration

Immigration is defined by political boundaries that bring the movement of peoples crossing borders to the attention of government authorities and their policies. Within the United States, people may move their residence, but they are not immigrating. For residents in the member nations of the European Union, free movement of people within the union is also protected.

Yet, increasingly, people recognize the need to think beyond national borders and national identity. As noted in Chapter 1, **globalization** is the world-wide integration of government policies, cultures, social movements, and financial markets through trade, movement of people, and the exchange of ideas. In this global framework, even immigrants are less likely to think of themselves as residents of only one country. For generations, immigrants have used foreign-language newspapers to keep in touch with events in their home countries. Today, cable channels carry news and variety programs from their home countries, and the Internet offers immediate access to the homeland and kinfolk thousands of miles away.

Although it helps in bringing the world together, globalization has also highlighted the dramatic economic inequalities between nations. Today, people in North America, Europe, and Japan consume 32 times more resources than the billions of people in developing nations. Thanks to tourism, media, and other aspects of globalization, the people of less-affluent countries are aware of such affluent lifestyles and, of course, often aspire to enjoy them (Diamond 2003).

**Transnationals** are immigrants who sustain multiple social relationships that link their societies of origin and settlement. Immigrants from the Dominican Republic, for example, not only identify themselves with Americans but also maintain very close ties to their Caribbean homeland. They return for visits, send remittances, and host extended stays of relatives and friends. Back in the Dominican Republic, villages reflect these close ties, as shown in billboards promoting special long-distance services to the United States and by the presence of household appliances sent by relatives. The volume of remittances worldwide is easily the most reliable source of foreign money going to poor countries, far outstripping foreign aid programs.

The presence of transnationals would be yet another example of pluralism, as illustrated in the Spectrum of Intergroup Relations.

The growing number of transnationals, as well as immigration in general, directly reflects the world systems analysis we considered in Chapter 1. Transnationals are not new, but the ability to communicate and transfer resources makes the immigration experience today different from that of

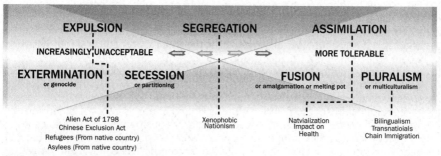

**Spectrum of Intergroup Relations**

the nineteenth century. The sharp contrast between the industrial "have" nations and the developing "have-not" nations only encourages movement across borders. The industrial haves gain benefits from such movement even when they seem to discourage it. The back-and-forth movement only serves to increase globalization and help create informal social networks between people who seek a better life and those already enjoying increased prosperity.

Transnationals' attempts to bridge their homeland and the United States can be found in everyday behavior. Food practices are always a challenge to immigrants, and Chinese Americans are no exception. But in Research Focus, we consider how a dietary preference has run afoul of environmentalists.

The transnationals themselves maintain a multithreaded relationship between friends and relatives in the United Sates, their home country, and perhaps other countries where relatives and friends have resettled. Besides the economic impact of remittances described above, scholars are increasingly giving attention to "social remittances" that include ideas, social norms, and practices (religious and secular) throughout this global social network (Levitt and Jaworsky 2007).

---

### RESEARCH FOCUS

## Challenge to Pluralism: The Shark's Fin

Popular among the Chinese generally and also Chinese Americans is the delicacy of shark's fin soup. Generally viewed as a luxury food item, it is often served at special occasions such as wedding and anniversary banquets.

However, not joining in the celebration are the growing numbers who feel that consumption of a soup using shark fins is contributing to the global decline of certain species of sharks. Curiously the fins themselves are virtually tasteless but are seen as the critical ingredient to this delicacy, which typically includes mushrooms, diced ham, other seafood, and chicken for taste.

In 2011, the California legislature introduced a bill banning both the sale and possession of shark fins, including shark's fin soup. Hawaii passed a similar law taking effect in 2011 and Washington State and Oregon are considering it. Taken together these four states account for 43 percent of the nation's Chinese American population.

To many in the Chinese American communities this represents a frontal assault on their culture. Scholars would see this as a case for **cultural relativism** where an action of a particular group is judged objectively within the context of a particular culture. However, even some Chinese Americans favor such a ban. California state legislator Paul Fong who grew up with shark's fin soup says he is "environmentally conscious" and takes "the scientists' side."

Cultural relativism often surfaces in the Untied States as a source of tension. Society and courts in particular refuse to recognize polygamous marriages even if perfectly legal in the immigrants' country. Shark's fin soup is yet another battleground for how much society is willing to accommodate cultural differences (Brown 2011; Forero 2006).

# The Environment and Immigration

At the beginning of the twenty-first century, the public expressed growing concern on a variety of environmental issues, from water quality to global warming. As with so many other aspects of life, the environment and immigration are tightly linked.

First, environmental factors are behind a significant amount of world migration. Famine, typhoons, rising sea levels, expanding deserts, chronic water shortages, earthquakes, and so forth lead to cross-border migration of what has been termed *climate refugees*. One estimate suggests up to 200 million people may move due to environmental factors between 2005 and 2050.

A particularly deadly aspect of this forced movement is that overwhelmingly the migration is by vulnerable poor people to developing countries ill-suited to accept the arrivals (International Organization for Migration 2009; Meyers 2005; Stern 2007).

Second, some environmentalists favor reducing or even ending U.S. population growth by imposing a much more restrictive immigration policy. The respected environmentalist group Sierra Club debated for several years whether to take an official position favoring restricting immigration. Thus far, the majority of the club's members have indicated a desire to keep a neutral position rather than enter the politically charged immigration debate.

Yet others still contend for the United States to finally address environmental problems at home and become global environmental citizens, and for the United States to stop population growth. Critics of this environmentalist approach counter that we should focus on consumption, not population (Barringer 2004; CaFaro and Staples 2009).

# Refugees

**Refugees** are people living outside their country of citizenship for fear of political or religious persecution. Enough refugees exist to populate an entire "nation." There are approximately 11 million refugees worldwide. That makes the nation of refugees larger than Belgium, Sweden, or Cuba. The United States has touted itself as a haven for political refugees. However, as we shall see, the welcome to political refugees has not always been unqualified.

The United States makes the largest financial contribution of any nation to worldwide assistance programs. The United States resettles about 70,000 refugees annually and served as the host to over one million refugees between 1990 and 2008. The post-9/11 years have seen the procedures become much more cumbersome for foreigners to acquire refugee status and gain entry to the United States. Many other nations much smaller and much poorer than the United States have many more refugees, with Jordan, Iran, and Pakistan

**Table 4.4 Top Sources of Refugees**

| | 2000 | | | 2010 | |
|---|---|---|---|---|---|
| 1 | Bosnia-Herzegovina | 22,699 | | Iraq | 18,016 |
| 2 | Yugoslavia (former) | 14,280 | | Burma | 16,693 |
| 3 | Vietnam | 9,622 | | Bhutan | 12,363 |
| 4 | Ukraine | 8,649 | | Somalia | 4,884 |
| 5 | Russia | 4,386 | | Cuba | 4,818 |
| | Total: | 85,076 | | | 73,293 |

*Source*: Martin 2011; Office of Immigration Statistics 2009:Table 14.

hosting more than one million refugees each (Martin 2011; United Nations High Commission on Refugees 2008).

The United States, insulated by distance from wars and famines in Europe and Asia, has been able to be selective about which and how many refugees are welcomed. Since the arrival of refugees uprooted by World War II, through the 1980s the United States had allowed three groups of refugees to enter in numbers greater than regulations would ordinarily permit: Hungarians, Cubans, and Southeast Asians.

Despite periodic public opposition, the U.S. government is officially committed to accepting refugees from other nations. In Table 4.4 we consider the major sources of refugees. According to the United Nations treaty on refugees, which our government ratified in 1968, countries are obliged to refrain from forcibly returning people to territories where their lives or liberty might be endangered. However, it is not always clear whether a person is fleeing for his or her personal safety or to escape poverty. Although people in the latter category may be of humanitarian interest, they do not meet the official definition of refugees and are subject to deportation.

Refugees are people who are granted the right to enter a country while still residing abroad. **Asylees** are foreigners who have already entered the United States and now seek protection because of persecution or a well-founded fear of persecution. This persecution may be based on the individual's race, religion, nationality, membership in a particular social group, or political opinion. Asylees are eligible to adjust to lawful permanent resident status after one year of continuous presence in the United States. Asylum is granted to about 12,000 people annually.

Because asylees, by definition, are already here, the outcome is either to grant them legal entry or to return them to their home country. It is the practice of deporting people who are fleeing poverty that has been the subject of criticism. There is a long tradition in the United States of facilitating the arrival of people leaving Communist nations, such as the Cubans. Mexicans who are refugees from poverty, Liberians fleeing civil war, and Haitians running from despotic

Haitian Americans often face uncertain futures. A dramatic exception is Wyclef Jean who moved to Brooklyn at the age of nine to be with his parents. Now a major rap star, he has not forgotten his roots as for years he spearheaded humanitarian aid to Haiti and became the celebrity face of the earthquake relief effort.

rule are not similarly welcomed. The plight of Haitians has become one of particular concern.

Haitians began fleeing their country, often on small boats, in the 1980s. The U.S. Coast Guard intercepted many Haitians at sea, saving some of these boat people from death in their rickety and overcrowded wooden vessels. The Haitians said they feared detentions, torture, and execution if they remained in Haiti. Yet both Republican and Democratic administrations viewed most of the Haitian exiles as economic migrants rather than political refugees and opposed granting them asylum and permission to enter the United States. Once apprehended, the Haitians are returned. In 1993, the U.S. Supreme Court, by an 8–1 vote, upheld the government's right to intercept Haitian refugees at sea and return them to their homeland without asylum hearings.

The devastating 2010 earthquake in Haiti has caused the government to reconsider this policy. Indeed, the United States halted all deportations of the 30,000 Haitians that was about to occur for at least 18 months. This moratorium would also apply to the more than 100,000 Haitians believed to be living in the United States. As more residents of Haiti with U.S. citizenship or dual citizenship arrived in the aftermath from the island nation, the Haitian community rose to 830,000 by 2009. Despite the continuing obstacles, the Haitian American community exhibits pride in those who have succeeded, from a Haitian American Florida state legislator and professional athletes to hip-hop musician Wyclef Jean. In fact the initial earthquake refugees tended to come from the middle class or higher and even expressed annoyance at the quality of the public schools their children now attended compared to the private ones in Haiti (Buchanan et al. 2010; Office of Immigration Statistics 2011; Preston 2010; Winerip 2011).

New foreign military campaigns often bring new refugee issues. The occupation of Iraq, beginning in 2003, had been accompanied by large movements of Iraqis throughout the country and the region. Hopefully, most will return home, but some clearly are seeking to relocate to the United States. As was true in Vietnam, many Iraqis who have aided the U.S.-led mission have increasingly sought refuge in the West, fearing for their safety if they were to remain in Iraq or even in the Middle East. Gradually, the United States has begun to offer refugee status to Iraqis; some 18,000 arrived in 2010 to join an Iraqi American community of 90,000. The diverse landscape of the United States takes on yet another nationality group in large numbers (Martin 2011).

# Conclusion

The immigrant presence in the United States can often be heard on the streets and the workplace as people speak in different languages. Check out your radio; as of 2011, radio stations broadcast in 35 languages other than English including Albanian, Creole, Welsh, Yiddish, and Oji, a language spoken in Ghana (Keen 2011).

Throughout the history of the United States, as we have seen, there has been intense debate over the nation's policies that bring immigrants that speak these and other languages to the country. In a sense, this debate reflects the deep value conflicts in the U.S. culture and parallels the "American dilemma" identified by Swedish social economist Gunnar Myrdal (1944). One strand of our culture—epitomized by the words "Give us your tired, your poor, your huddled masses"—has emphasized egalitarian principles and a desire to help people in their time of need. One could hardly have anticipated at the time the Statue of Liberty was dedicated in 1886 that more than a century later Barack Obama, the son of a Kenyan immigrant, would be elected president of the United States.

At the same time, however, hostility to potential immigrants and refugees—whether the Chinese in the 1880s, European Jews in the 1930s and 1940s, or Mexicans, Haitians, and Arabs today—reflects not only racial, ethnic, and religious prejudice but also a desire to maintain the dominant culture of the ingroup by keeping out those viewed as outsiders. The conflict between these cultural values is central to the American dilemma of the twenty-first century.

The current debate about immigration is highly charged and emotional. Some people see it in economic terms, whereas others see the new arrivals as a challenge to the very culture of our society. Clearly, the general perception is that immigration presents a problem rather than a promise for the future.

Today's concern about immigrants follows generations of people coming to settle in the United States. This immigration in the past produced a very diverse country in terms of both nationality and religion, even before the immigration of the last 60 years. Therefore, the majority of Americans today are not descended from the English, and Protestants are just more than half of all worshipers. This diversity of religious and ethnic groups is examined in Chapter 5.

# Summary

1. Immigration to the United States has been consistent since the country achieved its independence, but in the last 30 years the number of legal immigrants has even exceeded the numbers of the early 1900s.

2. Immigration has been regulated by the United States; the first significant restriction was the Chinese Exclusion Act in 1882.

3. Subsequent legislation through the national origins system favored northern and western Europeans. Not until 1965 were quotas by nation largely lifted.

4. Immigration policy is impacted by economic demands for workers who cannot be found among citizens. These workers may be professionals, but they also include large numbers of people who are prepared to do hard labor for wages deemed too low for most citizens but which are attractive to many people outside the United States.

5. Issues such as population growth, the environment, the brain drain, mixed-status households, and English-language acquisition influence contemporary immigration policy.

6. Illegal immigration remains formidable and heightened by new concerns about securing our borders since the September 11, 2001, terrorist attacks.

7. Economically, immigration impacts local communities differently, but the new arrivals typically pay taxes and energize the national economy.

8. Refugees present a special challenge to policymakers who balance humanitarian values against an unwillingness to accept all those who are fleeing poverty and political unrest.

## Key Terms

asylees  148
bilingual education  133
bilingualism  133
brain drain  130
chain immigration  119

globalization  144
mixed status  131
nativism  123
naturalization  139
refugees  147

remittances  142
sinophobes  124
transnationals  145
cultural relativism  146
xenophobia  123

## Review Questions

1. What are the functions and dysfunctions of immigration?

2. What were the social and economic issues when public opinion mounted against Chinese immigration to the United States?

3. Ultimately, what do you think is the major concern people have about contemporary immigration to the United States: the numbers of immigrants, their legal status, or their nationality?

4. What principles appear to guide U.S. refugee policy?

## Critical Thinking

1. What is the immigrant root story of your family? Consider how your ancestors arrived in the United States and also how your family's past has been shaped by other immigrant groups.
2. Can you find evidence of the brain drain in terms of the professionals with whom you come in contact? Do you regard this as a benefit? What groups in the United States may not have been encouraged to fill such positions by the availability of such professionals?
3. What challenge does the presence of people in the United States speaking languages other than English present for them? For schools? For the workplace? For you?

# 5 Ethnicity and Religion

## CHAPTER OUTLINE

{ HIGHLIGHTS }

The United States includes a multitude of ethnic and religious groups. Do they coexist in harmony or in conflict? How significant are they as sources of identity for their members? Because White is a race, significant attention has been given to the social construction of race as it applies to White people. Many White ethnic groups have transformed their ethnic status into Whiteness. In the 1960s and 1970s, there was a resurgence of interest in White ethnicity, partly in response to the renewed pride in the ethnicity of Blacks, Latinos, and Native Americans. We have an ethnic paradox in which White ethnics seem to enjoy their heritage but at the same time seek to assimilate into the larger society. This refers to the maintenance of one's ethnic ties in a way that can assist with assimilation in larger societies.

Major White ethnic groups such as German, Irish, Italian, and Polish Americans have experienced similar, yet distinctive, social circumstances in the United States. We can make some tentative comparisons from their experiences and what we could expect among today's immigrants. Religious diversity continues and expands with immigration and growth in the followings of non-Christian faiths. Religious minorities experience intolerance in the present as they have in the past. Constitutional issues such as school prayer, secessionist minorities, creationism, and public religious displays are regularly taken to the Supreme Court.

---

The very complexity of relations between dominant and subordinate groups in the United States today is partly the result of its heterogeneous population. No one ethnic origin or religious faith encompasses all the inhabitants of the United States. Even though our largest period of sustained immigration is three generations past, an American today is surrounded by remnants of cultures and practitioners of religions whose origins are foreign to this

The changing nature of ethnicity in America's cities was underscored when the 2010 census showed not a single Italian-born person living in New York City's Little Italy. While many people of Italian descent resided there, one was much more likely to find Chinese-born people than of any other nationality.

country. Ethnicity and religion continue to be significant in defining a person's identity.

New York City's Little Italy would seem to be the quintessential example of ethnicity. One problem, where are the Italians? In 1950, most in the 20-square-block area of Lower Manhattan were Italian-born and by 2000 it was 6 percent. Then, in 2010, census takers could not find a single resident born in Italy. Yes, Italian residents and shops are obvious, but the residents are more likely to be Chinese American. To unite the two communities of Italian and Chinese cultures, an annual Marco Polo Day has begun to honor the explorer from Venice who journeyed in the thirteenth century through Central Asia to China (Roberts 2011).

It's May, ready for the National Day of Prayer? Congress formalized this observance in 1952. While 83 percent of people in the United States indicate there is a God who answers prayers, the increasing diversity of believers makes even the observance of this event increasingly contentious. What kind of praying? Some more ecumenical prayers (no reference to Jesus Christ, for example, or even to a supreme being) affront many. Specific Biblical, Talmudic, or Qur'anic references have limited appeals across a nation tolerant of so many faiths. So are we too religious or not religious enough (Grossman 2010; Jones 2010)?

One's religious or ethnic experience is unlikely to be identical to the next person's, so it is this diversity that we consider in this chapter. We also consider with this diversity, how one goes about "fitting in" to a new society.

# Ethnic Diversity

The ethnic diversity of the United States at the beginning of the twenty-first century is apparent to almost everyone. Passersby in New York City were undoubtedly surprised once when two street festivals met head-to-head. The procession of San Gennaro, the patron saint of Naples, marched through Little Italy, only to run directly into a Chinese festival originating in Chinatown. Teachers in many public schools often encounter students who speak only one language, and it is not English. Students in Chicago are taught in Spanish, Greek, Italian, Polish, German, Creole, Japanese, Cantonese, or the language of a Native American tribe. In the Detroit metropolitan area, classroom instruction is conveyed in 21 languages, including Arabic, Portuguese, Ukrainian, Latvian, Lithuanian, and Serbian. In many areas of the United States, you can refer to special yellow pages and find a driving instructor who speaks Portuguese or a psychotherapist who will talk to you in Hebrew.

Germans are the largest ancestral group in the United States; the 2008 census showed about 17 percent of Americans saying they had at least some German ancestry. Although most German Americans are assimilated, it is possible to see the ethnic tradition in some areas, particularly in Milwaukee, whose population has 48 percent German ancestry. There, three Saturday schools teach German, and one can affiliate with 34 German American clubs and visit a German library that operates within the public library system. Just a bit to the south in River Forest, a Chicago suburb, *kinderwerkstatt* meets weekly to help parents and children alike to maintain German culture (American Community Survey 2009:Table B04003; Carvajal 1996; Johnson 1992; Usdansky 1992).

Germany is one of 20 European nations from which at least 1 million people claim to have ancestry. The numbers are striking when one considers the size of some of the sending countries. For example, there are more than 36 million Irish Americans, and the Republic of Ireland had a population of 4 million as of 2010. Similarly, more than 4 million people claim Swedish ancestry, and 9 million people live in Sweden today. Of course, many Irish Americans and Swedish Americans are of mixed ancestry, but not everyone in Ireland is Irish, nor is everyone in Sweden Swedish.

# Why Don't We Study Whiteness?

Race is socially constructed, as we learned in Chapter 1. Sometimes we come to define race in a clear-cut manner. A descendant of a Pilgrim is White, for example. But sometimes race is more ambiguous: People who are the children of an African American and Vietnamese American union are biracial or "mixed," or whatever they come to be seen by others. Our recognition that race is socially constructed has sparked a renewed interest in what it means to be White in the United States. Two aspects of White as a race are useful to consider: the historical creation of Whiteness and how contemporary White people reflect on their racial identity.

When the English immigrants established themselves as the political founders of the United States, they also came to define what it meant to be White. Other groups that today are regarded as White—such as Irish, Germans, Norwegians, or Swedes—were not always considered White in the eyes of the English. Differences in language and religious worship, as well as past allegiance to a king in Europe different from the English monarch, all caused these groups to be seen not so much as Whites in the Western Hemisphere but more as nationals of their home country who happened to be residing in North America.

The old distrust in Europe, where, for example, the Irish were viewed by the English as socially and culturally inferior, continued on this side of the Atlantic Ocean. Writing from England, Karl Marx reported that the average English worker looked down on the Irish the way poor Whites in the U.S. South looked down on Black people (Ignatiev 1994, 1995; Roediger 1994).

As European immigrants and their descendants assimilated to the English and distanced themselves from other oppressed groups such as American Indians and African Americans, they came to be viewed as White rather than as part of a particular culture. Writer Noel Ignatiev (1994:84), contrasting being White with being Polish, argues, "Whiteness is nothing but an expression of race privilege." This strong statement argues that being White, as opposed to being Black or Asian, is characterized by being a member of the dominant group. Whiteness, although it may often be invisible, is aggressively embraced and defended (Giroux 1997).

White people do not think of themselves as a race or have a conscious racial identity. The only occasions when a White racial identity emerges is when filling out a form asking for self-designation of race or when they are culturally or socially surrounded by people who are not White.

Many immigrants who were not "White on arrival" had to "become White" in a process long forgotten by today's White Americans. The long documented transparent racial divide that engulfed the South during slavery allowed us to ignore how Whiteness was constructed.

Therefore, contemporary White Americans generally give little thought to "being White." Consequently, there is little interest in studying "Whiteness" or considering "being White" except that it is "not being Black." Unlike non-Whites, who are much more likely to interact with Whites, take orders from Whites, and see Whites as leading figures in the mass media, Whites enjoy the privilege of not being reminded of their Whiteness.

Unlike racial minorities, Whites downplay the importance of their racial identity, although they are willing to receive the advantages that come from being White. This means that advocacy of a "color-blind" or "race-neutral" outlook permits the privilege of Whiteness to prevail (Bonilla-Silva 2002; Feagin and Cobas 2008; Yancey 2003).

The new scholarly interest seeks to look at Whiteness but not from the vantage point of a White supremacist. Rather, focusing on White people as a race or on what it means today to be White goes beyond any definition that implies superiority over non-Whites. It is also recognized that "being White" is not the same experience for all Whites any more than "being Asian American" or "being Black" is the same for all Asian Americans or all Blacks. Historian Noel Ignatiev observes that studying Whiteness is a necessary stage to the "abolition of whiteness"—just as, in Marxist analysis, class consciousness is a necessary stage to the abolition of class. By confronting Whiteness, society grasps the all-encompassing power that accompanies socially constructed race (Lewis 2004; McKinney 2003; Roediger 2006).

**White privilege**, introduced in Chapter 2, refers to the right granted as a benefit or favor of being White and can be an element of Whiteness. However, of course, many Whites consciously try to minimize the exercising of this privilege. Admittedly it is difficult when a White person is more likely than not to mostly see national leaders, celebrities, and role models who are also White. For every Barack Obama, there are hundreds of movers and shakers who are White.

When race is articulated or emphasized for Whites, it is more likely to be seen as threatening to Whites than allowing them to embrace their own race or national roots with pride. Behavioral economists Michael Norton and Samuel Sommers (2011) found that Whites view race as a zero-sum game, that is, decreases in bias against African Americans over the last 60 years are associated with increases in what they perceived as bias against Whites. While still seeing anti-Black bias as greater today than anti-White feeling in society, their analysis shows the two coming very close together in the minds of the White respondents. Black respondents also saw a marked decline in anti-Black bias during the same period but perceived only a modest increase in anti-White feelings. While their research deals only with perception of reality, it does suggest that race, and not just that of non-Whites, influences one's perception of society.

## The Rediscovery of Ethnicity

Robert Park (1950:205), a prominent early sociologist, wrote in 1913 that "a Pole, Lithuanian, or Norwegian cannot be distinguished, in the second generation, from an American, born of native parents." At one time, sociologists saw the end of ethnicity as nearly a foregone conclusion. W. Lloyd Warner and Leo Srole (1945) wrote in their often-cited *Yankee City* series that the future of ethnic groups seemed to be limited in the United States and that they would be quickly absorbed. Oscar Handlin's *The Uprooted* (1951) told of the destruction of immigrant values and their replacement by American culture. Although Handlin was among the pioneers in investigating ethnicity, assimilation was the dominant theme in his work.

Many writers have shown almost a fervent hope that ethnicity would vanish. The persistence of ethnicity was for some time treated by sociologists as dysfunctional because it meant a continuation of old values that interfered with the allegedly superior new values. For example, to hold on to one's language delayed entry into the larger labor market and the upward social mobility it afforded. Ethnicity was expected to disappear not only because of assimilation but also because aspirations to higher social class and status demanded that it vanish. Somehow, it was assumed that one could not be ethnic and middle class, much less affluent.

### Blended Identity

The process of being an ethnic to an ethnic who is a part of a larger society leads to what has been termed a **blended identity**. This is a self-image and worldview that is a combination of religious faith, cultural background based on nationality, and the status of being a resident of the United States.

Consider the example of a Pakistani American. As shown in Figure 5.1 Muslims often find their daily activities defined by their faith, their nationality, and their status as American, however defined in terms of citizenship. Younger Muslims especially can move freely among the different identities. In Chicago,

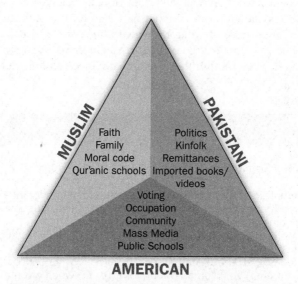

**Figure 5.1**  Blended Identity of Muslim Americans
Muslim Americans, as shown in this illustration representing the life/experience of a Pakistani Muslim living in the United States, form their identity by bringing together three different identities: their faith, their homeland, and the United States.

Muslim college students perform hip-hop in Arabic with lyrics like "La ilaha ila Allah" ("There is no God but Allah"). In Fremont, California, high school Muslim girls and some of their non-Muslim girlfriends hold an alternative prom, decked out in silken gowns, dancing to both 50 Cent and Arabic music, dining on lasagna, but pausing at sunset to face toward Mecca and pray (Abdo 2004a; Brown 2003; Mostofi 2003).

Multiple identities along ethnic, racial, and national lines can lead to confusion between how one sees themselves. In any ethnic or immigrant community, divisions arise over who can truly be counted as a member of the community. Sociologist Gary David (2003, 2007) developed the concept of the **deficit model of ethnic identity**. This states that others view one's identity as a factor of subtracting away characteristics corresponding to some ideal ethnic type. Each factor encompassing a perfect ethnic identity missing from a person's background or identity leads the person to be viewed by others as more assimilated and less ethnic. In the case of Arab Americans, if they are unable to speak Arabic, then they are less Arab to some people; if they are married to non-Arabs, then they are less ethnic; if they have never been to the home country, then they are less ethnic. Depending on one's perspective, an Arab American can come to regard another Arab American as either "too American" or "too Arab." Arab American organizations, magazines, and associations may seek to cater to the entire Arab American community, but, more likely, cater to certain segments based on nationality, religion, and degree of assimilation.

Groups that gravitated to one another may also form organizations because they share the same sense of what it means to be Arab American. As noted in the Research Focus, younger Arab Americans seem more willing to self-identify as Arab American even though they are actually more assimilated to U.S. culture than their parents.

## RESEARCH FOCUS

## Self-Identifying as "Arab American"

Racial and ethnic identities are important aspects of the immigrant experience. We have already considered how *blended identity* functions, but how might this change over time?

Sociologist Kristine Ajrouch and political scientist Amaney Jamal conducted a survey of Arab Americans in the Detroit metropolitan area. Overall in the United States, 80 percent of Arab Americans select "White" since the government does not offer "Arab" as an option for race. Yet when given that choice, Ajrouch and Jamal found many chose Arab American as a self-identifier but also considered themselves "White."

Being Arab American does not mean that you do not also see yourself as "American." Indeed 94 percent of Arab Americans who are citizens describe themselves as very or quite proud to be American, compared to 98 percent of the general population.

Interestingly, younger Arab Americans seem more willing to use the label of "Arab American." Researchers wonder if the post-9/11 world has given being Arab and/or Muslim American new meaning. Will younger people, as they become adults, embrace "Arab American" in a sense of unity or seek to distance themselves from it in a fear of being marginalized by society?

*Sources*: Abdulrahim 2009; Ajrouch 2011; Ajrouch and Jamal 2007; Brittingham and de la Cruz 2003.

## The Third-Generation Principle

Historian Marcus Hansen's (1952) **principle of third-generation interest** was an early exception to the assimilationist approach to White ethnic groups. Simply stated, Hansen maintained that in the third generation—the grandchildren of the original immigrants—ethnic interest and awareness would actually increase. According to Hansen, "What the son wishes to forget, the grandson wishes to remember."

Hansen's principle has been tested several times since it was first put forth. John Goering (1971), in interviewing Irish and Italian Catholics, found that ethnicity was more important to members of the third generation than it was to the immigrants themselves. Similarly, Mary Waters (1990)—in her interviews of White ethnics living in suburban San Jose, California, and suburban Philadelphia, Pennsylvania—observed that many grandchildren wanted to study their ancestors' language, even though it would be a foreign language to them. They also expressed interest in learning more of their ethnic group's history and a desire to visit their homeland.

Social scientists in the past were quick to minimize the ethnic awareness of blue-collar workers. In fact, ethnicity was viewed as merely another aspect of White ethnics' alleged racist nature, an allegation that is examined later in this chapter. Curiously, the very same intellectuals and journalists who bent over backward to understand the growing solidarity of Blacks, Hispanics, and Native Americans refused to give White ethnics the academic attention they deserved (Kivisto 2008; Wrong 1972).

The new assertiveness of Blacks and other non-Whites of their rights in the 1960s unquestionably presented White ethnics with the opportunity to reexamine their own position. "If solidarity and unapologetic self-consciousness might hasten Blacks' upward mobility, why not ours?" asked the White ethnics, who were often only a half step above Blacks in social status. The African American movement pushed other groups to reflect on their past. The increased consciousness of Blacks and their positive attitude toward African culture and the contributions worldwide of African Americans are embraced in what we called the *Afrocentric perspective* (see Chapter 1). Therefore, the mood was set in the 1960s for the country to be receptive to ethnicity. By legitimizing Black cultural differences from White culture, along with those of Native Americans and Hispanics, the country's opinion leaders legitimized other types of cultural diversity.

People express or self-identify with their ethnic origins in a variety of ways.
*Source*: ScienceCartoonsPlus.com.

## Ethnic Paradox

So, many nearly assimilated Whites are rediscovering their ethnicity (i.e., the principle of third-generation interest) while others are at least publicly acknowledging their ethnicity from time to time (i.e., symbolic ethnicity). Yet research confirms that preserving elements of one's ethnicity may actually advance economic success and further societal acceptance.

**Ethnic paradox** refers to the maintenance of one's ethnic ties in a manner that can assist with assimilation with larger society. Immigrant youth as well as adults who maintain their ethnicity tend to succeed better as indicated by health measures, educational attainment, and lower incidence of behavioral problems such as delinquency and truancy.

Researchers typically measure ethnic maintenance by facility in the mother language (not just conversational or "street" use) and living with others of the same ethnic background. These clear ethnic ties are not an automatic recipe for success. For example, residing with co-ethnics can lead to exploitation such as in neighborhoods where people steer their countrymen into dead-end, poor-paying, and even unhealthy working conditions. Yet for many ethnics, enclaves do offer a refuge, sort of a halfway house, between two different cultures. Language maintenance, as noted in the previous chapter, is often critical to being truly literate and comfortable with English (Desmond and Kubrin 2009).

## Symbolic Ethnicity

Observers comment on both the evidence of assimilation and the signs of ethnic identity that seem to support a pluralistic view of society. How can both be possible?

First, there is the visible evidence of **symbolic ethnicity**, which may lead us to exaggerate the persistence of ethnic ties among White Americans. According to sociologist Herbert Gans (1979), ethnicity today increasingly involves the symbols of ethnicity, such as eating ethnic food, acknowledging ceremonial holidays such as St. Patrick's Day, and supporting specific political issues or the issues confronting the old country. One example was the push in 1998 by Irish Americans to convince state legislatures to make it compulsory in public schools to teach about the Irish potato famine, which was a significant factor in immigration to the United States. This symbolic ethnicity may be more visible, but this type of ethnic heritage does not interfere with what people do, read, or say, or even whom they befriend or marry.

The ethnicity of the twenty-first century, embraced by English-speaking Whites, is largely symbolic. It does not include active involvement in ethnic activities or participation in ethnic-related organizations. In fact, sizable proportions of White ethnics have gained large-scale entry into almost all clubs, cliques, and fraternal groups. Such acceptance is a key indicator of assimilation. Ethnicity has become increasingly peripheral to the lives of the members of the ethnic group. Although today's White ethnics may not relinquish their ethnic identity, other identities become more important.

Second, the ethnicity that does exist may be more a result of living in the United States than actual importing of practices from the past or the old country. Many so-called ethnic foods or celebrations, for example, began in the United States. The persistence of ethnic consciousness, then, may not depend on foreign birth, a distinctive language, and a unique way of life. Instead, it may reflect the experiences in the United States of a unique group that developed a cultural tradition distinct from that of the mainstream. For example, in Poland, the *szlachta*, or landed gentry, rarely mixed socially with the peasant class. In the United States, however, even with those associations still fresh, *szlachta* and peasants interacted together in social organizations as they settled in concentrated communities segregated physically and socially from others (Lopata 1994; Winter 2008).

Third, maintaining ethnicity can be a critical step toward successful assimilation. This ethnicity paradox facilitates full entry into the dominant culture. The ethnic community may give its members not only a useful financial boost but also the psychological strength and positive self-esteem that will allow them to compete effectively in a larger society. Thus, we may witness people participating actively in their ethnic enclave while trying to cross the bridge into the wider community (Lal 1995).

Therefore, ethnicity gives continuity with the past in the form of an effective or emotional tie. The significance of this sense of belonging cannot be emphasized enough. Whether reinforced by distinctive behavior or by what Milton Gordon (1964) called a sense of *peoplehood*, ethnicity is an effective, functional source of cohesion. Proximity to fellow ethnics is not necessary for a person to maintain social cohesion and in-group identity. Fraternal organizations or sports-related groups can preserve associations between ethnics who are separated geographically. Members of ethnic groups may even maintain their feelings of in-group solidarity after leaving ethnic communities in the central cities for the suburban fringe.

Despite the diversity in the languages spoken among groups of Asian Americans and Asian Pacific Islanders, they have spent generations being treated as a monolithic group. Out of similar experiences have come panethnic identities in which people share a self-image, as do African Americans or Whites of European descent. As we noted in Chapter 1, **panethnicity** is the development of solidarity between ethnic subgroups. Are Asian Americans finding a panethnic identity? In Listen to Our Voices, New York–based writer Jean Han, born in the United States and the daughter of immigrants from Korea, tackles this question head on.

## LISTEN TO OUR VOICES

### Asian America Still Discovering Elusive Identity

It's not easy to figure out the collective identity of a community.

An annual lift in spirits comes around the month of May designated as APA Heritage Month, which has become an opportunity to observe the history of Asians in America through a calendar full of cultural events and celebrations.

But the month also serves as a springboard for many Asian Americans to grapple with identity on a personal and communal level outside of these organized events.

Having a political voice, for example, still remains a challenge for Asians, says Ann Surapruik, who serves on the Washington D.C. chapter board of the national Asian Pacific American Women's Forum. According to Surapruik, when groups of high-level people gather, very often Asian Americans are not represented. "Our biggest issue is visibility," she says.

Visibility also extends to the different deeds of ethnic groups within the "Asian Pacific Islander" description. For example, a February *Seattle Times* article details the battle against the misperception by potential scholarship funders that because Asian Pacific Islander students are doing well as a group, they do not need extra help—yet there are wide disparities in standardized test performance between Japanese American and Samoan American students.

And this may prove one of the ways APA Heritage Month can be most useful: to spotlight how the APA community is cohesive, but not homogeneous. Events that come and go, like APA Heritage Month, can seem "generic," says Ben de Guzman, national campaign coordinator for the Asian Pacific American Labor Alliance. "But I think the usefulness of it is our ability to say in an official way that this is [Asian America] in all of its diversity."

APA Heritage month can also create a diversity of public forums for important Asian American issues, says Deepa Iyer, executive director of South Asian Americans Leading Together, a nonprofit community-building organization in Maryland. "Different forums exist, whether it's a corporate affinity group or a local high school, or even [looking at] Asian American history," Iyer says. "There are many different ways in which we can take a closer look at our community."

The month can also be a time for more personal reflection. Attorney Courtney Chappell, a Korean American adoptee, says her questions of Asian identity did not surface fully until college. "I'm still sort of figuring out what it means," she adds.

Chappell recalls the difficulty of finding an Asian American role model or someone who could empathize with her identity struggles. "When I face racism and discrimination, it was hard to share that with my parents, who would try but couldn't relate," she explains.

For Chappell, celebrating a heritage that is mostly foreign to her is empowering: "I celebrate by being part of a movement that is larger than me."

What it means to be Asian American on a personal level, then, may often be placed within a larger context of community. At the same time, understanding what the larger community needs means identifying its smaller parts. "Our community is so diverse," de Guzman concludes, "it exceeds our ability to describe it."

*Source*: Han 2008.

# The German Americans

Germany is the largest single source of ancestry of people in the United States today, even exceeding the continents of either Africa or Asia. Yet except in a few big-city neighborhood enclaves, the explicit presence of German culture seems largely relegated to bratwurst, pretzels, beer, and Kris Kringle.

## Settlement Patterns

In the late 1700s, the newly formed United States experienced the arrival of a number of religious dissenters from Germany (such as the Amish) who were attracted by the proclamation of religious freedom as well as prospects for economic advancement. At the time of the American Revolution, immigrants from Germany (as well as German-speaking Swiss) accounted for about one in eight White residents. German colonial subjects split their loyalty between the revolutionaries and the British, but were united in their optimistic view of the opportunities the New World would present.

Although Pennsylvania was the center of early settlements, German Americans, like virtually all other Europeans, moved out west (Ohio, Michigan, and beyond), where land was abundant. In many isolated communities, they established churches and parochial schools and, in some instances, ethnic enclaves that in selected areas spoke of creating "New Germanys."

Beginning in the 1830s through 1890, Germans represented at least one-quarter of the immigration, ensuring their destiny in the settlement of the United States (see Figure 5.2). Their major urban presence was in Milwaukee, Chicago, Cleveland, Detroit, and Cincinnati.

Early in the history of America, German immigrant cultural influence was apparent. Although the new United States never voted on making German the national language, publications of the proceedings of the Continental Congress were published in German and English. Yet even in those early years, the fear of foreigners—that is, non-Anglos—prevented German, even temporarily, from ever getting equal footing with English.

German Americans, perhaps representing 10 percent of the population, established bilingual programs in many public schools, but the rise of Germany as a military foe in the twentieth century ended that movement (Harzig 2008; Nelsen 1973).

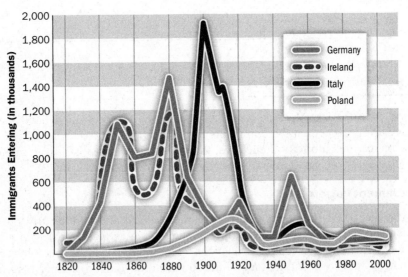

**Figure 5.2**   Immigration from Germany, Ireland, Italy, and Poland

Note: Immigration after 1925 from Northern Ireland is not included. No separate data is included for Poland from 1900 to 1920.

Source: Office of Immigration Statistics 2009:Table 2.

## Twentieth-Century German America

In 1901, the German-American National Alliance (Deutsche-Amerikanischer National-Bund) was founded to speak for all Germans in the United States, especially urban Protestant middle-class German Americans. As time passed, it sought to commemorate the contributions to the nation's development but also sought to block prohibition. With the rise of German military power, many German Americans sought to argue for U.S. neutrality. But these efforts ended quickly, and the organization actually disbanded after the United States declared war on Germany in 1917.

With World War I and especially the rise of the Nazi era and the war years of the 1930s and 1940s, most German Americans sought to distance themselves from the politics in their homeland. There were anti-German incidents of harassment and intimidation. About 11,000 German Americans (out of 5 million) were interned, but the stigmatization did not come close to that felt by Japanese Americans. By comparison, many more German Americans enlisted and played important roles (none more so than Dwight Eisenhower, whose ancestors immigrated to Pennsylvania from Germany in 1741).

Anti-German sentiment spread in the United States during World War I, escalating dramatically after the United States entered the war in April 1917. A wave of verbal and physical attacks on German Americans was accompanied by a campaign to repress German culture. In this photograph from 1917, a group of children stand in front of an anti-German sign posted in Chicago. As the sign suggests, some people in the United States questioned the loyalty of their German American neighbors.

German Americans made the group transition into core society. Indeed, Horace Kallen, who popularized the term *pluralism*, held up German America as a success in finding a place in the United States. With the end of wartime tensions, German Americans moved from having multiple identities that included being somewhat marginalized as "Germans" to an identity of "American" and, less explicitly, White (Carlson 2003; Kazal 2004; Krammer 1997).

By the latter half of the twentieth century, the animosity toward Germany seemed a part of the distant past. Germany and its people became emblematic of stalwart friends of the United States, as reflected with appearances beginning with John F. Kennedy in Berlin in 1963 and Ronald Reagan in 1987. Both spoke of the U.S. commitment to uniting Germany, and presidential candidate Barack Obama in 2008 spoke in Berlin of a united Europe.

In the last ten years, immigration from Germany, a country of 82 million, has fluctuated between 8,000 and 22,000 annually. The steady immigration for decades placed Germany in the 2000 census as the tenth largest source of foreign-born residents, with more than 700,000 (only about 170,000 behind Cuba and Korea). Yet the broad dispersion of these immigrants and their bilingual capability means the numbers are insufficient to create (or re-create) a German cultural presence. Rather, today's German American community is characterized by postwar and historical ties that have long since overshadowed the lingering bitterness of World Wars I and II (Harzig 2008; Office of Immigration Statistics 2009).

Famous German Americans include industrialist John D. Rockefeller, General John Pershing, baseball players Babe Ruth and Lou Gehrig, and actors Clark Gable and Kirsten Dunst.

## The Irish Americans

The Irish presence in the United States stretches back to the 1600s and reflects diversity based on time of entry, settlement area, and religion. Irish Americans have been visible both in a positive way in terms of playing a central role in American life and in a negative way at certain historical periods, being victimized like so many other immigrant groups.

### Irish Immigration

The Roman Catholics among the early immigrants were a diverse group. Some were extensions of the privileged classes seeking even greater prosperity. Protestant settlers of all national backgrounds including those coming from Ireland were united in their hatred of Catholicism. In most of the colonies, Catholics could not practice their faith openly and either struggled inwardly or converted to Anglicanism. Other Roman Catholics and some Protestants came from Europe as an alternative to prison or after signing articles of indenture and arriving bound to labor for periods of customarily three to five years and sometimes as long as seven years (Meagher 2005).

The American Revolution temporarily stopped the flow of immigration, but deteriorating economic conditions in Ireland soon spurred even greater movement to North America. British officials, by making passage to the newly formed republic of the United States expensive, diverted many immigrants to British North America (Canada). Yet the numbers to the United States remained significant and, although still primarily Protestant, drew from a broader spectrum of Ireland both economically and geographically.

Many people mistakenly overlook this early immigration and begin with Irish immigration during the Great Famine. Yet the Irish were the largest group after the English among immigrants during the colonial period. The historical emphasis on the famine immigrants is understandable, given the role it played in Ireland and its impetus for the massive transfer of population from Ireland to the United States.

In 1845, a fungus wiped out the potato crop of Ireland, as well as that of much of Western Europe and even coastal America. Potatoes were particularly central to the lives of the Irish, and the devastating starvation did not begin to recede until 1851. Mortality was high, especially among the poor and in the more agricultural areas of the island. Predictably, to escape catastrophe, some 2 million Irish fled mostly to England, but then many continued on to the United States. From 1841 through 1890, more than 3.2 million Irish arrived in the United States (see Figure 5.1).

This new migration fleeing the old country was much more likely to consist of families rather than single men. The arrival of entire households and extended kinship networks increased significantly the rapid formation of Irish social organizations in the United States. This large influx of immigrants led to the creation of ethnic neighborhoods, complete with parochial schools and parish churches serving as focal points. Fraternal organizations such as the Ancient Order of Hibernians, corner saloons, local political organizations, and Irish nationalist groups seeking the ouster of Britain from Ireland rounded out neighborhood social life.

Even in the best of times, the lives of the famine Irish would have been challenging in the United States, but they arrived at a very difficult time. Nativist—that is, anti-Catholic and anti-immigrant—movements were already emerging and being embraced by politicians. Antagonism was not limited to harsh words. From 1834 to 1854, mob violence against Catholics across the country led to death, the burning of a Boston convent, the destruction of a Catholic church and the homes of Catholics, and the use of Marines and state militia to bring peace to American cities as far west as St. Louis.

In retrospect, the reception given to the Irish is not difficult to understand. Many immigrated after the potato crop failure and famine in Ireland. They fled not so much to a better life as from almost certain death. The Irish Catholics brought with them a celibate clergy, who struck the New England

For many Irish American participants in a St. Patrick's Day parade, this is their most visible expression of symbolic ethnicity during the entire year.

aristocracy as strange and reawakened old religious hatreds. The Irish were worse than Blacks, according to the dominant Whites, because unlike the slaves and even the freed Blacks who "knew their place," the Irish did not suffer their maltreatment in silence. Employers balanced minorities by judiciously mixing immigrant groups to prevent unified action by the laborers. For the most part, nativist efforts only led the foreign born to emphasize their ties to Europe.

Mostly of peasant backgrounds, the Irish arriving were ill prepared to compete successfully for jobs in the city. Their children found it much easier to improve their occupational status over that of their fathers as well as experienced upward mobility in their own lifetimes.

## Becoming White

Ireland had a long antislavery tradition, including practices that prohibited Irish trade in English slaves. Some 60,000 Irish signed an address in 1841, petitioning Irish Americans to join the abolitionist movement in the United States. Many Irish Americans already opposed to slavery applauded the appeal, but they were soon drowned out by fellow immigrants who denounced or questioned the authenticity of the petition.

The Irish immigrants, subjected to derision and menial jobs, sought to separate themselves from the even lower classes, particularly Black Americans and especially the slaves. It was not altogether clear that the Irish were "White" during the antebellum period. Irish character was rigidly cast in negative racial typology. Although the shared experiences of oppression could have led Irish Americans to ally with Black Americans, they grasped for Whiteness at the margins of their lives in the United States. Direct competition was not common between the two groups. For example, in 1855, Irish immigrants made up 87 percent of New York City's unskilled laborers, whereas free Blacks accounted for only 3 percent (Greeley 1981; Ignatiev 1995; Roediger 1994).

As Irish immigration continued in the latter part of the nineteenth century until Irish independence in 1921, they began to see themselves favorably in comparison to the initial waves of Italian, Polish, and Slovak Roman Catholic immigrants. The Irish Americans began to assume more leadership positions in politics and labor unions. Loyalty to the Church still played a major role. By 1910, the priesthood was the professional occupation of choice for second-generation men. Irish women were more likely than their German and English immigrant counterparts to become schoolteachers. In time, Irish Americans' occupational profiles diversified, and they began to experience slow advancement and gradually were welcomed into the White working class as their identity as "White" overcame any status as "immigrant."

With mobility came social class distinctions within Irish America. The immigrants and their children who began to move into the more affluent urban areas were derogatorily referred to as the "lace-curtain Irish." The lower-class Irish immigrants they left behind, meanwhile, were referred to as the "shanty Irish." But as immigration from Ireland slowed and upward mobility quickened, fewer and fewer Irish qualified as the poor cousins of their predecessors.

For the Irish American man, the priesthood was viewed as a desirable and respected occupation. Irish Americans furthermore played a leadership role in the Roman Catholic Church in the United States. The Irish dominance persisted long after other ethnic groups swelled the ranks of the faithful (Fallows 1979; Lee and Bean 2007; Lee and Casey 2006).

## The Contemporary Picture

By 2009, 36.9 million people identified themselves as having Irish ancestry—second only to German ancestry and *eight* times the current population of Ireland itself. Massachusetts has the largest concentration of Irish Americans, with 24 percent of the state indicating Irish ancestry.

Irish immigration today is relatively slight, accounting for perhaps one out of 1,000 legal arrivals until, because of tough economic times, it climbed to 2,800 in 2010. About 122,000 people in the United States were born in Ireland.

Today's Irish American typically enjoys the symbolic ethnicity of food, dance, and music. Gaelic language instruction is limited to fewer than 30 colleges. Visibility as a collective ethnic group is greatest with the annual St. Patrick's Day celebrations, when everyone seems to be Irish, or with the occasional fervent nationalism aimed at curtailing Great Britain's role in Northern Ireland. Yet some stereotypes remain concerning excessive drinking despite available data indicating that alcoholism rates are no higher and sometimes lower among people of Irish ancestry compared to descendants of other European immigrant groups (Bureau of the Census 2011i; Chazan and Thomson 2011).

St. Patrick's Day celebrations, as noted previously, offer an example of how ethnic identity evolves over time. The Feast of St. Patrick has a long history, but public celebrations with parties, concerts, and parades originated in the United States, which were then exported to Ireland in the latter part of the twentieth century. Even today, the large Irish American population often defines what authentic Irish is globally. For example, participants in Irish step dancing in the United States have developed such clout in international competitions that they have come to define many aspects of cultural expression, much to the consternation of the Irish in Ireland (Bureau of the Census 2009c; Hassrick 2007).

Well-known or remembered Irish Americans can be found in all arenas of American society, including celebrity chef Bobby Flay, actor Philip Seymour Hoffman, comedian Conan O'Brien, and author Frank McCourt as well as the political dynasties of the Kennedys in Massachusetts and the Daleys in Chicago. Reflecting growing rates of intermarriage, Irish America also includes singer Mariah Carey (her mother Irish and her father African American and Venezuelan).

The Irish were the first immigrant group to encounter prolonged organized resistance. However, strengthened by continued immigration, facility with the English language, building on strong community and family networks, and familiarity with representative politics, Irish Americans became an integral part of the United States.

## The Italian Americans

Although each European country's immigration to the United States has created its own social history, the case of Italians, though not typical of every nationality, offers insight into the White ethnic experience. Italians immigrated even during the colonial period, coming from what was a highly differentiated land, because Italian states did not unify as one nation and escaped foreign domination until 1848.

### Early Immigration

From the beginning, Italian Americans played prominent roles during the American Revolution and the early days of the republic. Mass immigration began in the 1880s, peaking in the first 20 years of the twentieth century, when Italians accounted for one-fourth of European immigration (refer to Figure 5.1).

Italian immigration was concentrated not only in time but also by geography. The majority of the immigrants were landless peasants from rural southern Italy, the Mezzogiorno. Although many people in the United States assume that Italians are a nationality with a single culture, this is not true either culturally or economically. The Italian people recognize multiple geographic divisions reflecting sharp cultural distinctions. These divisions were brought with the immigrants to the New World.

Many Italians, especially in the early years of mass immigration in the nineteenth century, received their jobs through an ethnic labor contractor, the padrone. Similar arrangements have been used by Asian, Hispanic, and Greek immigrants, where the labor contractors, most often immigrants, have mastered sufficient English to mediate for their compatriots. Exploitation was common within the padrone system through kickbacks, provision of inadequate housing, and withholding of wages. By World War I, 90 percent of Italian girls and 99 percent of Italian boys in New York City were leaving school at age 14 to work, but by that time, Italian Americans were sufficiently fluent in English to seek out work on their own, and the padrone system had disappeared. Still, by comparison to the Irish, the Italians in the United States were slower to accept formal schooling as essential to success (Sassler 2006).

Along with manual labor, the Catholic Church was a very important part of Italian Americans' lives at that time. Yet they found little comfort in a Catholic Church dominated by an earlier immigrant group: the Irish. The traditions were different; weekly attendance for Italian Americans was overshadowed by the religious aspects of the feste (or festivals) held throughout the year in honor of saints (the Irish viewed the feste as practically a form of paganism). These initial adjustment problems were overcome with the establishment of ethnic parishes, a pattern repeated by other non-Irish immigrant groups. Thus, parishes would be staffed by Italian priests, sometimes imported for that purpose. Although the hierarchy of the Church adjusted more slowly, Italian Americans were increasingly able to feel at home in their local parish church. Today, more than 70 percent of Italian Americans identify themselves as Roman Catholics (Luconi 2001).

## Constructing Identity

As assimilation proceeded, Italian Americans began to construct a social identity as a nationality group rather than viewing themselves in terms of their village or province. As shown in Figure 5.3, over time, Italian Americans shed old identities for new ones. As immigration from Italy declined, the descendants' ties became more nationalistic. This move from local or regional to national identity was followed by Irish and Greek Americans. The changing identity of Italian Americans reflected the treatment they received in the United States, whereas non-Italians did not make those regional distinctions. However, they were not treated well. For example, in turn-of-the-century New Orleans, Italian Americans established special ties with the Black community because both

**Figure 5.3** Constructing Social Identity among Italian Immigrants
Over time, Italian Americans moved from seeing themselves in terms of their provincial or village identity to their national identity, and then they successfully became indistinguishable from other Whites.

groups were marginalized in Southern society. Gradually, Italian Americans became White and enjoyed all the privileges that came with it. Today, it would be inconceivable to imagine that Italian Americans of New Orleans would reach out to the African American community as their natural allies on social and political issues (Guglielmo and Salerno 2003; Luconi 2001; Steinberg 2007:126).

A controversial aspect of the Italian American experience involves organized crime, as typified by Al Capone (1899–1947). Arriving in U.S. society in the bottom layers, Italians lived in decaying, crime-ridden neighborhoods that became known as Little Italy. For a small segment of these immigrants, crime was a significant means of upward social mobility. In effect, entering and leading criminal activity was one aspect of assimilation, though not a positive one. Complaints linking ethnicity and crime actually began in colonial times with talk about the criminally inclined Irish and Germans, and they continue with contemporary stereotyping about groups such as Colombian drug dealers and Vietnamese street gangs. Yet the image of Italians as criminals has persisted from Prohibition-era gangsters to the view of mob families today. As noted earlier, it is not at all surprising that groups have been organized to counter such negative images.

The fact that Italians are often characterized as criminal, even in the mass media, is another example of what we have called respectable bigotry toward White ethnics. The persistence of linking Italians, or any other minority group, with crime is probably attributable to attempts to explain a problem by citing a single cause: the presence of perceived undesirables. Many Italian Americans still see their image tied to old stereotypes. A 2001 survey of Italian American teenagers found that 39 percent felt the media presented their ethnic group as criminal or gang members and 34 percent as restaurant workers (Girardelli 2004; Italian-Americans Against Media Stereotypes 2009; National Italian American Foundation 2006; Parrillo 2008).

The immigration of Italians was slowed by the national origins system, described in Chapter 4. As Italian Americans settled permanently, the mutual aid to provide basic social services to societies that had grown up in the 1920s began to dissolve. More slowly, education came to be valued by Italian Americans as a means of upward mobility. Even becoming more educated did not ward off prejudice, however. In 1930, for example, President Herbert Hoover rebuked Fiorello La Guardia, then an Italian American member of Congress from New York City, stating that "the Italians are predominantly our murderers and bootleggers" and recommending that La Guardia "go back to where you belong" because, "like a lot of other foreign spawn, you do not appreciate this country which supports you and tolerates you" (Baltzell 1964:30).

Although U.S. troops, including 500,000 Italian Americans, battled Italy during World War II, some hatred and sporadic violence emerged against Italian Americans and their property. However, they were not limited to actions against individuals. Italian Americans were even confined by the federal government in specific areas of California by virtue of their ethnicity alone, and 10,000 were relocated from coastal areas. In addition, 1,800 Italian Americans who were citizens of Italy were placed in an internment camp in Montana. The internees were eventually freed on Columbus Day 1942 as President Roosevelt lobbied the Italian American community to gain full support for the impending land invasion of Italy (Department of Justice 2001; Fox 1990).

## The Contemporary Picture

In politics, Italian Americans have been more successful, at least at the local level, where family and community ties can be translated into votes. However, political success did not come easily because many Italian immigrants anticipated returning to their homeland and did not always take neighborhood politics seriously. It was even more difficult for Italian Americans to break into national politics.

Not until 1962 was an Italian American named to a cabinet-level position. Geraldine Ferraro's nomination as the Democratic vice presidential candidate in 1984 was every bit as much an achievement for Italian Americans as it was for women. The opposition to the nomination of Judge Samuel Alito to the Supreme Court in 2006 struck many as bordering on anti–Italian American sentiments in the manner the opposition was advanced. Numerous critics used the phrase "Judge Scalito" in obvious reference to the sitting Italian American on the Court, Justice Antonio Scalia (Cornacchia and Nelson 1996).

While as a group Italian Americans are firmly a part of middle America, they frequently continue to be associated with crime. In 2009, three New Jersey mayors were indicted for corruption and not all of them were Italian; at the core of the scandal were five Syrian American rabbis. Yet newspapers quickly dubbed it "New Jersey's 'Italian' Problem." MTV's successful reality show *Jersey*

*Shore*, which seems to focus on drinking, hot tubbing, and brawling stars, did not help. Stereotypes and labeling do not go away and truth is no antidote (Cohen 2010a; McGurn 2009).

There is no paucity of well known or remembered Italian Americans. They include athletes such as Joe DiMaggio, politician Rudolph Giuliani, film director Francis Ford Coppola, singer Madonna, comedian Jay Leno, writer Mario Puzo, actor Nicholas Cage, chef Rachel Ray, and auto racing legend Mario Andretti.

Italian Americans still remain the seventh-largest immigrant group. Just how ethnically conscious is the Italian American community? Although the number is declining, 800,000 Americans speak Italian at home; only eight languages are spoken more frequently at home: Spanish, French, Chinese, Vietnamese, Russian, Tagalog (Philippines), German, and Japanese. For another 14-plus million Italian Americans, however, the language tie to their culture is absent, and, depending on their degree of assimilation, only traces of symbolic ethnicity may remain. In a later section, we look at the role that language plays for many immigrants and their children (Shin and Kominski 2010).

## The Polish Americans

Immigrants from Poland have had experiences similar to those of the Irish and Italians. They had to overcome economic problems and personal hardships just to make the journey. Once in the United States, they found themselves often assigned to the jobs many citizens had not wanted to do. They had to adjust to a new language and a familiar yet different culture. And they were always looking back to the family members left behind who either wanted to join them in the United States or, in contrast, never wanted them to leave in the first place.

Like other arrivals, many Poles sought improvement in their lives through migration that was known as *ZaChlebem* (For Bread). The Poles who came were, at different times, more likely than many other European immigrants to see themselves as forced immigrants and were often described by, and themselves adopted, the terminology directly reflecting their social roles—exiles, refugees, displaced persons, or émigrés. The primary force for this exodus was the changing political status of Poland through most of the nineteenth and twentieth centuries, which was as turbulent as the lives of the new arrivals.

### Early Immigration

Polish immigrants were among the settlers at Jamestown, Virginia, in 1608, who helped develop the colony's timber industry, but it was the Poles who came later in that century who made a lasting mark. The successful exploits of Polish immigrants such as cavalry officer Casimir Pulaski and military engineer Thaddeus Kosciuszko are still commemorated today in communities with large

Polish American populations. As we can see in Figure 5.1, it was not until the 1890s that Polish immigration was significant in comparison to some other European arrivals. Admittedly, it is difficult to exactly document the size of this immigration because at various historical periods Poland or parts of the country became part of Austria–Hungary, Germany (Prussia), and the Soviet Union, so that the migrants were not officially coming from a nation called "Poland."

Many of the Polish immigrants were adjusting not only to a new culture but also to a more urban way of life. Sociologists William I. Thomas and Florian Znaniecki, in their classic study *The Polish Peasant in Europe and America* ([1918] 1996), traced the path from rural Poland to urban America. Many of the peasants did not necessarily come directly to the United States but first traveled through other European countries. This pattern is not unique and reminds us that, even today, many immigrants have crossed several countries, sometimes establishing themselves for a period of time before finally settling in the United States (Abbott and Egloff 2008).

Like the Germans, Italians, and Irish, Poles arrived at the large port cities of the East Coast but, unlike the other immigrant groups, these were more likely

Richie Sambora, a guitarist with the rock group Bon Jovi, is one of many well-known Polish Americans.

to settle in cities further inland or work in mines in Pennsylvania. In such areas, they would join kinfolk or acquaintances through the process of chain migration (as described in Chapter 4).

The reference to coal mining as an occupation reflects the continuing tendency of immigrants to work in jobs avoided by most U.S. citizens because they paid little, were dangerous, or both. For example, in September 1897, a group of miners in Lattimer, Pennsylvania, marched to demand safer working conditions and an end to special taxes placed only on foreign-born workers. In the ensuing confrontation with local officials, police officers shot at the protesters, killing 19 people, most of who were Polish, the others Lithuanians and Slovaks (Duszak 1997).

## Polonia

With growing numbers, the emergence of Polonia (meaning Polish communities outside of Poland) became more common in cities throughout the Midwest. Male immigrants who came alone often took shelter through a system of inexpensive boarding houses called *tryzmaniebortnków* (brother keeping), which allowed the new arrival to save money and send it back to Poland to support his family. These funds eventually provided the financial means necessary to bring family members over, adding to the size of Polonia in cities such as Buffalo, Cleveland, Detroit, Milwaukee, Pittsburgh, and, above all, Chicago, where the population of Poles was second only to Warsaw, Poland.

Religion has played an important role among Polish immigrants and their descendants. Most of the Polish immigrants who came to the United States before World War I were Roman Catholic. They quickly established their own parishes where new arrivals could feel welcome. Although religious services at that time were in the Latin language, as they had been in Poland, the many service organizations around the parish, not to mention the Catholic schools, kept the immigrants steeped in the Polish language and the latest happenings back home. Jewish Poles began immigrating during the first part of the twentieth century to escape the growing hostility they felt in Europe, which culminated in the Holocaust. Their numbers swelled greatly until movement from Poland stopped with the invasion of Poland by Germany in 1939; it resumed after the war.

Although the Jewish–Catholic distinction may be the most obvious distinguishing factor among Polish Americans, there are other divisions as well. Regional subgroups such as the Kashubes, the Górali, and the Mazurians have often carried great significance. Some Poles emigrated from areas where German was actually the language of origin.

As with other immigrant groups, Polish Americans could make use of a rich structure of voluntary self-help associations that was already well established by the 1890s. Not all organizations smoothly cut across different generations of Polish immigrants. For example, the Poles who came immediately after World

War II as political refugees fleeing Soviet domination were quite different in their outlook than the descendants of the economic refugees from the turn of the century. These kinds of tensions in an immigrant community are not unusual, even if they go unnoticed by the casual observer who lumps all immigrants of the same nationality together (Jaroszyn'ska-Kirchmann 2004).

Like many other newcomers, Poles have been stigmatized as outsiders and also stereotyped as simple and uncultured—the typical biased view of working-class White ethnics. Their struggles in manual occupations placed them in direct competition with other White ethnics and African Americans, which occasionally led to labor disputes and longer-term tense and emotional rivalries. "Polish jokes" continue now to have a remarkable shelf life in casual conversation well into the twenty-first century. Jewish Poles suffer the added indignities of anti-Semitism (Dolan and Stotsky 1997).

## The Contemporary Picture

Today, Polonia in the United States is nearly 10 million. Although this may not seem significant in a country of more than 300 million, we need to recall that today Poland itself has a population of only about 39 million. Whether it was to support the efforts of Lech Walesa, the Solidarity movement leader who confronted the Soviet Union in the 1980s, or to celebrate the elevation of Karol József Wojtyla as Pope John Paul II in 1978, Polish Americans are a central part of the global Polish community.

Many Polish Americans have retained little of their rich cultural traditions and may barely acknowledge even symbolic ethnicity. Data released in 2010 show about 690,000 whose primary language is Polish, with 31 percent in Chicago and another 23 percent in New York City. Others are still immersed in Polonia, and their lives still revolve around many of the same religious and social institutions that were the center of Polonia a century ago. For example, 54 Roman Catholic churches in the metropolitan Chicago area still offer Polish-language masses. Although in many of these parishes there may be only one service in Polish serving a declining number of celebrants, a few traditional "Polish" churches actually still have Polish-speaking priests in residence. Even with the decline in Polish-language services, Pole seminarians are actively recruited by the Roman Catholic Church, although now English-language training is often emphasized.

In the latter part of the twentieth century, some of the voluntary associations relocated or built satellite centers to serve the outlying Polish American populations. To sustain their activities financially, these social organizations also reached out of the central cities in order to tap into the financial resources of suburban Poles. Increasingly, people of Polish descent also have now made their way into the same social networks populated by German, Irish, Italian, and other ethnic Americans (Bukowcyk 2007; Erdmans 1998, 2006; Lopata 1994; Mocha 1998; Polzin 1973; Shin and Kominski 2010; Stone 2006).

Except for immigrants who fled persecution in their homelands, immigration typically has back-and-forth movement. In the early years of the twenty-first century, there was an identifiable movement of Polish Americans from Polonia to Poland, especially as economic opportunity improved in the home country. One estimate of returnees places it at 50,000 from 2004 to 2009, which is a significant number in absolute numbers but is relatively small given the magnitude of the Polish American community (Hundley 2009).

Among the many Polish Americans well known or remembered today are actor Adrien Brody, home designer Martha (Kostyra) Stewart, comedian Jack Benny (Benjamin Kubelsky), guitarist Richie Sambora of the rock group Bon Jovi, actress Jane Kaczmarek of *Malcolm in the Middle*, entertainer Liberace, *Wheel of Fortune* host Pat Sajak, baseball star Stan Musial, football star Mike Ditka, novelist Joseph Conrad (Józef Korzeniowski), singer Bobby Vinton (Stanley Ventula, Jr.), polio vaccine pioneer Albert Sabin, and motion picture director Stanley Kubrick.

## Religious Pluralism

Religion plays a fundamental role in society, even affecting those who do not practice or even believe in organized religion. **Religion** refers to a unified system of sacred beliefs and practices that encompass elements beyond everyday life that inspire awe, respect, and even fear (Durkheim [1912] 2001).

In popular speech, the term *pluralism* has often been used in the United States to refer explicitly to religion. Although certain faiths figure more prominently in the worship scene, there has been a history of greater religious tolerance in the United States than in most other nations. Today there are more than 1,500 religious bodies in the United States, ranging from the more than 66 million members of the Roman Catholic Church to sects with fewer than 1,000 adherents. In virtually every region of the country, religion is being expressed in greater variety, whether it be the Latinization of Catholicism and some Christian faiths or the de-Europeanizing of some established Protestant faiths as with Asian Americans or the de-Christianizing of the overall religious landscape with Muslims, Buddhists, Hindus, Sikhs, and others (Roof 2007).

How do we view the United States in terms of religion? There is an increasingly non-Christian presence in the United States. In 1900, an estimated 96 percent of the nation was Christian; slightly more than 1 percent was nonreligious, and approximately 3 percent held other faiths. In 2010, it was estimated that the nation was 74 percent Christian, 14 percent nonreligious, and another 12 percent all other faiths. The United States has a long Jewish tradition, and Muslims number close to 5 million. A smaller but also growing number of people adhere to such Eastern faiths as Hinduism, Buddhism, Confucianism, and Taoism (Gallup 2010).

The Greek Orthodox Church is one of 25 Christian faiths with at least a million members.

Sociologists use the word **denomination** for a large, organized religion that is not linked officially with the state or government. By far, the largest denomination in the United States is Catholicism; yet at least 26 other Christian religious denominations have 1 million or more members as of 2011 (Table 5.1).

There are also at least four non-Christian religious groups in the United States whose numbers are comparable to any of these large denominations: Jews, Muslims, Buddhists, and Hindus. In the United States each numbers more than 1 million members. Within each of these groups are branches or sects that distinguish themselves from each other. For example, as we examine in greater detail later in this chapter, in the United States and the rest of the world, some Muslims are Sunni and others Shia. There are further divisions within these groups, just as there are among Protestants, and, in turn, among Baptists.

Islam in the United States has a long history stretching back to Muslim Africans who came as slaves to today's Muslim community, which includes immigrants and native-born Americans. President Obama, the son of a practicing Muslim and who lived for years in Indonesia, the country with the largest Muslim population, never sought to hide his roots. However, reflecting the prejudices of many toward non-Christians, his Christian upbringing was stressed throughout the campaign. Little wonder that a national survey showed that 55 percent believe the U.S. Constitution establishes the country as a "Christian nation" (Cose 2008; Thomas 2007).

## Table 5.1 Churches with More Than a Million Members

| Denomination Name | Inclusive Membership |
|---|---|
| Roman Catholic Church | 68,503,456 |
| Southern Baptist Convention | 16,160,088 |
| United Methodist Church | 7,774,931 |
| Church of Jesus Christ of Latter-Day Saints | 6,058,907 |
| Church of God in Christ | 5,499,875 |
| National Baptist Convention, U.S.A., Inc. | 5,000,000 |
| Evangelical Lutheran Church in America | 4,542,868 |
| National Baptist Convention of America, Inc. | 3,500,000 |
| Assemblies of God | 2,914,669 |
| Presbyterian Church (U.S.A.) | 2,770,730 |
| African Methodist Episcopal Church | 2,500,000 |
| National Missionary Baptist Convention of America | 2,500,000 |
| Lutheran Church—Missouri Synod (LCMS) | 2,312,111 |
| Episcopal Church | 2,006,343 |
| Churches of Christ | 1,639,495 |
| Greek Orthodox Archdiocese of America | 1,500,000 |
| Pentecostal Assemblies of the World, Inc. | 1,500,000 |
| African Methodist Episcopal Zion Church | 1,400,000 |
| American Baptist Churches in the U.S.A. | 1,310,505 |
| Jehovah's Witnesses | 1,162,686 |
| United Church of Christ | 1,080,199 |
| Church of God (Cleveland, TN) | 1,076,254 |
| Christian Churches and Churches of Christ | 1,071,616 |
| Seventh-Day Adventist Church | 1,043,606 |
| Progressive National Baptist Convention, Inc. | 1,010,000 |

Note: Most recent data as of 2011.

Source: Eileen Lindner (ed.) 2011. *Yearbook of American and Canadian Churches 2011*, Table 2, p. 12. Nashville, TN: Abingdon Press. Reprinted by permission from *Yearbook of American and Canadian Churches 2011*. Copyright © National Council of Churches of Christ in the USA.

Even if religious faiths have broad representation, they tend to be fairly homogeneous at the local church level. This is especially ironic, given that many faiths have played critical roles in resisting racism and in trying to bring together the nation in the name of racial and ethnic harmony.

Broadly defined faiths represent a variety of ethnic and racial groups. In Figure 5.4, we consider the interaction of White, Black, and Hispanic races with religions. Muslims, Pentecostals, and Jehovah's Witnesses are much

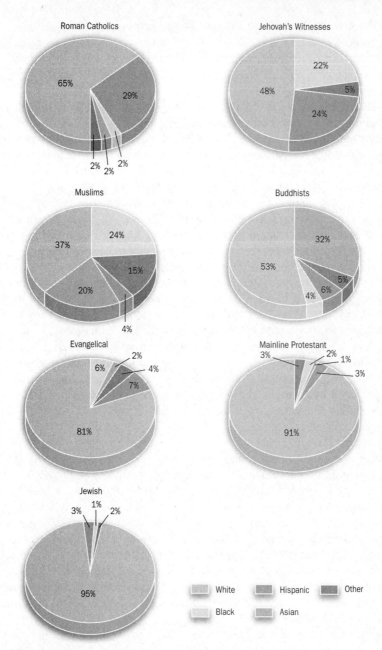

**Figure 5.4** Racial and Ethnic Makeup of Selected Religions in the United States

*Note*: "Other" includes self-identified mixed race. Evangelical includes Baptist, Lutheran (Missouri and Wisconsin Synods), and Pentecostal, among others. Mainline Protestant includes Methodist, Lutheran (ELCA), Presbyterian, Episcopal, and United Church of Christ, among others, but excludes historically Black churches. Based on a national survey of 35,556 adults conducted in August 2007.

*Source*: Pew Forum on Religion and Public Life 2008b:120.

more diverse than Presbyterians or Lutherans. Religion plays an even more central role for Blacks and Latinos than Whites. A national survey indicated that 65 percent of African Americans and 51 percent of Latinos attend a religious service every week, compared to 44 percent of White non-Hispanics (Winseman 2004).

It would also be mistaken to focus only on older religious organizations. Local churches that developed into national faiths in the 1990s, such as the Calvary Chapel, Vineyard, and Hope Chapel, have created a following among Pentecostal believers, who embrace a more charismatic form of worship devoid of many traditional ornaments, with pastors and congregations alike favoring informal attire. New faiths develop with increasing rapidity in what can only be called a very competitive market for individual religious faith. In addition, many people, with or without religious affiliation, become fascinated with spiritual concepts such as angels or become a part of loose-knit fellowships such as the Promise Keepers, an all-male movement of evangelical Christians founded in 1990. Religion in the United States is an ever-changing social phenomenon. Other nonmainstream faiths emerge in new arenas, as evidenced by the campaign of Mitt Romney, a Mormon, to win the Republican nomination for president in 2008 or the visible role of celebrities promoting the Church of Scientology (Dudley and Roozen 2001; Schaefer and Zellner 2011).

Divisive conflicts along religious lines are muted in the United States compared with those in, say, the Middle East. Although not entirely absent, conflicts about religion in the United States seem to be overshadowed by civil religion. **Civil religion** is the religious dimension in the United States that merges public life with sacred beliefs. It also reflects that no single faith is privileged over all others.

Sociologist Robert Bellah (1967) borrowed the phrase *civil religion* from eighteenth-century French philosopher Jean-Jacques Rousseau to describe a significant phenomenon in the contemporary United States. Civil religion exists alongside established religious faiths, and it embodies a belief system that incorporates all religions but is not associated specifically with any one. It is the type of faith to which presidents refer in inaugural speeches and to which American Legion posts and Girl Scout troops swear allegiance. In 1954, Congress added the phrase *under God* to the pledge of allegiance as a legislative recognition of religion's significance. Elected officials in the United States, beginning with Ronald Reagan, often concluded even their most straightforward speeches with "God bless the United States of America," which in effect evokes the civil religion of the nation.

Functionalists see civil religion as reinforcing central American values that may be more expressly patriotic than sacred in nature. Often, the mass media, following major societal upheavals, from the 1995 Oklahoma City bombing to the 2001 terrorist attacks, show church services with clergy praying and asking for national healing. Bellah (1967) sees no sign that the importance of civil religion has diminished in promoting collective identity, but he does acknowledge that it is more conservative than during the 1970s.

Beginning with the Clinton administration, the federal government has made explicit effort to include religious organizations. The 1996 welfare reform act President Clinton signed provided that religious groups could compete for grants. President George W. Bush created a White House Office of Faith-Based and Community Initiatives to provide for a significant expansion of charitable choice. President Barack Obama has continued the office, naming a Pentecostal minister to oversee it (Jacoby 2009).

In the following sections, we explore the diversity among the major Christian groups in the United States, such as Roman Catholics and Protestants, as well as how Islam has emerged as a significant religious force in the United States and can no longer be regarded as a marginal faith in terms of followers (Gorski 2010).

## Diversity among Roman Catholics

Social scientists have persistently tended to ignore the diversity within the Roman Catholic Church in the United States. Recent research has not sustained the conclusions that Roman Catholics are melding into a single group, following the traditions of the American Irish Catholic model, or even that parishioners are attending English-language churches. Religious behavior has been different for each ethnic group within the Roman Catholic Church. The Irish and French Canadians left societies that were highly competitive both culturally and socially. Their religious involvement in the United States is more relaxed than it was in Ireland and Quebec. However, the influence of life in the United States has increased German and Polish involvement in the Roman Catholic Church, whereas Italians have remained largely inactive. Variations by ethnic background continue to emerge in studies of contemporary religious involvement in the Roman Catholic Church (Eckstrom 2001).

Since the mid-1970s, the Roman Catholic Church in America has received a significant number of new members from the Philippines, Southeast Asia, and particularly Latin America. Although these new members have been a stabilizing force offsetting the loss of White ethnics, they have also challenged a church that for generations was dominated by Irish, Italian, and Polish parishes. Perhaps the most prominent subgroup in the Roman Catholic Church is the Latinos, who now account for one-third of all Roman Catholic parishioners. Some Los Angeles churches in or near Latino neighborhoods must schedule 14 masses each Sunday to accommodate the crowds of worshipers. In 2010, the Pope selected a Latino, Mexican-born Archbishop Jose H. Gomez, to lead the Los Angeles Archdiocese (Goodstein and Steinhauer 2010; Navarro-Rivera, Kosmin, and Keysar 2010).

The Roman Catholic Church, despite its ethnic diversity, has clearly been a powerful force in reducing the ethnic ties of its members, making it also

Reflecting the rising presence of Latinos among Roman Catholics nationwide and specifically in Los Angeles, the Pope selected a Latino, Mexican-born Archbishop Jose H. Gomez, to lead the Los Angeles Archdiocese.

a significant assimilating force. The irony in this role of Catholicism is that so many nineteenth-century Americans heaped abuse on Catholics in this country for allegedly being un-American and having a dual allegiance. The history of the Catholic Church in the United States may be portrayed as a struggle within the membership between the Americanizers and the anti-Americanizers, with the former ultimately winning. Unlike the various Protestant churches that accommodated immigrants of a single nationality, the Roman Catholic Church had to Americanize a variety of linguistic and ethnic groups. The Catholic Church may have been the most potent assimilating force after the public school system. Comparing the assimilationist goal of the Catholic Church and the current diversity in it leads us to the conclusion that ethnic diversity has continued in the Roman Catholic Church despite, not because of, this religious institution.

## Diversity among Protestants

Protestantism, like Catholicism, often is portrayed as a monolithic entity. Little attention is given to the doctrinal and attitudinal differences that sharply divide the various denominations in both laity and clergy. However, several studies document the diversity. Unfortunately, many opinion polls and surveys are content to learn whether a respondent is a Catholic, a Protestant, or a Jew. Stark and Glock (1968) found sharp differences in religious attitudes within Protestant churches. For example, 99 percent of Southern Baptists had no doubt that Jesus was the divine Son of God as contrasted to only 40 percent of Congregationalists. We can identify four "generic theological camps":

1. *Liberals*: United Church of Christ (Congregationalists) and Episcopalians
2. *Moderates*: Disciples of Christ, Methodists, and Presbyterians
3. *Conservatives*: American Lutherans and American Baptists
4. *Fundamentalists*: Missouri Synod Lutherans, Southern Baptists, and Assembly of God

Roman Catholics generally hold religious beliefs similar to those of conservative Protestants, except on essentially Catholic issues such as papal infallibility (the authority of the spiritual role in all decisions regarding faith and morals). Whether or not there are four distinct camps is not important: the point is that the familiar practice of contrasting Roman Catholics and Protestants is clearly not productive. Some differences between Roman Catholics and Protestants are inconsequential compared with the differences between Protestant sects.

Secular criteria as well as doctrinal issues may distinguish religious faiths. Research has consistently shown that denominations can be arranged in a hierarchy based on social class. Members of certain faiths, such as Episcopalians, Jews, and Presbyterians, have a higher proportion of affluent members. Members of other faiths, including Baptists, tend to be poorer. Of course, all Protestant groups draw members from each social stratum. Nonetheless, the social significance of these class differences is that religion becomes a mechanism for signaling social mobility. A person who is moving up in wealth and power may seek out a faith associated with a higher social ranking. Similar contrasts are shown in formal schooling.

Protestant faiths have been diversifying, and many of their members have been leaving them for churches that follow strict codes of behavior or fundamental interpretations of biblical teachings. This trend is reflected in the gradual decline of the five mainline churches: Baptist, Episcopalian, Lutheran, Methodist, and Presbyterian. In 2006, these faiths accounted for about 58 percent of total Protestant membership, compared with 65 percent in the 1970s. With a broader acceptance of new faiths and continuing immigration, it is unlikely that these mainline churches will regain their dominance in the near future (Davis, Smith, and Marsden 2007:171–172).

Although Protestants may seem to define the civil religion and the accepted dominant orientation, some Christian faiths feel they, too, experience the discrimination usually associated with non-Christians such as Jews and Muslims. For example, representatives of the liberal and moderate faiths dominate the leadership of the military's chaplain corps. There are 16 Presbyterian soldiers for every Presbyterian chaplain, 121 Full Gospel worshippers for every Full Gospel chaplain, and 339 Muslim soldiers for every Muslim chaplain (Cooperman 2005).

As another example of denominational discrimination, in 1998, the Southern Baptist Convention amended its basic theological statements of beliefs to include a strong statement on family life. However, the statement included a declaration that a woman should "submit herself graciously" to her husband's leadership. There were widespread attacks on this position, which many Baptists felt was inappropriate because they were offering guidance for their denomination's members. In some respects, Baptists felt this was a form of respectable bigotry. It was acceptable to attack them for their views on social issues even though such criticism would be much more muted for many more liberal faiths that seem free to tolerate abortion (Bowman 1998; Niebuhr 1998).

## Religion and the Courts

Religious pluralism owes its existence in the United States to the First Amendment declaration that "Congress shall make no law respecting an establishment of religion, or prohibiting the free exercise thereof." The U.S. Supreme Court has consistently interpreted this wording to mean not that government should ignore religion but that it should follow a policy of neutrality to maximize religious freedom. For example, the government may not help religion by financing a new church building, but it also may not obstruct religion by denying a church adequate police and fire protection. We examine four issues that continue to require clarification: school prayer, secessionist minorities and their rituals, creationism (including intelligent design), and the public display of religious (or sacred) symbols.

**School Prayer**    Among the most controversial and continuing disputes has been whether prayer has a role in the schools. Many people were disturbed by the 1962 Supreme Court decision in *Engel v. Vitale*, which disallowed a purportedly nondenominational prayer drafted for use in the New York public schools. The prayer was "Almighty God, we acknowledge our dependence upon Thee, and we beg Thy blessings upon us, our parents, our teachers, and our country." Subsequent decisions overturned state laws requiring Bible reading in public schools, laws requiring recitation of the Lord's Prayer, and laws permitting a daily one-minute period of silent meditation or prayer. Despite such judicial pronouncements, children in many public schools in the United States are led in regular prayer recitation or Bible reading.

What about prayers at public gatherings? In 1992, the Supreme Court ruled 5–4 in *Lee v. Weisman* that prayer at a junior high school graduation in Providence, Rhode Island, violated the U.S. Constitution's mandate of separation of church and state. A rabbi had given thanks to God in his invocation. The district court suggested that the invocation would have been acceptable without that reference. The Supreme Court did not agree with the school board that a prayer at a graduation was not coercive. The Court did say in its opinion that it was acceptable for a student speaker voluntarily to say a prayer at such a program (Marshall 2001).

Public schools and even states have mandated a "moment of silence" at the start of the school day in what critics contend is a transparent attempt to get around *Lee v. Weisman*. The Supreme Court had struck down such actions earlier, but then prayer was clearly intended by legislators when they created these "moments."

**Secessionist Minorities**    Several religious groups have been in legal and social conflict with the rest of society. Some can be called **secessionist minorities** in that they reject both assimilation and coexistence in some form of cultural pluralism. The Amish are one such group that comes into conflict with outside society because of its beliefs and way of life. The Old Order Amish shun most modern conveniences and maintain a lifestyle dramatically different from that of larger society.

Are there limits to the free exercise of religious rituals by secessionist minorities? Today, tens of thousands of members of Native American religions believe that ingesting the powerful drug peyote is a sacrament and that those who partake of peyote will enter into direct contact with God. In 1990, the Supreme Court ruled that prosecuting people who use illegal drugs as part of a religious ritual is not a violation of the First Amendment guarantee of religious freedom. The case arose because Native Americans were dismissed from their jobs for the religious use of peyote and were then refused unemployment benefits by the state of Oregon's employment division. In 1991, however, Oregon enacted a new law permitting the sacramental use of peyote by Native Americans (*New York Times* 1991).

In another ruling on religious rituals, in 1993, the Supreme Court unanimously overturned a local ordinance in Florida that banned ritual animal sacrifice. The High Court held that this law violated the free-exercise rights of adherents of the Santeria religion, in which the sacrifice of animals (including goats, chickens, and other birds) plays a central role. The same year, Congress passed the Religious Freedom Restoration Act, which said the government may not enforce laws that "substantially burden" the exercise of religion. Presumably, this action will give religious groups more flexibility in practicing their faiths. However, many local and state officials are concerned that the law has led to unintended consequences, such as forcing states to accommodate prisoners' requests for

The U.S. Department of Veterans Affairs eventually approved, after lobbying by Wiccans, the pentacle symbol for use on the cemetery markers of fallen soldiers who self-identify as Witches.

questionable religious activities or to permit a church to expand into a historic district in defiance of local laws (Greenhouse 1996).

The legal acceptance of different faiths has been illustrated in numerous decisions. For example, the courts have allowed Wiccan organizations to enjoy nonprofit status. In addition, the U.S. Department of Veterans Affairs' approval of the pentacle symbol for use on the cemetery markers of fallen soldiers buried in any of the national cemeteries who self-identify as Witches.

**Creationism and Intelligent Design**   The third area of contention has been whether the biblical account of creation should be or must be presented in school curricula and whether this account should receive the same emphasis as scientific theories. In the famous "monkey trial" of 1925, Tennessee schoolteacher John Scopes was found guilty of teaching the scientific theory of evolution in public schools. Since then, however, Darwin's evolutionary theories have been presented in public schools with little reference to the biblical account in Genesis. People who support the literal interpretation of the Bible, commonly known as **creationists**, have formed various organizations to crusade for creationist treatment in U.S. public schools and universities.

In a 1987 Louisiana case, *Edwards v. Aguillard*, the Supreme Court ruled that states may not require the teaching of creationism alongside evolution in public schools if the primary purpose of such legislation is to promote a religious viewpoint. Nevertheless, the teaching of evolution and creationism has remained a controversial issue in many communities across the United States (Applebome 1996).

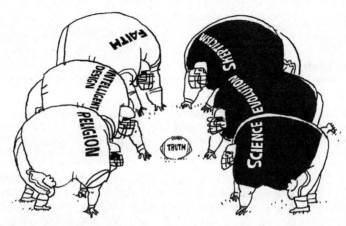

Competing interests argue over the inclusion of intelligent design as a valid aspect of science curriculum in public schools.

*Source*: The Mike Lester Studio, Inc.

Beginning in the 1980s, those who believe in a divine hand in the creation of life have advanced **intelligent design** (ID), the idea that life is so complex it could only have been created by a higher intelligence. Although not explicitly drawn on the biblical account, creationists feel comfortable with ID and advocate that it is a more accurate account than Darwinism or, at the very least, that it be taught as an alternative alongside the theory of evolution. In 2005, a federal judge in *Kitzmiller v. Dove Area School District* ended a Pennsylvania school district intention to require the presentation of ID. In essence, the judge found ID to be "a religious belief" that was only a subtler way of finding God's fingerprints in nature than traditional creationism. Because the issue continues to be hotly debated, future court cases are certain to come (Clemmitt 2005; Goodstein 2005).

**Public Displays**    The fourth area of contention has been a battle over public displays that depict symbols of religion or appear to others to be sacred representations. Can manger scenes be erected on public property? Do people have a right to be protected from large displays such as a cross or a star atop a water tower overlooking an entire town? In a series of decisions in the 1980s through 1995, the Supreme Court ruled that tax-supported religious displays on public government property may be successfully challenged but may be permissible if made more secular. Displays that combine a crèche, the Christmas manger scene depicting the birth of Jesus, or the Hanukkah menorah and also include

Frosty the Snowman or even Christmas trees have been ruled secular. These decisions have been dubbed "the plastic reindeer rules." In 1995, the Court clarified the issue by stating that privately sponsored religious displays may be allowed on public property if other forms of expression are permitted in the same location (Bork 1995; Hirsley 1991; Mauro 1995).

## Conclusion

Considering ethnicity and religion reinforces our understanding of the spectrum of intergroup relations first presented in Chapter 1. The Spectrum of Intergroup Relations figure shows the rich variety of relationships as defined by people's ethnic and religious identities. The profiles of German, Irish, Italian, and Polish Americans reflect the variety of White ethnic experiences.

Any study of life in the United States, especially one that focuses on dominant and subordinate groups, cannot ignore religion and ethnicity. The two are closely related, as certain religious faiths predominate in certain nationalities. Both religious activity and interest by White ethnics in their heritage continue to be prominent features of the contemporary scene. People have been and continue to be ridiculed or deprived of opportunities solely because of their ethnic or religious affiliation. To get a true picture of people's place in society, we need to consider both ethnicity and social class in association with their religious identification.

Religion is changing in the United States. As one commercial recognition of this fact, Hallmark created its first greeting card in 2003 for the Muslim holiday Eid-al-fitr, which marks the end of the month-long fast of Ramadan. The issue of the persistence of ethnicity is an intriguing one. Some people may only casually exhibit their ethnicity and practice what has been called symbolic ethnicity. However, can people immerse themselves in their ethnic culture without society punishing them for their will to be different? The tendency to put down White ethnics through respectable bigotry continues. Despite this intolerance, ethnicity remains a viable source of identity for many citizens today. There is also the ethnic paradox, which finds that practicing one's ethnic heritage often strengthens people and allows them to move successfully into the larger society.

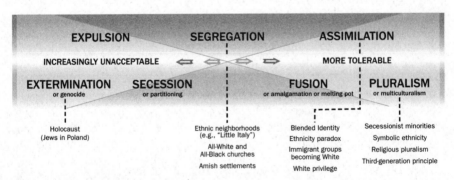

**Spectrum of Intergroup Relations**

The social significance of identity is a reoccurring theme in this chapter. We consider how identity may change as immigrants remain longer in the United States and how identity may differ between the adult immigrant and their children born in the United States. Even among second- and third-generation immigrants, identity may not be straightforward as they employ multiple identities and hold an identity, which others may not readily identify in the same manner.

The issue of religious expression in all its forms also raises a variety of intriguing questions. How can a country that is increasingly populated by diverse and often non-Christian faiths maintain religious tolerance? How might this change in the decades ahead? How will the courts and society resolve the issues of religious freedom? This is a particularly important issue in areas such as school prayer, secessionist minorities, creationism, intelligent design, and public religious displays. Some examination of religious ties is fundamental to completing an accurate picture of a person's social identity.

Ethnicity and religion are a basic part of today's social reality and of each individual's identity. The emotions, disputes, and debate over religion and ethnicity in the United States are powerful indeed.

## Summary

1. While considering race and ethnicity in the United States, we often ignore how White people come to see themselves as a group and in relationship to others.

2. Feelings of ethnicity may be fading among the descendants of Europeans, but it may reemerge as reflected in either the third-generation principle or, in a more limited fashion, through symbolic ethnicity.

3. Maintaining or remaining networked to one's ethnic roots can actually facilitate success and eventually assimilation, as has been documented in the study of the ethnic paradox.

4. Even though the historical circumstances and settlement patterns differ, there are definite similarities in the experiences of German, Irish, Italian, and Polish Americans.

5. Research shows that historically, at least, a generation passes before immigrants experienced upward mobility. Contemporary immigrants seem to follow the same pattern, with most speaking English fluently by the second generation and virtually all third-generation members doing so.

6. The ethnic diversity of the United States is matched by the many denominations among Christians as well as the sizable Jewish and Muslim presence.

7. In its interpretation of the First Amendment, the Supreme Court has tried to preserve religious freedom, but critics have argued that the Court has served to stifle religious expression.

## Key Terms

blended identity  159
civil religion  184
creationists  190
deficit model of ethnic
  identity  160
denomination  181

ethnic paradox  162
intelligent design  191
panethnicity  164
principle of third-generation
  interest  161
religion  180

secessionist minority  189
symbolic ethnicity  163
White privilege  158

## Review Questions

1. In what respects are ethnic and religious diversity in the United States related to each other?
2. Is assimilation automatic within any given ethnic group?
3. Apply "Whiteness" to German, Irish, Italian, and Polish Americans.
4. To what extent has a non-Christian tradition been developing in the United States?
5. How have court rulings affected religious expression?

## Critical Thinking

1. When do you see ethnicity becoming more apparent? When does it appear to occur only in response to other people's advancing their own ethnicity? From these situations, how can ethnic identity be both positive and perhaps counterproductive or even destructive?
2. Why do you think we are so often reluctant to show our religion to others? Why might people of certain faiths be more hesitant than others?
3. How does religion reflect conservative and liberal positions on social issues? Consider services for the homeless, the need for childcare, the acceptance or rejection of gay men and lesbians, and a woman's right to terminate a pregnancy versus the fetus's right to survive.

# 6 The Nation as a Kaleidoscope

**CHAPTER OUTLINE**

———————————————⟨ HIGHLIGHTS ⟩———————————————

The nation is likened to a kaleidoscope because the diverse population has not fused into a melting pot, nor is the future composition apt to be as static as a salad bowl. Although nationally there is considerable, growing diversity, this mosaic varies considerably from one state to another. Racial and ethnic subordinate groups are making progress economically and educationally, but so are Whites. Even relatively successful Asian Americans are undeserving of their model-minority stereotype.

That is not the only stereotype widely expressed as one considers the notion that African Americans avoid success in school for fear of "acting White." We consider whether our face-to-face interaction takes advantage of our diverse society or whether we interpret our social surroundings to conform to more intolerant views of one another.

What metaphor do we use to describe a nation whose racial, ethnic, and religious minorities are now becoming numerical majorities in cities coast to coast, as already seen in the states of California, Hawaii, New Mexico, Texas, and about one-tenth of all counties within the United States (refer to Figure 1.2)? The outpouring of statistical data and personal experience documents the racial and ethnic diversity of the entire nation. The mosaic may be different in different regions and different communities; the tapestry of racial and ethnic groups is always close at hand wherever one is in the United States.

Although *E Pluribus Unum* may be reassuring, it does not describe what a visitor sees along the length of Fifth Avenue in Manhattan or in Monterey Park outside Los Angeles. It is apparent in the increasing numbers of Latinos in the rural river town of Beardstown, Illinois, and the emerging Somali immigrant population in Lewiston, Maine.

For several generations, the melting pot has been used as a convenient description of our culturally diverse nation. The analogy of an alchemist's cauldron was clever, even if a bit jingoistic—in the Middle Ages, the alchemist attempted to change less costly metals into gold and silver.

The phrase *melting pot* originated as the title of a 1908 play by Israel Zangwill. In this play, a young Russian Jewish immigrant to the United States composes a symphony that portrays a nation that serves as a crucible (or pot) where all ethnic and racial groups dissolve into a new, superior stock.

The belief of the United States as a melting pot became widespread in the first part of the twentieth century, particularly because it suggested that the United States had an almost divinely inspired mission to destroy artificial divisions and create a single humankind. However, the dominant group had indicated its unwillingness to welcome Native Americans, African Americans, Hispanics, Jews, and Asians, among many others, into the melting pot.

Although the metaphor of the melting pot is still used today, observers recognize that it hides as much about a multiethnic United States as it discloses. Therefore, the metaphor of the salad bowl emerged in the 1970s to portray a country that is ethnically diverse. As we can distinguish the lettuce from the tomatoes from the peppers in a tossed salad, we can see the increasing availability of ethnic restaurants and the persistence of "foreign" language newspapers. The dressing over the ingredients is akin to the shared value system and culture covering, but not hiding, the different ingredients of the salad.

Yet even the notion of a salad bowl is wilting. Like its melting-pot predecessor, the picture of a salad is static—certainly not what we see in the United States. It also hardly calls to mind the myriad cultural pieces that make up the fabric or mosaic of our diverse nation.

The kaleidoscope offers another familiar, yet more useful, analogy. Patented in 1817 by Scottish scientist Sir David Brewster, the kaleidoscope is both a toy and increasingly a table artifact of upscale living rooms. Users of this optical device are aware that when they turn a set of mirrors, the colors and patterns reflected off pieces of glass, tinsel, or beads seem to be endless. The growing popularity of the phrase "people of color" seems made for the kaleidoscope that is the United States. The changing images correspond to the often-bewildering array of groups found in the United States.

How easy is it to describe the image to someone else as we gaze into the eyepiece of a kaleidoscope? It is a challenge similar to that faced by educators who toil with what constitutes the ethnic history of the United States. We can forgive the faux pas by the *Washington Post* writer who described the lack of Hispanic-speaking (rather than Spanish-speaking) police as a factor contributing to the recent hostilities in the capital. Little wonder, given the bewildering ethnic patterns, that Chicago politicians, who sought to maintain the "safe" Hispanic congressional district after the results of the 2010 Census, found themselves scrutinized by Blacks fearful of losing their "safe" districts and critiqued by Latinos for not creating a second or even third safe seat. We can forgive Marlon Brando for sending a Native American woman to refuse his Oscar, thus protesting Hollywood's portrayal of Native Americans. Was he unaware of Italian Americans' disbelief when his award-winning performance was in *The Godfather*? We can understand why the African Americans traumatized by Hurricane Katrina would turn their antagonism from the White power structure that they perceived as ignoring their needs to the Latinos who took advantage of reconstruction projects in New Orleans.

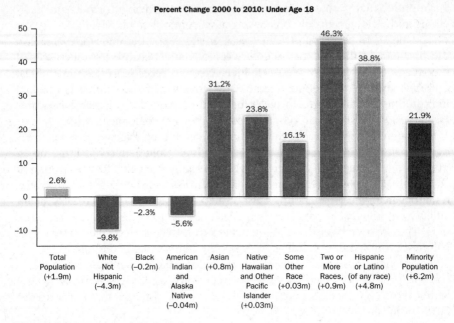

**Figure 6.1**   Youth and Diversity

For the last ten years, the growth in the population has been in the minority population with White non-Hispanics actually declining almost 10 percent.

*Source*: Bureau of the Census 2011d:slide 42.

It is difficult to describe the image created by a kaleidoscope because it changes dramatically with little effort. As we can see in Figure 6.1, the last decade has seen a rapid increase in the number of racial and ethnic minorities and an actual decline in the number of White non-Hispanics. Similarly, in the kaleidoscope of the United States, we find it a challenge to describe the multiracial nature of this republic. Perhaps in viewing the multiethnic, multiracial United States as a kaleidoscope, we may take comfort that the Greek word *kalos* means "beautiful" (Schaefer 1992).

In order to develop a better understanding of the changing image through the kaleidoscope, we will first try to learn what progress has taken place and why miscommunication among our diverse peoples seems to be the rule rather than the exception.

## The Glass Half Empty

A common expression makes reference to a glass half full or half empty. If one is thirsty, it is half empty and in need of being replenished. If one is attempting to clear dirty dishes, it is half full. For many people, especially Whites, the progress of subordinate groups or minorities makes it difficult to understand calls for more programs and new reforms and impossible to understand when minority neighborhoods erupt in violence.

In absolute terms, the glass has been filling up, but people in the early twenty-first century do not compare themselves with people in the 1960s. For example, Latinos and African Americans regard the appropriate reference group to be Whites today; compared with them, the glass is half empty at best.

In Figure 6.2, we have shown the current picture and recent changes by comparing African Americans and Hispanics with Whites as well as contemporary data for Native Americans (American Indians). We see that the nation's largest minority groups—African Americans and Hispanics—have higher household income, complete more schooling, and enjoy longer life expectancy today than in 1975. White Americans have made similar strides in all three areas. The gap remains and, if one analyzes it closely, has actually increased in some instances. Both Blacks and Latinos in 2009 had just edged out the income level that Whites had exceeded back in 1975, more than three decades behind! Also, Black Americans today have barely matched the life expectancy that Whites had a generation earlier. Similarly, many minority Americans remain entrenched in poverty: nearly one out of four Hispanics and African Americans.

Little has changed since 1975. We have chosen 1975 because that was a year for which we have comparable data for Latinos, Whites, and African Americans. However, the patterns would be no different if we considered 1950, 1960, or 1970.

## Is There a Model Minority?

"Asian Americans are a success! They achieve! They succeed! There are no protests, no demands. They just do it!" This is the general image that people in the United States so often hold of Asian Americans as a group. They constitute a **model or ideal minority** because, although they have experienced prejudice and discrimination, they seem to have succeeded economically, socially, and educationally without resorting to political or violent confrontations with Whites. Some observers point to the existence of a model minority as a reaffirmation that anyone can get ahead in the United States. Proponents of the model-minority view declare that because Asian Americans have achieved success, they have ceased to be subordinate and are no longer disadvantaged. This is only a variation of blaming the victim; with Asian Americans, it is "praising the victim." An examination of aspects of their socioeconomic status will allow a more thorough exploration of this view (Chang and Demyan 2007; Sakamoto et al. 2009).

Despite this widespread belief that they constitute a model minority, Asian Americans are victims of both prejudice and violence. Reports released annually have chronicled incidents of suspected and proven anti–Asian American incidents. After the terrorist attacks of September 11, 2001, anti-Asian violence increased dramatically for several months in the United States. The first fatality was an Asian Indian American who was shot and killed by a gunman in Mesa, Arizona, shouting, "I stand for America all the way" (National Asian Pacific American Legal Consortium 2002).

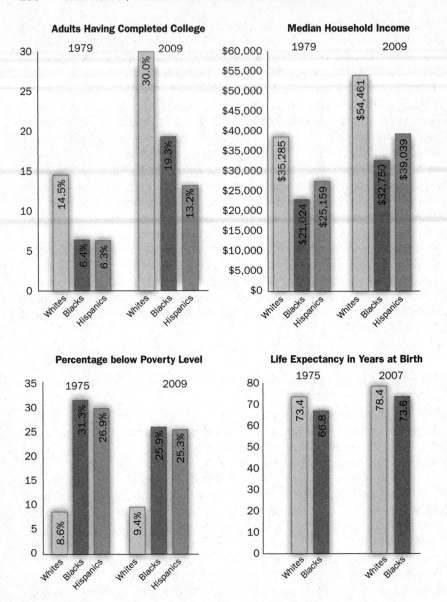

**Figure 6.2**  Changes in Schooling, Income, and Life Expectancy

*Note*: Native American data are for 2000. Education data include people age 25 and over. Data for 1975 Hispanic education estimated by author from data for 1970 and 1980. White data are for non-Hispanic (except in education).

*Sources*: Bureau of the Census 1988:167; Bureau of the Census 2010a; DeNavas-Walt et al. 2010:Tables A-1, B-1.

The model minority myth asserts that all Asian Americans succeed. Reality is much more complex.

Asian Americans, as a group, have impressive school enrollment rates in comparison to the total population. In 2010, half of Asian Americans age 25 or older held bachelor's degrees, compared with 33 percent of the non-Hispanic White population. These rates vary among Asian American groups, with Asian Indians, Korean Americans, and Chinese Americans having higher levels of educational achievement than others (Bureau of the Census 2011c).

This encouraging picture does have some qualifications, however, which call into question the optimistic model-minority view. According to a study of California's state university system, although Asian Americans often are viewed as successful overachievers, they have unrecognized and overlooked needs and experience discomfort and harassment on campus. As a group, they also lack Asian faculty and staff members to whom they can turn for support. They confront many identity issues and have to do a "cultural balancing act" along with all the usual pressures faced by college students. The report noted that an "alarming number" of Asian American students appear to be experiencing intense stress and alienation, problems that have often been "exacerbated by racial harassment" (Ohnuma 1991; Teranishi 2010).

Even the positive stereotype of Asian American students as "academic stars" or "whiz kids" can be burdensome to the people so labeled. Asian Americans who do only modestly well in school may face criticism from their parents or teachers for their failure to conform to the "whiz kid" image. Some Asian American youths disengage from school when faced with these expectations or receive little support for their interest in vocational pursuits or athletics (Kibria 2002; Leung et al. 2008).

That Asian Americans as a group work in the same occupations as Whites suggests that they have been successful, and many have. However, the pattern shows some differences. Asian immigrants, like other minorities and immigrants before them, are found disproportionately in the low-paying service occupations. At the same time, they are also concentrated at the top in professional and managerial positions. Yet as we will see, they rarely reach the very top. They hit the glass ceiling (as described in Chapter 3) or, as some others say, try to "climb a broken ladder," before they reach management. In 2007, only 1.5 percent of 5,563 people who serve on the boards of the nation's 500 largest corporations were Asian American (Committee of 100:2009).

The absence of Asian Americans as top executives also indicates that their success is not complete. Asian Americans have done well in small businesses and modest agricultural ventures. Although self-employed and managing their own businesses, Asian Americans have had very modest-sized operations. Because of the long hours of work, the income from such a business may be below prevailing wage standards. So even when they are business owners, they may still constitute cheap labor despite earning the profits. Chinese restaurants, Korean American cleaning businesses and fruit and vegetable stores, and motels, gasoline stations, and newspaper vending businesses operated by Asian Indians fall into this category.

Another misleading sign of the apparent success of Asian Americans is their high incomes as a group. Like other elements of the image, however, this deserves closer inspection. Asian American family income approaches parity with that of Whites because of their greater achievement than Whites in formal schooling. In other words, incomes of Asian Americans are lower than they should be given their high level of education.

If we look at specific educational levels, Whites earn more than their Asian counterparts of the same age. Asian Americans' average earnings increased by at least $2,300 for each additional year of schooling whereas Whites gained almost $3,000. Asian Americans as a group have significantly more formal schooling but, actually, have lower household family income. We should note that, to some degree, some Asian Americans' education is from overseas and, therefore, may be devalued by U.S. employers. Yet in the end, educational attainment does pay off as much if you are of Asian descent as it does for White non-Hispanics (Sakamoto et al. 2009; Zeng and Xie 2004).

There are striking contrasts among Asian Americans. Nevertheless, for every Asian American family in 2009 with an annual income of $150,000 or more, another earns less than $23,000 a year. Almost every Asian American group has a higher poverty rate than non-Hispanic Whites; the lone exception is Filipinos who tend to live in the relatively high income states of Hawaii and California (DeNavas-Walt Proctor, and Smith 2010:37; Omi 2008; Sakamoto et al. 2009).

**SECRET ASIAN MAN** by Tak Toyoshima

Discussions of race and ethnicity often leave out Asian Americans, yet Asian Americans too are subject to stereotypes today such as the model-minority image.

*Source*: Secret Asian Man © Tak Toyoshima, distributed by United Features Syndicate, Inc.

At first, one might be puzzled to see criticism of a positive generalization such as "model minority." Why should the stereotype of adjusting without problems be a disservice to Asian Americans? The answer is that this incorrect view helps to exclude Asian Americans from social programs and conceals unemployment and other social ills. When representatives of Asian groups do seek assistance for those in need, those who have accepted the model-minority stereotype resent them. If a minority group is viewed as successful, it is unlikely that its members will be included in programs designed to alleviate the problems they encounter as minorities. The positive stereotype reaffirms the United States' system of mobility. New immigrants as well as established subordinate groups ought to achieve more merely by working within the system. At the same time, viewed from the conflict perspective outlined in Chapter 1, this becomes yet another instance of "blaming the victim"; if Asian Americans have succeeded, Blacks and Latinos must be responsible for their own low status (Bascara 2008; Choi and Lahey 2006; Leung et al. 2008; Ryan 1976).

For young Asian Americans, life in the United States often is a struggle for one's identity when their heritage is so devalued by those in positions of influence. It has little relevance to the substantial number of working- and lower-middle class people of Asian descent. And for young successful second- and third-generation Asian Americans, they still feel compelled to justify their presence in a nation of immigrants.

In Listen to Our Voices, we follow the trek of a young Japanese-born woman coming of age in the Midwest, which underscores the path that most Asian Americans take far from the model-minority stereotype. Sometimes identity means finding a role in White America; other times, it involves finding a place among Asian Americans collectively—as in the panethnicity we spoke of in Chapter 1—and then locating oneself within one's own racial or ethnic community. Now we turn to the issue of identity and quite a different stereotype.

## LISTEN TO OUR VOICES

### From Kawasaki to Chicago

*Miku Ishii*

I was born a citizen of Japan in an area named Kawasaki, which is basically the suburbs of Tokyo. My parents raised me in a small apartment in Kawasaki until I was six years old. From then, my father's company decided to transfer him to the U.S. and my mother, my father and my brother all moved to Illinois. Japanese is my native language and as I came to America, I was forced to learn English. It took me four years in bilingual school to fully be able to speak English and get sent off to the "regular" school where there were no foreigners like me. Since we moved to the Northwest suburbs of Chicago, I grew up with mostly Caucasian kids and a mediocre percentage of Asians. There were hardly any African American people in the town of Schaumburg. In elementary school, I was mistreated so badly at my "regular" school that I hardly spoke and was incredibly shy.

The very first time I had experienced the excruciating pain of pure racism was when I was only in the second grade. A Caucasian girl with big bright blue eyes and short bouncy blonde hair had a habit of picking at me constantly. She said it was because of my slanted slim slits of an eye. It was because of my dark jet-black pigtails that hung thick as horses' tails around my face. One afternoon during recess, I climbed up a dome that she also happened to be on. As she saw me coming near, she jumped back down on the ground and ran to the teacher. The next thing I knew, my teacher was punishing me, saying that I should not be pushing this grinning blonde-haired blue-eyed girl. At the time, I was only a beginner in bilingual class so I was barely able to say anything but "Where is the bathroom?" and "I don't know." I tried to explain to the teacher. But all that came out were words in Japanese. Of course they looked at me wide eyed, as I tried to speak broken English with Japanese. Finally, the teacher, who could not understand me to hear my self-defense, banned me from going out to recess for a week. I was furious and embarrassed and felt ashamed of my race.

Even the bus ride to school and back could not be near peaceful for me. The back of the bus was where all the cool white kids sat. When I would try to sit in the back because there were no other seats, those kids would call me Chinese or chink and make that obnoxious sound which clearly mocked the language. Some days they threw chewed gum at me. Not because I did anything to them. But because I was a chink and they wanted to see how crazy I would react. I would always just ignore it and stay quiet. I wanted to make it seem like it did not bother me, but inside, it was breaking my heart. Heck, I was not even

Chinese but I was always called that in such disdainful manner. Going to school became something I feared. I remember I felt so miserable and ashamed to death for being born "Chinese." All I wanted was to be white.

I stand here today still remembering those days very vividly. In all essence, those experiences have molded me into the person that I am today. I like to think that I am very open-minded and I love diversity. I love to learn about other cultures and I have a very ethnic variety of friends. I would say relative to others, my multicultural experience has been rich because of the fact that I am an immigrant, a minority. And as I have expressed before, for many years when I first came to the United States, I have experienced so much hate and prejudice for just being born my race. I am still a citizen of Japan to this day and I go back to Kawasaki about every two years. I feel that I have grown up in two different worlds. The experiences that I have undergone have made me accept people at face value. A lot of times for me, I forget about color because I never judge by race but I am also not oblivious or blind to the fact that racism does exist. I think, as sad as it sounds, that it is an evil that will never go away.

*Source*: Ishii 2006.

## Acting White, Acting Black, or Neither

A common view advanced by some educators is that the reason African Americans, especially males, do not succeed in school is that they do not want to be caught "**acting White**." That is, they avoid taking school seriously at all costs and do not accept the authority of teachers and administrators. Whatever the accuracy of such a generalization, acting White clearly shifts the responsibility of low school attainment from the school to the individual and, therefore, can be seen as yet another example of blaming the victim (Ferguson 2007; Fordham and Ogbu 1986; Fryer 2006; Fryer and and Torelli 2010; Ogbu 2004; Ogbu with Davis 2003; Tyson 2011).

To what extent do Blacks not want to act White in the context of high achievers? Many scholars have noted that individuals' efforts to avoid looking like they want an education have a long history and are hardly exclusive to any one race. Back in the 1950s, one heard disparaging references to "teacher's pet" and "brown nosing." Does popularity come to high school debaters and National Honor Society students or to cheerleaders and athletes? Academic-oriented classmates are often viewed as social misfits, nerds, and geeks, and are seen as socially inept even if their skill building will later make them more economically independent and often more socially desirable. For minority children, including African Americans, to take school seriously means they must overcome their White classmates' same desire to be cool and not a nerd. In addition, Black youth must also come to embrace a curriculum and respect teachers who are much less likely to look or sound like them (Chang and Demyan 2007; Tyson 2011; Tyson, Darity, and Castellino 2005).

Thus far, few but now growing in numbers, African Americans are entering positions that few people of any color reach. Dr. Mae Jemison successfully completed her astronaut-training program in August 1988; she became the fifth black astronaut and the first Black female astronaut in NASA history.

The "acting White" thesis overemphasizes personal responsibility rather than structural features such as quality of schools, curriculum, and teachers. Therefore, it locates the source of Black miseducation—and by implication, the remedy—in the African American household. As scholar Michael Dyson (2005) observes, "When you think the problems are personal, you think the solutions are the same." If we could only get African American parents to encourage their children to work a little harder and act better (i.e., White), everything would be fine. As Dyson notes, "It's hard to argue against any of these things in the abstract; in principle such suggestions sound just fine."

Of course, not all Whites "act White." To equate "acting White" with high academic achievement has little empirical or cultural support. Although more Whites between ages 18 and 19 are in school, the differences are hardly dramatic—67 percent of Whites compared to 58 percent of Blacks. Studies comparing attitudes and performance show that Black students have the same attitudes—good and bad—about achievement as their White counterparts. Too often we tend to view White slackers who give a hard time to the advanced placement kids as "normal," but when low-performing African Americans do the same thing, it becomes a systemic pathology undermining everything good about schools. The primary stumbling block is not acting White or acting Black but being presented with similar educational opportunities (Bureau of the Census 2010a:Table 220; Downey 2008; Tough 2004; Tyson et al. 2005).

## Persistence of Inequality

Progress has occurred. Indignities and injustices have been eliminated, allowing us to focus on the remaining barriers to equity. But why do the gaps in income, living wages, education, and even life expectancy persist? Especially perplexing is this glass half full or half empty, given the numerous civil rights laws, study commissions, favorable court decisions, and efforts by nonprofits, faith-based organizations, and private sectors.

In trying to comprehend the persistence of inequality among racial and ethnic groups, sociologists and other social scientists have found it useful to think in terms of the role played by social and cultural capital. Popularized by French sociologist Pierre Bourdieu, these concepts refer to assets that are not necessarily economic but do impact economic capital for one's family and future. Less cultural and social capital may be passed on from one generation to the next, especially when prejudice and discrimination make it difficult to overcome deficits. Racial and ethnic minorities reproduce disadvantage while Whites are more likely to reproduce privilege (Bourdieu 1983; Bourdieu and Passeron 1990).

**Cultural capital** refers to noneconomic forces such as family background and past investments in education that is then reflected in knowledge about the arts and language. It is not necessarily book knowledge but the kind of education valued by the elites. African Americans and Native Americans have in the past faced significant restrictions in receiving a quality education. Immigrants have faced challenges due to English not being spoken at home. Muslim immigrants face an immediate challenge in functioning in a culture that advantages a different form of spirituality and lifestyle. The general historical pattern has been for immigrants, especially those who came in large numbers and settled in ethnic enclaves, to take two or three generations to reach educational parity. Knowledge of hip-hop and familiarity with Polish cuisine is culture, but it is not the culture that is valued and prestigious. Society privileges or values some lifestyles over others. This is not good, but it is social reality. Differentiating between *perogies* will not get you to the top of corporate America as fast as will differentiating among wines. This is, of course, not unique to the United States. Someone settling in Japan would have to deal with cultural capital that includes knowledge of Noh Theatre and tea ceremonies. In most countries, you are much better off following the run-up to the World Cup rather than the contenders for the next Super Bowl (DiMaggio 2005).

**Social capital** refers to the collective benefit of durable social networks and their patterns of reciprocal trust. Much has been written about the strength of family and friendship networks among all racial and ethnic minorities. Family reunions are major events. Family history and storytelling is rich and full. Kinfolk are not merely acquaintances but truly living assets upon which one depends or, at the very least, feels comfortable to call upon repeatedly. Networks outside the family are critical to coping in a society that often seems to be determined to keep anyone who looks like you down. But given past as well as current discrimination and prejudice, these social networks may help you become a construction worker, but they are less likely to get you into a boardroom. Residential and school segregation make developing social capital more difficult. Immigrant professionals find that their skills or advanced degrees are devalued, and they are shut out of networks of the educated and influential. Working-class Latino and Black workers have begun to develop informal social ties with their White coworkers and neighbors. Professional

Racial and ethnic minorities may not have the cultural and social capital of privileged Whites, but they treasure their rich heritage. The growing Black middle class owes part of its momentum to African American entrepreneurs. Pictured here is Glenn Harrell in front of his Silverlake, California, business.

immigrants, in time, become accepted as equals, but racial and ethnic minority communities continue to resist institutional marginalization (Coleman 1988; Cranford 2005; Portes and Vickstrom 2011).

As the ranks of the powerful and important have been reached by all racial and ethnic groups, social capital is more widely shared, but this process has proven to be slower than advocates of social equality would wish. Perhaps accelerating it will be the tendency for successful minority members to be more likely to network with up and coming members of their own community while Whites are more likely to be more comfortable, even complacent, with the next generation making it on their own. We are increasingly appreciative of the importance of aspirations and motivations that are often much more present among people with poor or immigrant backgrounds than those born of affluence. We know that bilingualism is an asset not a detriment. Children who have translated for their parents develop "real-world" skills at a much earlier age than their monolingual English counterparts (Bauder 2003; Monkman, Ronald, and Théraméne 2005; Portes 1998; Yosso 2005).

Considering cultural and social capital does leave room for measured optimism. Racial and ethnic groups have shared their cultural capital, whether it be the music we dance to or the food we eat. As the barriers to privilege weaken and eventually fall, people of all colors will be able to advance. The particular strength that African Americans, tribal people, Latinos, Asian Americans, and arriving immigrants bring to the table is that they also have the ability to resist and to refuse to accept second-class status. The role that cultural and social capital play also points to the need to embrace strategies of intervention that will increasingly acknowledge the skills and talents found in a pluralistic society.

## Talking Past One Another

African Americans, Italian Americans, Korean Americans, Puerto Ricans, Native Americans, Mexican Americans, and many others live in the United States and interact daily, sometimes face-to-face and constantly through the media. But communication does not mean we listen to, much less understand, one another. Sometimes we assume that, as we become an educated nation, we will set aside our prejudices. Yet, in recent years, our college campuses have been the scenes of tension, insults, and even violence. Fletcher Blanchard and his colleagues (1991) conducted an experiment at Smith College and found that even overheard statements can influence expressions of opinion on the issue of racism.

The researchers asked a student who said she was conducting an opinion poll for a class to approach seventy-two White students as each was walking across the campus. Each time she did so, she also stopped a second White student—actually a confederate working with the researchers—and asked her to participate in the survey as well. Both students were asked how Smith College should respond to anonymous racist notes actually sent to four African American students in 1989. However, the confederate was always instructed to answer first. In some cases, she condemned the notes; in others, she justified them. Blanchard and his colleagues (1991) concluded that "hearing at least one other person express strongly antiracist opinions produced dramatically more strongly antiracist public reactions to racism than hearing others express equivocal opinions or opinions more accepting of racism" (pp. 102–103). However, a second experiment demonstrated that when the confederate expressed sentiments justifying racism, the subjects were much less likely to express antiracist opinions than were those who heard no one else offer opinions. In this experiment, social control (through the

People of different races, religions, and ethnic backgrounds talk to each other, but do we talk past one another?

process of conformity) influenced people's attitudes and the expression of those attitudes.

Why is there so much disagreement and tension? There is a growing realization that people do not mean the same thing when they are addressing problems of race, ethnicity, gender, or religion. A husband regularly does the dishes and feels he is an equal partner in doing the housework, not recognizing that the care of his infant daughter is left totally to his wife. A manager is delighted that he has been able to hire a Puerto Rican salesperson but makes no effort to see that the new employee will adjust to an all-White, non-Hispanic staff.

We talk, but do we talk past one another? Surveys regularly show that different ethnic and racial groups have different perceptions, whether on immigration policies, racial profiling, or whether discrimination occurs in the labor force. Sociologist Robert Blauner (1969, 1972) contends that Blacks and Whites see racism differently. Minorities see racism as central to society, as ever present, whereas Whites regard it as a peripheral concern and a national concern only when accompanied by violence or involving a celebrity. African Americans and other minorities consider racist acts in a broader context: "It is racist if my college fails to have Blacks significantly present as advisers, teachers, and administrators." Whites would generally accept a racism charge if there had been an explicit denial of a job to an appropriately qualified minority member. Furthermore, Whites would apply the label "racist" only to the person or the few people who were actually responsible for the act. Members of minority groups would be more willing to call most of the college's members racist for allowing racist practices to persist. For many Whites, the word *racism* is a red flag, and they are reluctant to give it the wide use typically employed by minorities, that is, those who have been oppressed by racism (Lichtenberg 1992).

With an African American elected President, were people more relaxed to openly discuss race? Curiously, Barack Obama made speeches dedicated to revisiting the issue of race but none of his White opponents did. There certainly was initial optimism about a new era of race; however, people today evoke a color-blind racism and see little evidence of intolerance except when confronted by a horrendous hate crime. Others contend that racism is often couched in a "backstage" manner through discussions of immigration, affirmative action, anti-poverty programs, and profiling for national security (Kershaw 2009).

Is one view correct—the broader minority perspective or the more limited White outlook? No, but both are a part of the social reality in which we all live. We need to recognize both interpretations.

As we saw when we considered Whiteness in Chapter 5, the need to confront racism, however perceived, is not to make Whites guilty and absolve Blacks, Asians, Hispanics, and Native Americans of any responsibility for their present plight. Rather, to understand racism, past and present, is to understand how its impact has shaped both a single person's behavior and that of the entire society (Bonilla-Silva and Baiocchi 2001; Duke 1992).

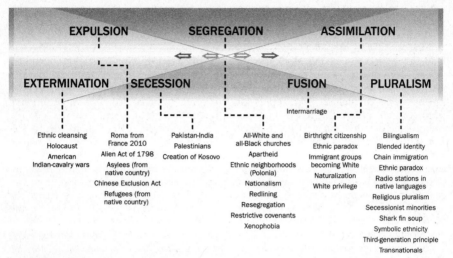

| EXPULSION | SEGREGATION | ASSIMILATION |
| --- | --- | --- |

| EXTERMINATION | SECESSION | FUSION | PLURALISM |
| --- | --- | --- | --- |

Intermarriage

| Ethnic cleansing | Roma from | Pakistan-India | All-White and | Birthright citizenship | Bilingualism |
| --- | --- | --- | --- | --- | --- |
| Holocaust | France 2010 | Palestinians | all-Black churches | Ethnic paradox | Blended identity |
| American | Alien Act of 1798 | Creation of Kosovo | Apartheid | Immigrant groups | Chain immigration |
| Indian-cavalry wars | Asylees (from | | Ethnic neighborhoods | becoming White | Ethnic paradox |
| | native country) | | (Polonia) | Naturalization | Radio stations in |
| | Chinese Exclusion Act | | Nationalism | White privilege | native languages |
| | Refugees (from | | Redlining | | Religious pluralism |
| | native country) | | Resegregation | | Secessionist minorities |
| | | | Restrictive covenants | | Shark fin soup |
| | | | Xenophobia | | Symbolic ethnicity |
| | | | | | Third-generation principle |
| | | | | | Transnationals |

**Spectrum of Intergroup Relations**

# Conclusion

As the United States promotes racial, ethnic, and religious diversity, it strives also to impose universal criteria on employers, educators, and realtors so that subordinate racial and ethnic groups can participate fully in the larger society. In some instances, to bring about equality of results—not just equality of opportunity—programs have been developed to give competitive advantages to women and minority men. Only more recently have similar strides been made on behalf of people with disabilities. These latest answers to social inequality have provoked much controversy over how to achieve the admirable goal of a multiracial, multiethnic society, undifferentiated in opportunity and rewards.

Relations between racial, ethnic, or religious groups take two broad forms, as situations characterized by either consensus or conflict. Consensus prevails where assimilation or fusion of groups has been completed. Consensus also prevails in a pluralistic society in the sense that members have agreed to respect differences between groups. By eliminating the contending group, extermination

and expulsion also lead to a consensus society. In the study of intergroup relations, it is often easy to ignore conflict where there is a high degree of consensus because it is assumed that an orderly society has no problems. In some instances, however, this assumption is misleading. Through long periods of history, misery inflicted on a racial, ethnic, or religious group was judged to be appropriate, if not actually divinely inspired.

In recent history, harmonious relations between all racial, ethnic, and religious groups have been widely accepted as a worthy goal. The struggle against oppression and inequality is not new. It dates back at least to the revolutions in England, France, and the American colonies in the seventeenth and eighteenth centuries. The twentieth century was unique in the extension of equality to the less-privileged classes, many of whose members are racial and ethnic minorities. Conflict along racial and ethnic lines is especially bitter now because it evokes memories of slavery, colonial oppression, and overt discrimination. Today's African Americans are much more aware of slavery than contemporary poor people are of seventeenth-century debtors' prison.

Unquestionably, the struggle for justice among racial and ethnic groups has not completely met its goals. Many people are still committed to repression, although they may see it only as the benign neglect of those less privileged. Such repression leads to the dehumanization of both the subordinated individual and the oppressor. Growth in equal rights movements and self-determination for Third World countries largely populated by non-White people has moved the world onto a course that seems irreversible. The old ethnic battle lines now renewed in Iran, Kenya, Sudan, and Chechnya in Russia have only added to the tensions.

Self-determination, whether for groups or individuals, often is impossible in societies as they are currently structured. Bringing about social equality, therefore, will entail significant changes in existing institutions. Because such changes are not likely to come about with everyone's willing cooperation, the social costs will be high. However, if there is a trend in racial and ethnic relations in the world today, it is the growing belief that the social costs, however high, must be paid to achieve self-determination.

It is naive to foresee a world of societies in which one person equals one vote and all are accepted without regard to race, ethnicity, religion, gender, age, disability status, or sexual orientation. It is equally unlikely to expect to see a society, let alone a world, that is without a privileged class or prestigious jobholders. Contact between different peoples, as we have seen numerous times, precedes conflict. Contact also may initiate mutual understanding and appreciation.

Assimilation, even when strictly followed, does not necessarily bring with it acceptance as an equal, nor does it even mean that one will be tolerated. Segregation persists. Efforts toward pluralism can be identified, but we can also easily see the counterefforts, whether they are the legal efforts to make English the official language or acts of intimidation by activists patroling the nation's borders, such as Klansmen, skinheads, and others. However, the sheer changing population of the United States guarantees that we will learn, work, and play in a more diverse society.

The task of making this kaleidoscope image of diverse cultures, languages, colors, and religions into a picture of harmony is overwhelming. But the images of failure in this task, some of which we have witnessed in our news media, are even more frightening. We can applaud success and even take time to congratulate ourselves, but we must also review the unfinished agenda.

## Summary

1. Like the image viewed in a kaleidoscope, the diversity of the American population is constantly changing with what has been often called "minority groups" accounting for increasing proportions of the population.

2. There is an agreement that racial and ethnic minority groups have made great strides during the last two generations in the United States, but typically the gap between them and White men and women has remained the same.

3. Often Asian Americans are labeled as a model minority, which overlooks the many problems they face and serves to minimize the challenges of succeeding despite prejudice and discrimination.

4. African Americans have made gains in all levels of formal schooling but still fall behind the gains made by others. Debate continues over the appropriateness of the notion that Black youths avoid appearances of acting White.

5. Inequality persists despite visible improvement because most racial and ethnic groups are unable to accumulate social and cultural capital.

6. While interaction across racial and ethnic lines occurs with increasing significance, it is less clear whether we are all listening to what each other has to say.

7. White people generally apply the charge of racism when it is operating very explicitly whereas members of racial and ethnic groups are more likely to apply it more generally where disadvantages persist.

## Key Terms

acting White 205
cultural capital 207

model or ideal minority 200
social capital 207

## Review Questions

1. What contributes to the changing image of diversity in the United States?
2. Pose views of some issue facing contemporary society that takes the position of "half full" and then "half empty."
3. Why is it harmful to be viewed as a model minority?
4. Is one view of racism the correct one?
5. Why are White Americans less likely to be concerned with social and cultural capital?

## Critical Thinking Questions

1. Considering the stereotypes that persist, how does it affect both the people who are stereotyped as well as those who express them?
2. Consider conversations you have with people very different than yourself. Why do you feel those people are very different? To what degree did you talk to them or past them? To what degree do they talk to you or past you?
3. How have places where you have worked, even part time, been different from those of your parents or grandparents in terms of diversity of the workforce? What explains these changes?

# Internet Resource Directory

The following is a sample of the thousands of Web sites that offer information on race, ethnicity, religion, and other related topics. They have been grouped by broad areas because most sites touch on a number of areas and subjects. Web sites have been selected that have stable URLs and are in English (or are multilingual and include English). Most of these Web sites, in turn, have links to other useful information.

## GENERAL

**All of Us Are Related, Each of Us Is Unique (Syracuse University)**

http://allrelated.syr.edu

**Death Penalty Information Center**

http://www.deathpenaltyinfo.org

**Ethnic Media: New America Media**

http://news.newamericamedia.org/news

**FBI Uniform Crime Reports (data on hate crimes)**

http://www.fbi.gov/ucr/ucr.htm#hate

**Hate Crimes Laws (Anti-Defamation League)**

http://adl.org/99hatecrime/intro.asp

**Lutheran Immigration and Refugee Service**

http://www.lirs.org

**Migration News**

http://migration.ucdavis.edu/mn/

**Minorities in Medicine (Association of American Medical Colleges)**

http://www.aamc.org/students/minorities

**The Prejudice Institute**

http://www.prejudiceinstitute.org

**Race Traitor (constructing Whiteness)**

http://www.racetraitor.org

**Southern Poverty Law Center (tolerance education)**

http://splcenter.org

**Teaching Tolerance (Southern Poverty Law Center)**

http://tolerance.org

**Understanding Katrina (Hurricane Katrina)**

http://understandingKatrina.ssrc.org

**U.S. Census Bureau**

http://www.census.gov

**U.S. Census Bureau Revisions to the Standards for the Classification of Federal Data on Race and Ethnicity (Office of Management and Budget)**

http://www.census.gov/population/www/socdemo/race/Ombdir15.html

**U.S. Citizenship and Immigration Services**

http://www.uscis.gov

**U.S. Commission on Civil Rights**

http://www.www.usccr.gov

**U.S. Commission on Immigration Reform**

http://www.utexas.edu/lbj/uscir

**U.S. Committee for Refugees and Immigrants**

http://www.refugees.org

**U.S. Equal Employment Opportunity Commission**

http://www.eeoc.gov

## AFRICAN AMERICANS

**African American History and Culture (The Smithsonian)**

http://www.si.edu/Encyclopedia_Si/History_and_Culture/AfricanAmerican_History.htm

**African American Research (National Archives)**

http://www.archives.gov/research/african-americans/index.html

**The Black Collegian Online**

http://www.black-collegian.com

**BlackSeek**

http://blackseek.com

**MelaNET (The UnCut Black Experience)**

http://www.melanet.com

**Official Kwanzaa Web Site**

http://www.officialkwanzaawebsite.org

**Rainbow/PUSH Coalition**

http://www.rainbowpush.org

**Southern Christian Leadership Conference (SCLC)**

http://www.sclcnational.org

## ASIAN AMERICANS AND PACIFIC ISLANDERS

**Asian American Net**

http://www.asianamerican.net

**Asians and Pacific Islanders (National Education Association)**

http://www.nea.org/tools/LessonPlans.html [search for "Asian Americans"]

**Chinese Immigration Records (National Archives)**

http://www.archives.gov/genealogy/heritage/chinese-immigration.html

**Densho: The Japanese American Legacy Project**

http://www.densho.org

**Hmong Home Page**

http://www.stolaf.edu/people/cdr/hmong

**Internment Archives**

http://www.internmentarchives.com

**Japanese American Citizens League**

http://www.jacl.org

**Japanese American National Museum**

http://www.janm.org

**Little India (magazine)**

http://www.littleindia.com

**Little Saigon Net**

http://www.littlesaigon.com

**Nation of Hawai'i**

http://hawaii-nation.org

**National Japanese American Historical Society**

http:/www.njahs.org

**National Japanese American Memorial Foundation**

http://www.njamf.com

**Of Civil Wrongs and Rights: The Fred Korematsu Story (by Eric Paul Fornier)**

http://www.pbs.org/pov/pov2001/ofcivilwrongsandrights/index.html

**Southeast Asia Resource Action Center**

http://www.searac.org

## HISPANICS AND LATINOS

**AfroCubaWeb (Afro Cubans as well as Cuba and the Caribbean)**

http://www.afrocubaweb.com

**Department of Mexican American Studies (University of Arizona)**

http://masrc.arizona.edu

**International Boundaries Research Unit**

http://www.dur.ac.uk/ibru

**Julian Samora Research Institute (Michigan State University)**

http://www.jsri.msu.edu

**Latin American Network Information Center**

http://lanic.utexas.edu

**Mexican Migration Project**

http://mmp.opr.princeton.edu

**Mexico–U.S. Binational Migration Study Report (U.S. Commission on Immigration Reform)**

http://www.utexas.edu/lbj/uscir/binational.html

**National Council of La Raza**

http://www.nclr.org

**Nijmegen Centre for Border Research**

http://www.ru.nl/ncbr

**Pew Hispanic Center (Pew Research Center)**

http://pewhispanic.org

**Puerto Rico and the American Dream**

http://prdream.com

## JEWS AND JUDAISM

**American Jewish Committee**

http://www.ajc.org

**Anti-Defamation League**

http://www.adl.org

**Hebrew Immigrant Aid Society (HIAS)**

http://www.hias.org

**Judaism and Jewish Life**

http://myjewishlearning.com

**Shamash: The Jewish Network (Judaism and Jewish Resources)**

http://shamash.org

## MUSLIMS AND ARAB AMERICANS

**American–Arab Anti-Discrimination Committee**

http://www.adc.org

**American Muslim Perspective**

http://ampolitics.ghazali.net

**Arab American Institute**

http://www.aaiusa.org

**Council on American–Islamic Relations**

http://www.cair.com

## NATIVE AMERICANS

**American Indian Higher Education Consortium (AIHEC)**

http://www.aihec.org

**National Congress of American Indians**

http://www.ncai.org

**National Indian Youth Council, Inc.**

http://www.niyc-alb.org

**Native American Records (National Archives)**

http://archives.gov/research/native-americans/index.html

**National Museum of the American Indian (The Smithsonian)**

http://www.nmai.si.edu

**NativeWeb**

http://www.nativeweb.org

**U.S. Department of The Interior: Indian Affairs**

http://www.bia.gov

## ETHNIC GROUPS AND OTHER SUBORDINATE GROUPS

**American Institute of Polish Culture, Inc.**

http://www.ampolinstitute.org

**American Irish Historical Society**

http://www.aihs.org

**Catholics for Choice**

http://www.cath4choice.org

**Ellis Island Immigration Museum**

http://www.ellisisland.org

**German Missions in the United States (German Embassy site)**

http://www.germany.info

**Immigration and Ethnic Group Experience in the 20th Century U.S. (Thomas J. Archdeacon at University of Wisconsin)**

http://history.wisc.edu/archdeacon/404tja

**Norwegian-American Historical Association**

http://www.stolaf.edu/naha

**Polish American Association**

http://www.polish.org

**Sons of Norway (Norwegian Americans)**

http://www.sofn.com

**Swedish American Museum**

www.swedishamericanmuseum.org

**Vesterheim: Norwegian-American Museum**

http://vesterheim.org

## THE AUTHOR

**Richard T. Schaefer**

(for e-mail correspondence)

schaeferrt@aol.com

http://www.schaefersociology.net

# Glossary

*Parenthetical numbers refer to the pages on which the term is introduced.*

**absolute deprivation** The minimum level of subsistence below which families should not be expected to exist. (83)

**acting White** Taking school seriously and accepting the authority of teachers and administrators. (205)

**affirmative action** Positive efforts to recruit subordinate-group members, including women, for jobs, promotions, and educational opportunities. (100)

**Afrocentric perspective** An emphasis on the customs of African cultures and how they have pervaded the history, culture, and behavior of Blacks in the United States and around the world. (35)

**amalgamation** The process by which a dominant group and a subordinate group combine through intermarriage to form a new group. (31)

**assimilation** The process by which a subordinate individual or group takes on the characteristics of the dominant group. (31)

**asylees** Foreigners who have already entered the United States and now seek protection because of persecution or a well-founded fear of persecution. (148)

**authoritarian personality** A psychological construct of a personality type likely to be prejudiced and to use others as scapegoats. (51)

**bilingual education** A program designed to allow students to learn academic concepts in their native language while they learn a second language. (133)

**bilingualism** The use of two or more languages in places of work or education and the treatment of each language as legitimate. (133)

**biological race** The mistaken notion of a genetically isolated human group. (11)

**blaming the victim** Portraying the problems of racial and ethnic minorities as their fault rather than recognizing society's responsibilities. (21)

**blended identity** Self-image and worldview that is a combination of religious faith, cultural background based on nationality, and current residency. (159)

**Bogardus scale** Technique to measure social distance toward different racial and ethnic groups. (69)

**brain drain** Immigration to the United States of skilled workers, professionals, and technicians who are desperately needed in their home countries. (130)

**chain immigration** Immigrants that sponsor several other immigrants who, on their arrival, may sponsor still more. (119)

**civil religion** The religious dimension in American life that merges the state with sacred beliefs. (184)

**class** As defined by Max Weber, people who share similar levels of wealth. (18)

**colonialism** A foreign power's maintenance of political, social, economic, and cultural dominance over people for an extended period. (25)

**color-blind racism** Use of race-neutral principles to defend the racially unequal status quo. (57)

**conflict perspective** A sociological approach that assumes that the social structure is best understood in terms of conflict or tension between competing groups. (20)

**contact hypothesis** Intergroup contact between people of equal status in noncompetitive circumstances will reduce prejudice. (69)

**creationists** People who support a literal interpretation of the biblical book of Genesis on the origins of the universe and argue that evolution should not be presented as established scientific thought. (190)

**cultural capital** Noneconomic forces such as family background and past investments in education that are then reflected in knowledge about the arts and language. (207)

**cultural relativism** An action of a particular group is judged objectively within the context of a particular culture. (146)

**deficit model of ethnic identity** One's ethnicity is viewed by others as a factor of subtracting away the characteristics corresponding to some ideal ethnic type. (160)

**denomination** A large, organized religion not officially linked with the state or government. (181)

**discrimination** The denial of opportunities and equal rights to individuals and groups because of prejudice or for other arbitrary reasons. (44, 82)

**dysfunction** An element of society that may disrupt a social system or decrease its stability. (20)

**emigration** Leaving a country to settle in another. (24)

**environmental justice** Efforts to ensure that hazardous substances are controlled so that all communities receive protection regardless of race or socioeconomic circumstances. (98)

**ethnic cleansing** Forced deportation of people accompanied by systematic violence. (27)

**ethnic group** A group set apart from others because of its national origin or distinctive cultural patterns. (8)

**ethnic paradox** The maintenance of one's ethnic ties in a way that can assist with assimilation in larger society. (162)

**ethnocentrism** The tendency to assume that one's culture and way of life are superior to all others. (43)

**ethnophaulism** Ethnic or racial slurs, including derisive nicknames. (44)

**exploitation theory** A Marxist theory that views racial subordination in the United States as a manifestation of the class system inherent in capitalism. (52)

**functionalist perspective** A sociological approach emphasizing how parts of a society are structured to maintain its stability. (19)

**fusion** A minority and a majority group combining to form a new group. (30)

**genocide** The deliberate, systematic killing of an entire people or nation. (27)

**glass ceiling** The barrier that blocks the promotion of a qualified worker because of gender or minority membership. (109)

**glass escalator** The male advantage experienced in occupations dominated by women. (111)

**glass wall** A barrier to moving laterally in a business to positions that are more likely to lead to upward mobility. (110)

**globalization** Worldwide integration of government policies, cultures, social movements, and financial markets through trade, movement of people, and the exchange of ideas. (25, 144)

**hate crime** Criminal offense committed because of the offender's bias against a race, religion, ethnic or national origin group, sexual orientation group, or disability status. (86)

**immigration** Coming into a new country as a permanent resident. (24)

**income** Salaries, wages, and other money received. (97)

**institutional discrimination** A denial of opportunities and equal rights to individuals or groups resulting from the normal operations of a society. (88)

**intelligence quotient (IQ)** The ratio of a person's mental age (as computed by an IQ test) to his or her chronological age, multiplied by 100. (12)

**intelligent design** View that life is so complex that it must have been created by a higher intelligence. (191)

**Islamophobia** A range of negative feelings toward Muslims and their religion that ranges from generalized intolerance to hatred. (47)

**labeling theory** A sociological approach introduced by Howard Becker that attempts to explain why certain people are viewed as deviants and others engaging in the same behavior are not. (22)

**marginality** The status of being between two cultures at the same time, such as the status of Jewish immigrants in the United States. (17)

**matrix of domination** Cumulative impact of oppression because of race, gender, and class as well as sexual orientation, religion, disability status, and age. (36)

**melting pot** Diverse racial or ethnic groups or both, forming a new creation or a new cultural entity. (31)

**migration** A general term that describes any transfer of population. (24)

**minority group** A subordinate group whose members have significantly less control or power over their own lives than do the members of a dominant or majority group. (5)

**mixed status** Families in which one or more members are citizens and one or more are noncitizens. (131)

**model or ideal minority** A group that, despite past prejudice and discrimination, succeeds economically, socially, and educationally without resorting to political or violent confrontations with Whites. (200)

**nativism** Beliefs and policies favoring native-born citizens over immigrants. (123)

**naturalization** Conferring of citizenship on a person after birth. (139)

**normative approach** The view that prejudice is influenced by societal norms and situations that encourage or discourage the tolerance of minorities. (52)

**panethnicity** The development of solidarity between ethnic subgroups as reflected in the terms Hispanic and Asian American. (17, 164)

**pluralism** Mutual respect for one another's culture, a respect that allows minorities to express their own culture without suffering prejudice or discrimination. (33)

**prejudice** A negative attitude toward an entire category of people such as a racial or ethnic minority. (44)

**principle of third-generation interest** Marcus Hansen's contention that ethnic interest and awareness increase in the third generation, among the grandchildren of immigrants. (161)

**racial formation** A sociohistorical process by which racial categories are created, inhibited, transformed, and destroyed. (14)

**racial group** A group that is socially set apart because of obvious physical differences. (7)

**racial profiling** Any arbitrary police-initiated action based on race, ethnicity, or natural origin rather than a person's behavior. (56)

**racism** A doctrine that one race is superior. (14)

**redlining** The pattern of discrimination against people trying to buy homes in minority and racially changing neighborhoods. (95)

**refugees** People living outside their country of citizenship for fear of political or religious persecution. (147)

**relative deprivation** The conscious experience of a negative discrepancy between legitimate expectations and present actualities. (82)

**religion** A unified system of sacred beliefs and practices that encompasses elements beyond everyday life that inspire awe, respect, and even fear. (180)

**remittances** The monies that immigrants return to their countries of origin. (142)

**resegregation** The physical separation of racial and ethnic groups reappearing after a period of relative integration. (30)

**reverse discrimination** Actions that cause better-qualified White men to be passed over for women and minority men. (106)

**scapegoating theory** A person or group blamed irrationally for another person's or group's problems or difficulties. (50)

**secessionist minority** Groups, such as the Amish, that reject both assimilation and coexistence. (189)

**segregation** The physical separation of two groups, often imposed on a subordinate group by the dominant group. (29)

**self-fulfilling prophecy** The tendency to respond to and act on the basis of stereotypes, a predisposition that can lead one to validate false definitions. (23)

**sinophobes** People with a fear of anything associated with China. (124)

**social capital** Collective benefits of durable social networks and their patterns of reciprocal trust. (207)

**social distance** Tendency to approach or withdraw from a racial group. (69)

**sociology** The systematic study of social behavior and human groups. (18)

**stereotypes** Unreliable, exaggerated generalizations about all members of a group that do not take individual differences into account. (22, 53)

**stratification** A structured ranking of entire groups of people that perpetuates unequal rewards and power in a society. (18)

**symbolic ethnicity** Herbert Gans's term that describes emphasis on ethnic food and ethnically associated political issues rather than deeper ties to one's heritage. (163)

**total discrimination** The combination of current discrimination with past discrimination created by poor schools and menial jobs. (83)

**transnationals** Immigrants who sustain multiple social relationships that link their societies of origin and settlement. (145)

**wealth** An inclusive term encompassing all of a person's material assets, including land, stocks, and other types of property. (97)

**White privilege** Rights or immunities granted as a particular benefit or favor for being White. (49, 158)

**world systems theory** A view of the global economic system as divided between nations that control wealth and those that provide natural resources and labor. (27)

**xenophobia** The fear or hatred of strangers or foreigners. (123)

# References

ABBOTT, ANDREW AND RANIER EGLOFF. 2008. The Polish Peasant in Oberlin and Chicago. The Intellectual Trajectory of W. I. Thomas. *American Sociologist* 39: 217–258.

ABDO, GENEIVE. 2004a. A Muslim Rap Finds Voice. *Chicago Tribune* (June 30): 1, 19.

ABDULRAHIM, RAJA. 2009. UC urged to expand ethnic labels. *Los Angeles Times* (March 31): A4.

ADORNO, T. W., ELSE FRENKEL-BRUNSWIK, DANIEL J. LEVINSON, AND R. NEVITT SANFORD. 1950. *The Authoritarian Personality*. New York: Wiley.

AJROUCH, KRISTINE J. AND AMANEY JAMAL. 2007. Assimilating to a White Identity: The Case of Arab Americans. *International Migration Review* (Winter): 860–879.

——— AND ———. 2011. Correspondence with author. June 12.

ALLIANCE FOR BOARD DIVERSITY. 2009. *Women and Minorities on Fortune 100 Boards*. New York: Catalyst, the Executive Leadership Council, and the Hispanic Association on Corporate Responsibility.

ALLPORT, GORDON W. 1979. *The Nature of Prejudice*, 25th anniversary ed. Reading, MA: Addison-Wesley.

AMERICAN COMMUNITY SURVEY. 2009. *American Community Survey 2008*. Released August 2009 from www.census.gov.

———. 2010. *American Community Survey 2009*. Released August 2010 from www.census.gov.

———. 2011. *American Community Survey 2010*. Released August 2011 from www.census.gov.

ANSELL, AMY E. 2008. Color Blindness. Pp. 320–322 in vol. 1, *Encyclopedia of Race, Ethnicity, and Society*, Richard T. Schaefer, ed. Thousand Oaks, CA: Sage.

APPLEBOME, PETER. 1996. 70 Years after Scopes Trial, Creation Debate Lives. *New York Times* (March 10): 1, 22.

ARCHIBOLD, RANDAL C. 2007. A City's Violence Feeds on Black-Hispanic Rivalry. *New York Times* (January 17): A1, A15.

ARIEL/HEWITT. 2009. *401(K) Plans in Living Color*. Chicago, IL: Ariel Education Institute and Ariel Investments/Hewitt Associates.

ASANTE, MOLEFI KETE. 2007. *An Afrocentric Manifesto: Toward an African Renaissance*. Cambridge, UK: Polity.

———. 2008. Afrocentricity. Pp. 41–42 in vol. 1, *Encyclopedia of Race, Ethnicity, and Society*, Richard T. Schaefer, ed. Thousand Oaks, CA: Sage.

BADGETT, M. V. LEE, AND HEIDI I. HARTMANN. 1995. The Effectiveness of Equal Employment Opportunity Policies. In *Economic Perspectives in Affirmative Action*, ed. Margaret C. Simms, 55–83. Washington, DC: Joint Center for Political and Economic Studies.

BALTZELL, E. DIGBY. 1964. *The Protestant Establishment: Aristocracy and Caste in America*. New York: Vintage Books.

BAMSHAD, MICHAEL J. AND STEVE E. OLSON. 2003. Does Race Exist? *Scientific American* (December): 78–85.

BANTON, MICHAEL. 2008. The Sociology of Ethnic Relations. *Ethnic and Racial Studies* (May): 1–19.

BARRINGER, FELICITY. 2004. Bitter Division for Sierra Club on Immigration. *New York Times* (March 14): A1, A16.

BASCARA, VICTOR. 2008. Model Minority. Pp. 910–912 in vol. 2, *Encyclopedia of Race, Ethnicity, and Society*, Richard T. Schaefer, ed. Thousand Oaks, CA: Sage.

BASH, HARRY M. 2001. If I'm So White, Why Ain't I Right? Some Methodological Misgivings on Taking Identity Ascriptions at Face Value. Paper presented at the annual meeting of the Midwest Sociological Society, St. Louis.

BAUDER, HARALD. 2003. Brain Abuse, or the Devaluation of Immigrant Labour in Canada. *Antipode* 35 (September): 699–717.

BEISEL, NICOLA AND TAMARA KAY. 2004. Abortion: Race and Gender in Nineteenth Century America. *American Sociological Review* 69 (August): 498–518.

BELL, DERRICK. 1994. The Freedom of Employment Act. *The Nation* 258 (May 23): 708, 710–714.

BELL, WENDELL. 1991. Colonialism and Internal Colonialism. Pp. 52–53 in 4th ed., *The Encyclopedic Dictionary of Sociology*, Richard Lachmann, ed. Guilford, CT: Dushkin Publishing Group.

BELLAH, ROBERT. 1967. Civil Religion in America. *Daedalus* 96 (Winter): 1–21.

BELTON, DANIELLE C. 2009. Blacks in Space. *American Prospect* (June): 47–49.

BENNETT, BRIAN. 2008. Coming to America. *Time* 171 (February 4).

BENNETT, NATALIE. 2008. Caribbean Americans. Pp. 241–244 in vol. 1, *Encyclopedia of Race, Ethnicity, and Society*, Richard T. Schaefer, ed. Thousand Oaks, CA: Sage.

BEST, JOEL. 2001. Social Progress and Social Problems: Toward a Sociology of Gloom. *Sociological Quarterly* 42 (1): 1–12.

BJERK, DAVID. 2008. Glass Ceilings or Sticky Floors? Statistical Discrimination in a Dynamic Model of Hiring and Promotion. *The Economic Journal* 118 (530): 961–982.

BLANCHARD, FLETCHER A., TERI LILLY, AND LEIGH ANN VAUGHN. 1991. Reducing the Expression of Racial Prejudice. *Psychological Science* (March 2): 101–105.

BLAUNER, ROBERT. 1969. INTERNAL COLONIALISM AND GHETTO REVOLT. *Social Problems* 16 (Spring): 393–408.

———. 1972. *Racial Oppression in America*. New York: Harper & Row.

BLAZAK, RANDY. 2011. Isn't Every Crime a Hate Crime? The Case for Hate Crime Laws. *Sociology Compass* 5 (4): 244–255.

BLOOM, LEONARD. 1971. *The Social Psychology of Race Relations*. Cambridge, MA: Schenkman Publishing.

BOCIAN, DEBBIE GRUENSTEIN, KEITH S. ERNST, AND WEI LI. 2006. *Unfair Lending: The Effect of Race and Ethnicity on the Price of Subprime Mortgages*. Oakland, CA: Center for Responsible Lending.

BOGARDUS, EMORY. 1968. Comparing Racial Distance in Ethiopia, South Africa, and the United States. *Sociology and Social Research* 52 (January): 149–156.

BOHMER, SUSANNE AND KAYLEEN V. OKA. 2007. Teaching Affirmative Action: An Opportunity to Apply, Segregate, and Reinforce Sociological Concepts. *Teaching Sociology* 35 (October): 334–349.

BONILLA-SILVA, EDUARDO. 1996. Rethinking Racism: Toward a Structural Interpretation. *American Sociological Review* 62 (June): 465–480.

———. 2002. The Linguistics of Color Blind Racism: How to Talk Nasty about Blacks without Sounding Racist. *Critical Sociology* 28 (1–2): 41–64.

———. 2006. *Racism without Racists*, 2nd ed. Lanham, MD: Rowman & Littlefield.

———. 2008. *Will Change Happen in Obamerica?* Accessed November 16, 2010, at http://contexts.org/obama/author/bonilla-silva.

——— AND GIANPAOLO BAIOCCHI. 2001. Anything but Racism: How Sociologists Limit the Significance of Racism. *Race and Society* 4: 117–131.

——— AND DAVID DIETRICH. 2011. The Sweet Enchantment of Color-Blind Racism in Obamerica. *The ANNALS of the American Academy of Political and Social Science* 634 (March): 190–206.

——— AND DAVID G. EMBRICK. 2007. "Every Place Has a Ghetto . . .": The Significance of Whites' Social and Residential Segregation. *Symbolic Interaction* 30 (3): 323–345.

BORDT, REBECCA L. 2005. Using a Research Article to Facilitate a Deep Structure Understanding of Discrimination. *Teaching Sociology* 33 (October): 403–410.

BORJAS, GEORGE J., JEFFERY GROGGER, AND GORDON H. HANSON. 2006. *Immigration and African-American Employment Opportunities: The Response of Wages, Employment, and Incarceration to Labor Supply Shocks*. Working Paper 12518. Cambridge, MA: National Bureau of Economic Research.

BORK, ROBERT H. 1995. What to Do about the First Amendment. *Commentary* 99 (February): 23–29.

BOSMAN, JULIE. 2007. Plan for Arabic School in Brooklyn Arouses Protests. *New York Times* (May 4): A22.

BOURDIEU, PIERRE. 1983. The Forms of Capital. Pp. 241–258 in *Handbook of Theory and Research for the Sociology of Education*, ed. J. G. Richardson. Westport, CT: Greenwood.

——— AND JEAN-CLAUDE PASSERON. 1990. *Reproduction in Education, Society and Culture*, 2nd ed. London: Sage. (Originally published as *La Reproduction* 1970.)

BOWLES, SCOTT. 2000. Bans on Racial Profiling Gain Steam. *USA Today* 2 (June): 3A.

BOWMAN, SCOTT WM. 2011. Multigenerational Interactions in Black Middle Class Wealth and Asset Decision Making. *Journal of Family and Economic Issues* 32: 15–26.

BOWMAN, TOM. 1998. Evangelicals Allege Bias in U.S. Navy, Marine Chaplain Corps. *Baltimore Sun* 23 (August): A12.

BRAXTON, GREGORY. 2009. "Reality Television" in More Ways than One. *Los Angeles Times* (February 17): A1, A15.

BOWSER, BENJAMIN AND RAYMOND G. HUNT, EDS. 1996. *Impacts of Racism on White Americans*. Beverly Hills, CA: Sage Publications.

BRANDS, H. W., T. H. BREEN, R. HAL WILLIAMS, AND ARIELA J. GROSS. 2009. *American Stories: A History of the United States*. New York: Pearson Longman.

BRITTINGHAM, ANGELA AND G. PATRICIA DE LA CRUZ. 2005. *We the People of Arab Ancestry in the United States*. CENSR-21. Washington, DC: U.S. Government Printing Office.

BROOKS-GUNN, JEANNE, PAMELA K. KLEBANOV, AND GREG J. DUNCAN. 1996. Ethnic Differences in Children's Intelligence Test Scores: Role of Economic Deprivation,

Home Environment, and Maternal Characteristics. *Child Development* 67 (April): 396–408.

BROWN, PATRICIA LEIGH. 2003. For the Muslim Prom Queen, There Are No Kings Allowed. *New York Times* 9 (June): A1, A24.

——. 2011. Soup without Fins? Some Californians Simmer. *New York Times* (March 5).

BROWNE, IRENE, ED. 2001. *Latinas and African American Women at Work: Race, Gender, and Economic Inequality.* New York: Russell Sage Foundation.

BRULLIARD, KARIN. 2006. A Proper Goodbye: Funeral Homes Learn Immigrants' Traditions. *Washington Post National Weekly Edition* (May 7): 31.

BUCHANAN, ANGELA B., NORA G. ALBERT, AND DANIEL BEAULIEU. 2010. *The Population with Haitian Ancestry in the United States: 2009.* ACSR/09-18. Accessed at www.census.gov.

BUDIG, MICHELLE J. 2002. Male Advantage and the Gender Composition of Jobs: Who Rides the Glass Escalator? *Social Problems* 49 (2): 258–277.

BUKOWCYK, JOHN J. 2007. *A History of Polish Americans.* New Brunswick, NJ: Transaction Books.

BUREAU OF THE CENSUS. 2008c. *Families and Living Arrangements: 2007.* Accessed at www.census.gov/population/www/socdemo/hh-fam/cps2007.html.

——. 2009c. *Irish-American Heritage Month (March) and St. Patrick's Day (March 17th): 2009.* Washington, DC: U.S. Census Bureau.

——. 2010a. *Statistical Abstract of the United States, 2011.* Washington, DC: U.S. Government Printing Office.

——. 2010b. *U.S. Population Projections.* Accessed at http://www.census.gov/population/www/projections/2009projections.html.

——. 2011c. *Asian/Pacific American Heritage Month May 2011.* CB11-FF.06. Accessed at www.census.gov.

——. 2011d. *2010 Center of Population.* Accessed at http://2010.census.gov/news/pdf/03242011_pressbrf_slides230pm.pdf.

——. 2011i. *Irish-American Heritage Month (March) and St. Patrick's Day (March 17): 2011.* Census Brief CB11-FF, 03, January 13.

BUREAU OF JUSTICE STATISTICS. 2004. *First Release from State Prisons 2001.* Washington, DC: Bureau of Justice Statistics.

CAFARO, PHILIP AND WINTHROP STAPLES III. 2009. *The Environmental Argument for Reducing Immigration to the United States.* Washington DC: Center for Immigration Studies.

CALAVITA, KITTY. 2007. Immigration Law, Race, and Identity. *Annual Reviews of Law and Social Sciences* 3: 1–20.

CAMAROTA, STEVEN A. 2007a. *Immigrants in the United States, 2007: A Profile of America's Foreign-Born Population.* Washington, DC: Center for Immigrant Statistics.

—— AND KAREN JENSNENUS. 2009. *A Shifting Tide: Recent Trends in the Illegal Immigrant Population.* Washington DC: Center for Immigration Studies.

CAPPS, RANDY, KU LEIGHTON, AND MICHAEL FIX. 2002. *How Are Immigrants Faring after Welfare Reform? Preliminary Evidence from Los Angeles and New York City.* Washington, DC: Urban Institute.

CARLSON, ALLAN C. 2003. The Peculiar Legacy of German-Americans. *Society* (January/February): 77–88.

CARR, JAMES H. AND NANDINEE K. KUTTY, EDS. 2008. *Segregation: The Rising Costs for America.* New York: Routledge.

CARROLL, JOSEPH. 2006. Public National Anthem Should Be Sung in English. *The Gallup Poll* (May): 3.

CARVAJAL, DOREEN. 1996. Diversity Pays Off in a Babel of Yellow Pages. *New York Times* (December 3): 1, 23.

CATALYST. 2001. Women Satisfied with Current Job in Financial Industry but Barriers Still Exist. Press release July 25, 2001. Accessed January 31, 2002, at www.catalystwomen.org.

CENTER FOR CONSTITUTIONAL RIGHTS. 2011. *Stop-and-Frisks of New Yorkers in 2010 Hit All-Time High at 600, 601; 87 percent of Those Stopped Black and Latino.* Accessed March 2, 2011, at http://ccrjustice.org.

CHANG, DORIS F. AND AMY DEMYAN. 2007. Teachers' Stereotypes of Asian, Black and White Students. *School Psychology Quarterly* 22 (2): 91–114.

CHAZAN, GUY AND AINSLEY THOMSON. 2011. Tough Irish Economy Turns Migration Influx to Exodus. *Wall Street Journal* (January 21): A8.

CHIROT, DANIEL AND JENNIFER EDWARDS. 2003. Making Sense of the Senseless: Understanding Genocide. *Contexts* 2 (Spring): 12–19.

CHOI, YOONSUN AND BENJAMIN B. LAHEY. 2006. Testing the Model Minority Stereotype: Youth Behaviors across Racial and Ethnic Groups. *Social Science Review* (September): 419–452.

CITRIN, JACK, AMY LERMAN, MICHAEL MURAKAMI, AND KATHRYN PEARSON. 2007. Testing Huntington: Is Hispanic Immigration a Threat to American Identity? *Perspectives on Politics* 5 (March): 31–48.

CLARK, KENNETH B. AND MAMIE P. CLARK. 1947. Racial Identification and Preferences in Negro Children. Pp. 169–178 in *Readings in Social Psychology*, Theodore M. Newcomb and Eugene L. Hartley, eds. New York: Holt, Rinehart & Winston.

CLEMMITT, MARCIA. 2005. Intelligent Design. *CQ Researcher* 95 (July 29): 637–660.

COGNARD-BLACK, ANDREW J. 2004. Will They Stay, or Will They Go? Sex—Atypical among Token Men Who Teach. *Sociological Quarterly* 45 (1): 113–139.

COHEN, PATRICIA. 2010a. Discussing That Word That Prompts Either a Fist Pump or a Scowl. *New York Times* (January 23): C1, C5.

COKER, TUMAINI, ET AL. 2009. Perceived Racial/Ethnic Discrimination among Fifth-Grade Students and Its Association with Mental Health. *American Journal of Public Health* 99 (5): 878–884.

COLBURN, DAVID R., CHARLES E. YOUNG, AND VICTOR M. YELLEN. 2008. Admissions and Public Higher Education in California, Texas, and Florida: The Post-Affirmative Action Era. *InterActions: UCLA Journal of Education and Information Studies* 4 (1): 2. Accessed April 20, 2008, at repositories.cdib.org/gseis/interactions/vol4/iss1/art2.

COLEMAN, JAMES S. 1988. Social Capital in the Creation of Human Capital. *American Journal of Sociology*, 94 (Suppl.): S95–S120.

COLLINS, PATRICIA HILL. 2000. *Black Feminist Thought: Knowledge, Consciousness, and the Politics of Empowerment*, 2nd ed. New York: Routledge.

COLLURA, HEATHER. 2007. Roommate Concerns Fed by Facebook. *USA Today* (August 8): 6D.

COMMISSION ON CIVIL RIGHTS. 1976. *Fulfilling the Letter and Spirit of the Law: Desegregation of the Nation's Public Schools*. Washington, DC: U.S. Government Printing Office.

———. 1981. *Affirmative Action in the 1980s: Dismantling the Process of Discrimination*. Washington, DC: U.S. Government Printing Office.

COMMITTEE OF 100. 2009. *Still the "Other"? Public Attitudes toward Chinese and Asian Americans*. New York: Committee of 100.

CONYERS, JAMES L., JR. 2004. The Evolution of Africology: An Afrocentric Appraisal. *Journal of Black Studies* 34 (May): 640–652.

COONTZ, STEPHANIE. 2010. *A Strange Stirring: "The Feminine Mystique" and American Women at the Dawn of the 1960s*. New York: Basic Books.

COOPER, MARY H. 2004. Voting Rights. *CQ Researcher* 14 (October 29): 901–924.

COOPERMAN, ALAN. 2005. One Way to Pray? *Washington Post National Weekly Edition* 22 (September 5): 10–11.

CORNACCHIA, EUGENE J. AND DALE C. NELSON. 1992. Historical Differences in the Political Experiences of American Blacks and White Ethnics: Revisiting an Unresolved Controversy. *Ethnic and Racial Studies* (January 15): 102–124.

——— AND ———. 1996. The Variable Ties that Bind: Content and Circumstance in Ethnic Processes. *Ethnic and Racial Studies* 19 (April): 265–289.

CORRELL, JOSHUA, BERNADETTE PARK, CHARLES M. JUDD, BERND WITTENBRINK, MELODY S. SADLER, AND TRACIE KEESEE. 2007a. Across the Thin Blue Line: Police Officers and Racial Bias in the Decision to Shoot. *Journal of Personality and Social Psychology*, 92 (6): 1006–1023.

———, ———, ———, ———, ———, AND ———. 2007b. The Influence of Stereotypes and Decisions to Shoot. *European Journal of Social Psychology* 37: 1102–1117.

COSE, ELLIS. 1993. *The Rage of a Privileged Class*. New York: HarperCollins.

———. 2008. So What if He Were Muslim? *Newsweek* (September 1): 37.

COX, OLIVER C. 1942. The Modern Caste School of Social Relations. *Social Forces* 21 (December): 218–226.

CRANFORD, CYNTHIA J. 2005. Networks of Exploitation: Immigrant Labor and the Restructuring of the Los Angeles Janitorial Industry. *Social Problems* 52 (3): 379–397.

DACOSTA, KIMBERLY MCCLAIN. 2007. *Making Multiracials: State, Family, and Market in the Redrawing of the Color Line*. Stanford, CA: Stanford University Press.

DALY, MATHEW. 2011. Tribes React with Shock Say Bin Laden Code Name another Insult. *News from Indian Country* 25 (May): 14.

DAVID, GARY C. 2003. Rethinking Who's an Arab American: Arab-American Studies in the New Millennium. *Al-Jadid* (Fall): 9.

———. 2007. The Creation of "Arab American": Political Activism and Ethnic (Dis)Unity. *Critical Sociology* 32: 833–862.

DAVIDSON, JAMES D. AND RALPH E. PYLE. 2011. *Ranking Faiths: Religious Stratification in America*. Lanham MD: Rowman and Littlefield.

DAVIS, JAMES A., TOM W. SMITH, AND PETER V. MARSDEN. 2007. *General Social Surveys, 1972–2006: Cumulative Codebook*. Chicago, IL: NORC.

DAVIS, MICHELLE R. 2008. Checking Sources: Evaluating Web Sites Requires Careful Eye. *Education Week* (March 6). Accessed June 20, 2008, at www.edweek.org.

DE ANDA, ROBERTO M. 2004. *Chicanas and Chicanos in Contemporary Society*, 2nd ed. Lanham, MD: Rowman & Littlefield & Bacon.

DE LA GARZA, RODOLFO O., LOUIS DESIPIO, F. CHRIS GARCIA, JOHN GARCIA, AND ANGELO FALCON. 1992. *Latino Voices: Mexican, Puerto Rican, and Cuban Perspectives on American Politics*. Boulder, CO: Westview Press.

DEL OLMO, FRANK. 2003. Slow Motion Carnage at the Border. *Los Angeles Times* (May 18): M5.

DENAVAS-WALT, CARMAN, BERNADETTE D. PROCTOR, AND JESSICA C. SMITH. 2010. *Income, Poverty, and Health Insurance Converge in the United States: 2009*. Washington, DC: U.S. Government Printing Office.

———, ———, AND ——— 2011. Income, Poverty, and Health Insurance Coverage in the United States: 2010. *Current Population Reports*: 60–239. Washington, DC: U.S. Government Printing Office.

DEPARTMENT OF HOMELAND SECURITY. 2009. *New Nationalization Test*. Accessed July 13, 2010, at http://www.usas.gov/files/nativedocuments/M-623-red.pdf.

DEPARTMENT OF JUSTICE. 2001. *Report to the Congress of the United States: A Review of Restrictions on Persons of Italian Ancestry during World War II*. Accessed February 1, 2002, at www.house.gov/judiciary/Italians.pdf.

————. 2011 *Hate Crime Statistics, 2010*. Accessed at www.fbi.gov.

DEPARTMENT OF STATE. 2008a. *Dual Nationality*. Accessed February 6, 2008, at travel.state.gov/travel/cis_pa_tw/cis/cis_1753.html#.

DESMOND, SCOTT A., AND CHARISE E. KUBRIN. 2009. The Power of Place: Immigrant Communities and Adolescent Violence. *Sociological Quarterly* 50: 581–607.

DEUTSCHER, IRWIN, FRED P. PESTELLO, AND H. FRANCES PESTELLO. 1993. *Sentiments and Acts*. New York: Aldine de Gruyter.

DEWAN, SHAILA AND ROBBIE BROWN. 2009. Black Member Tests Message of Masons in Georgia Lodges. *New York Times* (July 3): A13.

DEY, JUDY GOLDBERG AND CATHERINE HILL. 2007. *Behind the Pay Gap*. Washington, DC: American Association of University Women.

DIAMOND, JARED. 2003. Globalization, Then. *Los Angeles Times* (September 14): M1, M3.

DiMAGGIO, PAUL. 2005. Cultural Capital. Pp. 167–170 in *Encyclopedia of Social Theory*, George Ritzer, ed. Thousand Oaks, CA: Sage Publications.

DiTOMASO, NANCY, CORINNE POST, AND ROCHELLE PARKS-YANCY. 2007. Workforce Diversity and Inequality: Power, Status, and Numbers. *Annual Review of Sociology* 33: 473–501.

DOBBIN, FRANK, ALEXANDRA KALEV, AND ERIN KELLY. 2007. Diversity Management in Corporate America. *Contexts* 6 (4): 21–27.

————, SOOHAN KIM, AND ALEXANDRA KALEV. 2011. You Can't Always Get What You Need: Organizational Determinants of Diversity Programs. *American Sociological Review* 76 (3): 386.

DOLAN, SEAN AND SANDRA STOTSKY. 1997. *The Polish Americans*. New York: Chelsea House.

DOLNICK, SAM. 2010. A Bitter Divide as Immigrants Share a Church. *New York Times* (December 29): A1, A18.

DOWNEY, DOUGLAS B. 2008. Black/White Differences in School Performance: The Oppositional Culture Explanation. *Annual Review of Sociology* 34: 107–126.

DU BOIS, W. E. B. 1903. *The Souls of Black Folks: Essays and Sketches* (reprint). New York: Facade Publications, 1961.

————. 1969a. *An ABC of Color* [1900]. New York: International Publications.

DUDLEY, CARL S. AND DAVID A. ROOZEN. 2001. *Faith Communities Today*. Hartford, CT: Hartford Seminary.

DUKE, LYNNE. 1992. You See Color-Blindness, I See Discrimination. *Washington Post National Weekly Edition* 9 (June 15): 33.

DURKHEIM, ÉMILE. 2001. *The Elementary Forms of Religious Life* [1912]. New translation by Carol Cosman. New York: Oxford University Press.

DUSZAK, THOMAS. 1997. Lattimer Massacre Centennial Commemoration. *Polish American Journal* (August). Accessed June 4, 2008, at www.polamjournal.com/Library/APHistory/Lattimer/lattimer.html.

DYSON, MICHAEL ERIC. 2005. *Is Bill Cosby Right?* New York: Basic Civitas, Perseus Books.

ECKSTROM, KEVIN. 2001. New, Diverse Take Spot on Catholic Altars. *Chicago Tribune* (August 31): 8.

ECONOMIC MOBILITY PROJECT. 2007. *Economic Mobility of Black and White Families*. Washington, DC: Pew Charitable Trust.

EL-HAJ, NADIA ABU. 2007. The Genetic Reinscription of Race. *Annual Review of Anthropology* 16: 283–300.

ENNIS, SHARON R., MERARYS RIOS-VARGAS, AND NORA G. ALBERT. 2011. *The Hispanic Population: 2010*. C2010BR-404. Accessed at http://www.census.gov/prod/cen2010/briefs/c2010br-04.pdf.

EPSTEIN, CYNTHIA FUCHS. 1999. The Major Myth of the Women's Movement. *Dissent* (Fall): 83–111.

ERDMANS, MARY PATRICE. 1998. *Opposite Poles: Immigrants and Ethnics in Polish Chicago, 1976–1990*. University Park, PA: Pennsylvania State University.

————. 2006. New Chicago Polonia: Urban and Suburban. Pp. 115–127 in *The New Chicago*, John Koval, Larry Bennett, Michael Bennett, Fassil Demissie, Roberta Garner, Kiljoong Kim, eds. Philadelphia, PA: Temple University Press.

ESPINOZA, GALINA. 2011. That Latinos "Wave" Is Very Much American. *USA Today* (April 15): 9A.

ESPIRITU, YEN LE. 1992. *Asian American Panethnicity: Bridging Institutions and Identities*. Philadelphia, PA: Temple University Press.

EUROPEAN ROMA RIGHTS CENTRE. 2008. *Ostravis Case: D. H. and Others v. The Czech Republic*. Accessed June 29, 2008, at www.errc.org.

FALLOWS, MARJORIE R. 1979. *Irish Americans: Identity and Assimilation*. Englewood Cliffs, NJ: Prentice Hall.

FARKAS, STEVE. 2003. *What Immigrants Say about Life in the United States*. Washington, DC: Migration Policy Institute.

FAVREAULT, MELISSA. 2008. *Discrimination and Economic Mobility*. Washington, DC: Economic Mobility Project, Pew Charitable Trusts.

FEAGIN, JOE R. AND EILEEN O'BRIEN. 2003. *White Men on Race, Power, Privilege, and the Shaping of Cultural Consciousness*. Boston, MA: Beacon Press.

————, HERNÁN VERA, AND PINAR BATUR. 2000. *White Racism*, 2nd ed. New York: Routledge.

———— AND JOSÉ A. COBAS. 2008. Latinos/as and White Racial Frame: The Procrustean Bed of Assimilation. *Sociological Inquiry* 78 (February): 39–53.

——— AND KARYN D. MCKINNEY. 2003. *The Many Costs of Racism.* Lanham, MD: Rowan and Littlefield.

FELDMAN, MARCUS W. 2010. The Biology of Race. Pp. 136–159 in *Doing Race*, Hazel Rose Markus and Paula M. L. Moya, eds. New York: W. W. Norton.

FELSENTHAL, CAROL. 2009. The Making of a First Lady. *Chicago Magazine* (February).

FERBER, ABBY L. 2008. Privilege. Pp. 1073–1074 in vol. 3, *Encyclopedia of Race, Ethnicity, and Society*, Richard T. Schaefer, ed. Thousand Oaks, CA: Sage.

FERGUSON, RONALD. 2007. Parenting Practices, Teenage Lifestyles, and Academic Achievement among African-American Children. *Focus* 25 (Spring–Summer): 18–26.

FERNANDEZ, MANNY AND KAREEM FAHIM. 2006. Five on Plane Are Detained at Newark but Later Freed. *New York Times* (May 5): 29.

FERNANDEZ-ARMESTO, FELOPE. 2007. *The World: A History.* Upper Saddle River, NJ: Prentice Hall.

FINE, GARY. 2008. *Robber's Cave.* Pp. 1163–1164 in vol. 3, *Encyclopedia of Race, Ethnicity, and Society*, Richard T. Schaefer, ed. Thousand Oaks, CA: Sage.

FIX, MICHAEL E. AND JEFFERY S. PASSEL. 2001. *The Integration of Immigrant Families in the United States.* Washington, DC: The Urban Institute.

FOERSTRER, AMY. 2004. Race, Identity, and Belonging: "Blackness" and the Struggle for Solidarity in a Multiethnic Labor Union. *Social Problems* 51 (3): 386–409.

FORDHAM, SIGNITHIA AND JOHN U. OGBU. 1986. Black Students' School Success: Coping with the "Burden of 'Acting White.'" *Urban Review* 18 (3): 176–206.

FORERO, JUAN. 2006. Hidden Cost of Shark Fin Soup: Its Source May Vanish. *New York Times* (January 5).

FOX, STEPHEN. 1990. *The Unknown Internment.* Boston, MA: Twayne.

FRANK, REANNE, ILANA REDSTONE A. KRECH, AND BOB LU. 2010. Latino Immigrants and the U.S. Racial Order: How and Where Do They Fit In? *American Sociological Review* 75 (3): 378–401.

FREY, WILLIAM H. 2011. *Census Data: Blacks and Hispanics Take Different Segregation Paths* (February 24). Accessed at http://www.brookings.edu.

FRYER, RONALD G. 2006. Acting White. *Education Next* (Winter): 53–59.

——— AND PAUL TORELLI. An Empirical Analysis of "Acting White." *Journal of Public Econmics* 94 (June): 380–396.

FULLER, CHEVON. 1998. Service Redlining. *Civil Rights Journal* 3 (Fall): 33–36.

GALLUP. 2010. *Religion.* Accessed April 17, 2011, at http://www.gallup.com/poll/1690/Religion.aspx.

GANS, HERBERT J. 1979. Symbolic Ethnicity: The Future of Ethnic Groups and Cultures in America. *Ethnic and Racial Studies* 2 (January): 1–20.

GERTH, H. H. AND C. WRIGHT MILLS. 1958. *From Max Weber: Essays in Sociology.* New York: Galaxy Books.

GHOSH, BOBBY. 2010. Islam in America. *Time* (August 30): 20–26.

GIAGO, TIM. 2001. National Media Should Stop Using Obscene Words. *The Denver Post* (January 21).

GIBSON, CAMPBELL AND KAY JUNG. 2006. *Historical Census Statistics on the Foreign-Born Population of the United States: 1850 to 2000.* Working Paper No. 81. Washington, DC: Bureau of the Census.

GIRARDELLI, DAVIDE. 2004. Commodified Identities: The Myth of Italian Food in the United States. *Journal of Communication Inquiry* 28 (October): 307–324.

GIROUX, HENRY A. 1997. Rewriting the Discourse of Racial Identity: Towards a Pedagogy and Politics of Whiteness. *Harvard Educational Review* 67 (Summer): 285–320.

GITTELL, MARILYN AND BILL MCKINNEY. 2007. *The Economic Status of Working Women in New York.* New York: Howard Samuels Center.

GLASCOCK, STUART. 2008. A Town Confronts the Language Barrier. *Los Angeles Times* (May 25): A20.

GLEASON, PHILIP. 1980. American Identity and Americanization. Pp. 31–58 in *Harvard Encyclopedia of American Ethnic Groups*, Stephan Thernstrom, ed. Cambridge, MA: Belknap Press of Harvard University Press.

GOERING, JOHN M. 1971. The Emergence of Ethnic Interests: A Case of Serendipity. *Social Forces* 48 (March): 379–384.

GOLDIN, IAN, GEOFFREY CAMERON, AND MEERA BALARAJAN. 2011. *Exceptional People. How Migration Shaped Our World and Will Define Our Future.* Princeton: Princeton University Press.

GOMEZ, ALAN. 2010. Rise Seen in Births to Illegal Dwellers. *USA Today* (August 12): A1.

GONZALEZ, DAVID. 2009. A Family Divided by 2 Worlds, Legal and Illegal. *New York Times* (April 26): 1, 20–21.

GOODSTEIN, LAURIE. 2005. Issuing Rebuke: Judge Rejects Teaching of Intelligent Design. *New York Times* (December 21): A1, A21.

GOODSTEIN, LAURIE AND JENNIFER STEINHAUER. 2010. Pope Picks Latino to Lead Los Angeles Archdiocese. *New York Times* (April 7): A17.

GORDON, MILTON M. 1964. *Assimilation in American Life: The Role of Race, Religion, and National Origins.* New York: Oxford University Press.

GORSKI, PHILLIP S. 2010. *Civil Religion Today* (ARDA Guiding Paper Series). State College, PA: Association of Religion Data Archives at The Pennsylvania State University. Accessed at http://www.thearda.com/rrh/papers/guidingpapers.asp.

GRAY-LITTLE, BERNADETTE AND HAFDAHL, ADAM R. 2000. Factors Influencing Racial Comparisons of Self-Esteem: A Qualitative Review. *Psychological Bulletin* 126 (1): 26–54.

GREATER NEW ORLEANS FAIR HOUSING ACTION CENTER. 2007. *For Rent, Unless You're Black.* New Orleans, LA: Greater New Orleans Fair Housing Action Center.

————. 2011. *Enough is Enough.* Accessed April 12, 2011, at www.gnofairhousing.org/enoughisenough.html.

GREELEY, ANDREW M. 1981. *The Irish Americans: The Rise to Money and Power.* New York: Harper & Row.

GREENHOUSE, LINDA. 1996. Case on Government Interface in Religion Tied to Separation of Powers. *New York Times* (October 16): C23.

GRIECO, ELIZABETH M. AND EDWARD N. TREVELYAN. 2010. *Place of Birth of the Foreign-Born Population: 2009.* Washington DC: US Government Printing Office.

GRIECO, ELIZABETH M. AND RACHEL C. CASSIDY. 2001. *Overview of Race and Hispanic Origin.* Current Population Reports. Ser. CENBR/01-1. Washington, DC: U.S. Government Printing Office.

GROSSMAN, CATHY LYNN. 2010. Day of Prayer Divides Some. *USA Today* (May 5): 6D.

GUGLIELMO, JENNIFER AND SALVATORE SALERNO, EDS. 2003. *Are Italians White?* New York: Routledge.

HACEK, MIRO. 2008. Roma. Pp. 1168–1170 in vol. 3, *Encyclopedia of Race, Ethnicity, and Society,* Richard T. Schaefer, ed. Thousand Oaks, CA: Sage.

HALSTEAD, MARK L. 2008. Islamophobia. Pp. 762–764 in vol. 2, *Encyclopedia of Race, Ethnicity, and Society,* Richard T. Schaefer, ed. Thousand Oaks, CA: Sage.

HAN, JEAN. 2008. Asian America Still Discovering Elusive Identity. *AsianWeek* (May 16): 19.

HANDLIN, OSCAR. 1951. *The Uprooted: The Epic Story of the Great Migrations That Made the American People.* New York: Grossett and Dunlap.

HANSEN, MARCUS LEE. 1952. The Third Generation in America. *Commentary* (November 14): 493–500.

HARLOW, CAROLINE WOLF. 2005. *Hate Crime Reported by Victims and Police.* Bureau of Justice Statistics Special Report (November). Accessed May 8, 2008, at www.ojp.usdoj.gov/bjs/pub/pdf/hcrvp.pdf.

HARZIG, CHRISTINE. 2008. German Americans. Pp. 540–544 in vol. 1, *Encyclopedia of Race, Ethnicity, and Society,* Richard T. Schaefer, ed. Thousand Oaks, CA: Sage.

HASSRICK, ELIZABETH McGHEE. 2007. *The Transnational Production of White Ethnic Symbolic Identities.* Paper presented at the Annual Meeting of the American Sociological Association.

HERBERT, BOB. 2010. Jim Crow Policy. *New York Times* (February 2): A27.

HERRNSTEIN, RICHARD J. AND CHARLES MURRAY. 1994. *The Bell Curve: Intelligence and Class Structure in American Life.* New York: Free Press.

HIRSLEY, MICHAEL. 1991. Religious Display Needs Firm Count. *Chicago Tribune* 2 (December 20): 10.

HISNANICK, JOHN J. AND KATHERINE G. GIEFER. 2011. *Dynamics of Economic Well-Being: Fluctuations in the U.S. Income Distribution 2004–2007.* Washington, DC: U.S. Government Printing Office.

HOLZER, HARRY J. 2008. *The Effects of Immigration on the Employment Outcomes of Black Americans. Testimony before the U.S. Commission on Civil Rights.* Accessed December 6, 2011, at http://www.urban.org/publications/901159.html.

HONDAGNEU-SOTELO, PIERETTE, ED. 2003. *Gender and U.S. Immigration: Contemporary Trends.* Berkeley, CA: University of California Press.

HOOKS, BELL. 1984. *Feminist Theory: From Margin to Center.* Boston: South End Press.

HUGHLETT, MIKE. 2006. Judge: Craigslist Not Liable for Ad Content. *Chicago Tribune* 3 (November 16): 1.

HUMES, KAREN R., NICHOLAS A. JONES, AND ROBERTO R. RAMIREZ. 2011. Overview of Race and Hispanic Organization. *2010 Census Briefs.* C2010 BR-02.

HUNDLEY, TOM. 2009. Return Trip. *Chicago Tribune Magazine* (January 18): 8–14.

HUNTINGTON, SAMUEL P. 1993. The Clash of Civilizations? *Foreign Affairs* 73 (no. 3, Summer): 22–49.

————. 1996. *The Clash of Civilizations and the Remaking of World Order.* New York: Simon & Schuster.

IGNATIEV, NOEL. 1994. Treason to Whiteness Is Loyalty to Humanity. Interview with Noel Ignatiev. *Utne Reader* (November–December): 83–86.

————. 1995. *How the Irish Became White.* New York: Routledge.

INTERNATIONAL ORGANIZATION FOR MIGRATION. 2009. *Migration, Climate Change and the Environment.* Geneva, Switzerland: IOM.

ISHII, MIKU. 2006. Multicultural Autobiography. Unpublished Paper. Chicago: DePaul University.

ITALIAN-AMERICANS AGAINST MEDIA STEREOTYPES. 2009. *Italian-Americans against Media Stereotypes.* Accessed January 4, 2011, at http://iaams.blogspot.com.

JACOBS, TOM. 2008. Patriarchy and Paychecks. *Miller-McCune* 1 (2): 18–19.

JACOBY, SUSAN. 2009. Keeping the Faith, Ignoring the History. *New York Times* (March 1): 11.

JAROSZYNSKA-KIRCHMANN. 2004. *The Exile Mission: The Polish Political Diaspora and Polish Americans, 1939–1956.* Athens, OH: Ohio University Press.

JEFFERIES, SIERRA M. 2007. Environmental Justice and the Skull Valley Goshute Indians' Proposal to Store Nuclear Waste. *Journal of Land, Resources, and Environmental Law* 27 (2): 409–429.

JIMÉNEZ, TOMÁS R. 2007. The Next Americans. *Los Angeles Times* (May 27): M1, M7.

JOHNSON, KEVIN. 1992. German Ancestry Is Strong Beneath Milwaukee Surface. *USA Today* (August 4): 9A.

———. 2004. *Immigration and Civil Rights*. Philadelphia, PA: Temple University Press.

JOHNSTON, TIM. 2008. Australia to Apologize to Aborigines for Past Mistreatment. *New York Times* (January 31).

JONES, ADELE. 2008. A Silent but Mighty River: The Costs of Women's Economic Migration. *Signs: Journal of Women in Culture and Society* 33 (4): 761–769.

JONES, JEFFREY M. 2010. *Few Americans Oppose National Day of Prayer. May 5*. Accessed April 16, 2011, at http://www.gallup.com/poll.127721/Few-Americans-Oppose-National_Day_Prayer.aspx.

JONES, NICHOLAS AND AMY SYMENS SMITH. 2001. *The Two or More Races Population: 2000*. Series C2KBR/01-6. Washington, DC: U.S. Government Printing Office.

———. 2011. Americans' View on Immigration Holding Steady, June 21. Accessed at www.gallup.com.

JORDAN, MIRIAM. 2011. More "Silent Raids" Over Immigration. *Wall Street Journal* (June 10): A1, A2.

KAGAN, JEROME. 1971. The Magical Aura of the IQ. *Saturday Review of Literature* 4 (December 4): 92–93.

KAHLENBERG, RICHARD D. 2010. 10 Myths about Legacy Preference in College Admissions. *Chronicle of Higher Education* (October 1): A23–A25.

KANG, JERRY AND KRISTEN LANE. 2010. Seeing Through Colorblindness: Implicit Bias and the Law. *UCLA Law Review* 58: 465–520.

KAZAL, RUSSELL A. 2004. The Interwar Origins of the White Ethnic: Race, Residence, and German Philadelphia, 1917–1939. *Journal of American Ethnic History* (Summer): 78–131.

KEEN, JUDY. 2011. Transmitting the Immigrant Life. *USA Today* (June 16): 3A.

KENNEDY, RANDALL. 2010. The Enduring Relevance of Affirmative Action. *American Prospect* (September): 31–33.

KERSHAW, SARAH. 2009. Talk About Race? Relax, It's O.K. *New York Times* (January 15): Sect. E, 1, 5.

KIBRIA, NAZLI. 2002. *Becoming Asian American: Second-Generation Chinese and Korean American Identities*. Baltimore, MD: Johns Hopkins Press.

KINLOCH, GRAHAM C. 1974. *The Dynamics of Race Relations: A Sociological Analysis*. New York: McGraw-Hill.

KIVISTO, PETER. 2008. *Third Generation Principle*. Pp. 1302–1304 in vol. 3, *Encyclopedia of Race, Ethnicity, and Society*, Richard T. Schaefer, ed. Thousand Oaks, CA: Sage.

KOCH, WENDY. 2006b. Push for 'Official' English Heats Up. *USA Today* (October 9): 1A.

KOCHHAR, RAKESH. 2006. *Growth in the Foreign-Born Workforce and Employment of the Native Born*. Washington, DC: Pew Hispanic Center.

———, RICHARD FRY, AND PAUL TAYLOR. 2011. *Wealth Gaps Rise to Record Highs between Whites, Blacks and Hispanics*. Washington, DC: Pew Research Center.

KOTKIN, JOEL. 2010. Ready Set Grow. *Smithsonian* (July/August): 61–73.

KRAMMER, ARNOLD. 1997. *Undue Process: The Untold Story of America's German Alien Internees*. Lanham, MD: Rowman & Littlefield.

KRISTOF, NICHOLAS D. 2010. America's History of Fear. *New York Times* (September 5): A10.

KROEGER, BROOKE. 2004. When a Dissertation Makes a Difference. *New York Times* (March 20). Accessed January 15, 2005, at www.racematters.org/devahpager.htm.

KRYSAN, MARIA, REYNOLDS FARLEY, AND MICK P. COUPER. 2008. In the Eye of the Beholder. *DuBois Review* 5 (1): 5–26.

LAL, BARBARA BALLIS. 1995. Symbolic Interaction Theories. *American Behavioral Scientist* 38 (January): 421–441.

LAPIERE, RICHARD T. 1934. Attitudes vs. Actions. *Social Forces* (October 13): 230–237.

———. 1969. Comment of Irwin Deutscher's Looking Backward. *American Sociologist* 4 (February): 41–42.

LATTANZIO, VINCE. 2009. Swim Club Members: "Nothing to Do with Race" Campers Left Sad and Confused by the Whole Situation. *Philadelphia Inquirer* (July 10).

LAUTZ, JESSICA. 2011. *Race/Ethnicity of Home Buyers, 2003–2010*. Accessed at economistoutlookblogs.realtor.org/2011/03/16/race-ethnicity-of-home-buyers-2003-2010.

LEAVITT, PAUL. 2002. Bush Calls Agent Kicked Off Flight "Honorable Fellow." *USA Today* (January 8).

LEE, J. J. AND MARION R. CASEY. 2006. *Making the Irish American*. New York: New York University Press.

LEE, JAMES. 2011. *U.S. Naturalizations: 2010*. Washington, DC: Office of Immigration Statistics.

LEE, JENNIFER AND FRANK D. BEAN. 2007. Redrawing the Color Line. *City and Community* 6 (March): 49–62.

LEEHOTZ, ROBERT. 1995. Is Concept of Race a Relic? *Los Angeles Times* (April 15): A1, A14.

LEUNG, ANGELA KA-YEE, WILLIAM W. MADDUX, ADAM D. GALINSKY, AND CHI-YUE CHIU. 2008. Multicultural Experience Enhances Creativity. *American Psychologist* 63 (April): 169–181.

LEV-ARI, SHARI AND BOAZ KEYSAR. 2010. Why Don't We Believe Non-native Speakers? The Influence of Accent on Credibility. *Journal of Experimental Social Psychology* 46: 1093–1096.

LEVITT, PEGGY AND B. NADYA JAWORSKY. 2007. Transnational Migration Studies: Past Developments and Future Trends. *Annual Review of Sociology* 33: 129–156.

LEVIN, JACK AND JIM NOLAN. 2011. *The Violence of Hate*, 3rd ed. Boston: Allyn and Bacon.

LEWIN, TAMAR. 2006. Campaign to End Race Preferences Splits Michigan. *New York Times* (October 31): A1, A19.

LEWIS, AMANDA E. 2004. "What Group?" Studying Whites and Whiteness in the Era of "Color-Blindness." *Sociological Theory* 22 (December): 623–646.

LICHTENBERG, JUDITH. 1992. Racism in the Head, Racism in the World. *Report from the Institute for Philosophy and Public Policy* 12 (Spring-Summer): 3–5

LINDNER, EILEEN. 2011. *Yearbook of American and Canadian Churches*. Nashville, TN: Abingdon Press.

LIPMAN, FRANCINE J. 2008. *The Undocumented Immigrant Tax: Enriching Americans from Sea to Shining Sea*. Chapman University Law Research Paper No. 2008. Accessed at http://papers.ssrn.com.

LOPATA, HELENA ZNANIECKI. 1994. *Polish Americans*, 2nd ed. New Brunswick, NJ: Transaction Books.

LOPEZ, DAVID AND YEN ESPIRITU. 1990. Panethnicity in the United States: A Theoretical Framework. *Ethnic and Racial Studies* (April 13): 198–224.

LOPEZ, JULIE AMPARANO. 1992. Women Face Glass Walls as Well as Ceilings. *Wall Street Journal* (March 3).

LUCONI, STEFANO. 2001. *From Peasant to White Ethnics: The Italian Experience in Philadelphia*. Albany, NY: State University Press of New York.

LUGO, LUIS ET AL. 2010. *Public Remains Conflicted Over Islam*. Washington, DC: Pew Forum on Religion and Public Life.

LYONS, CHRISTOPHER J. AND BECKY PETTIT. 2011. Compounded Disadvantage: Race, Incarceration, and Wage Growth. *Social Problems* 58 (2): 257–280.

MACK, RAYMOND W. 1996. Whose Affirmative Action? *Society* 33 (March–April): 41–43.

MACLEAN, VICKY M., AND JOYCE E. WILLIAMS. 2008. Shifting Paradigms: Sociological Presentations of Race. *American Behavioral Scientist* 51 (January): 599–624.

MALHOTRA, NEI AND YOTAM MARGALIT. 2009. State of the Nation: Anti-Semitism and the Economic Crisis. *Boston Review* (May/June). Accessed at http://bostonreview.net/BR34.3/malhotra_margalit.php.

MANING, ANITA. 1997. Troubled Waters: Environmental Racism Suit Makes Waves. *USA Today* (July 31): A1.

MANNING, ROBERT D. 1995. Multiculturalism in the United States: Clashing Concepts, Changing Demographics, and Competing Cultures. *International Journal of Group Tensions* (Summer): 117–168.

MARSHALL, PATRICK. 2001. Religion in Schools. *CQ Research* 11 (July 12): 1–24.

MARTIN, DANIEL C. 2011. *Refugees and Asylees: 2010.* Washington, DC: Office of Immigration Statistics.

MARTIN, PHILIP AND ELIZABETH MIDGLEY. 2010. Immigration in America 2010. *Population Bulletin Update* (June).

MARUBBIO, M. ELISE. 2006. *Killing the Indian Maiden: Images of Native American Women in Film*. Lexington: University Press of Kentucky.

MARX, KARL, AND FREDERICK ENGELS. 1955. *Selected Works in Two Volumes*. Moscow: Foreign Languages Publishing House.

MASSEY, DOUGLAS AND MARGARITA MOONEY. 2007. The Effects of America's Three Affirmative Action Programs on Academic Performance. *Social Problems* 54 (1): 99–117.

——— AND NANCY A. DENTON. 1993. *American Apartheid: Segregation and the Making of the Underclass*. Cambridge, MA: Harvard University Press.

——— AND ———. 2011. The Past and Future of American Civil Rights. *Daedalus* 140 (no. 2, Spring): 37–54.

MATHER, MARK, KEVIN POLLARD, AND LINDA A. JACOBSEN. 2011. *First Results from the 2010 Census*. Washington DC: Population Reference Bureau.

MAURO, TONY. 1995. Ruling Helps Communities Set Guidelines. *USA Today* (December 21): A1, A2.

MAZZOCCO, PHILIP J., TIMOTHY C. BROCK, GREGORY J. BROCK, KRISTEN R. OLSON, AND MAHZARIN, R. BANAJI. 2006. The Cost of Being Black: White Americans' Perceptions and the Question of Reparations. *DuBois Review* 3 (2): 261–297.

MCGURN, WILLIAM. 2009. New Jersey's 'Italian' Problem. *Wall Street Journal* (July 28): A15.

MCINTOSH, PEGGY. 1988. *White Privilege: Unpacking the Invisible Knapsack*. Wellesley, MA: Wellesley College Center for Research on Women.

MCKINNEY, KARYN D. 2003. I Feel "Whiteness" When I Hear People Blaming Whites: Whiteness as Cultural Victimization. *Race and Society* 6: 39–55.

MCKINNEY, KARYN D. 2008. Confronting Young People's Perceptions of Whiteness: Privilege or Liability? *Social Compass* 2. Accessed at www.blackwell-compass.com/subject/ sociology.

MEAGHER, TIMOTHY J. 2005. *The Columbia Guide to Irish American History*. New York: Columbia University Press.

MERTON, ROBERT K. 1949. Discrimination and the American Creed. Pp. 99–126 in *Discrimination and National Welfare*, Robert M. MacIver, ed. New York: Harper & Row.

———. 1968. *Social Theory and Social Structure*. New York: Free Press.

———. 1976. *Sociological Ambivalence and Other Essays*. New York: Free Press.

MEYERS, DOWELL. 2007. *Immigrants and Boomers: Forging a New Social Contract for the Future of America*. New York: Russell Sage.

MEYERS, NORMA. 2005. *Environment Refugees: An Emergent Security Issue*. Paper presented at the 13th Economic Forum, May 2005, Prague.

MIGRATION NEWS. 2011. *Remittances Up. and South Africa* (January). Accessed January 2011, at migration. ucdavis.edu.mn.

MILLER, NORMAN. 2002. Personalization and the Promise of Contact Theory. *Journal of Social Issues* 58 (Summer): 387–410.

MOCHA, FRANK, ED. 1998. *American "Polonia" and Poland*. New York: Columbia University Press.

MOHAMED, BESHEER AND JOHN O'BRIEN. 2011. Ground Zero of Misunderstanding. *Contexts* (Winter): 62–64.

MONG, SHERRY N. AND VINCENT J. ROSCIGNO. 2010. African American Men and the Experience of Employment Discrimination. *Qualitative Sociology* 33: 1–21.

MONGER, RANDALL AND JAMES YANKAY. 2011. *U.S. legal Permanent Residents: 2010*. Washington, DC: Department of Homeland Security.

MONKMAN, KAREN, MARGARET RONALD, AND FLORENCE DÉLIMON THÉRAMÉNE. 2005. Social and Cultural Capital in an Urban Latino School Community. *Urban Education* 40 (January): 4–33.

MONTAGU, ASHLEY. 1972. *Statement on Race*. New York: Oxford University Press.

MOSISA, ABRAHAM T. 2006. Foreign-Born Workforce, 2004: A Visual Essay. *Monthly Labor Review* 129 (July): 48–56.

MOSTOFI, NILOU. 2003. Who We Are: The Perplexity of Iranian-American Identity. *Sociological Quarterly* 44 (Fall): 681–703.

MOULDER, FRANCES V. 1996. *Teaching about Race and Ethnicity: A Message of Despair or a Message of Hope?* Paper presented at annual meeting of the American Sociological Association, New York.

MUELLER, JENNIFER C., DANIELLE DIRKS, AND LESLIE HOUTS PICCA. 2007. Unmasking Racism: Halloween Costuming and Engagement of the Racial Other. *Qualitative Sociology* 30: 315–335.

MULLEN, FITZHUGH. 2005. The Metrics of the Physician Brain Drain. *New England Journal of Medicine* 353 (October 27): 1810–1818.

MYERS, DOWELL, JOHN PITKIN, AND JULIE PARK. 2004. *California's Immigrants Turn the Corner. Urban Initiative Policy Relief*. Los Angeles, CA: University of Southern California.

MYRDAL, GUNNAR. 1944. *An American Dilemma: The Negro Problem and Modern Democracy*. New York: Harper & Row.

NAIMARK, NORMAN M. 2004. Ethnic Cleansing, History of. Pp. 4799–4802 in *International Encyclopedia of Social and Behavioral Sciences*, N. J. Smelser and P. B. Baltes, eds. New York: Elsevier.

NASH, MANNING. 1962. Race and the Ideology of Race. *Current Anthropology* 3 (June): 285–288.

NATIONAL ASIAN PACIFIC AMERICAN LEGAL CONSORTIUM. 2002. *Backlash: When America Turned on its Own*. Washington DC: NAPALC.

NATIONAL CENTER FOR EDUCATION STATISTICS. 2009. *Digest of Education Statistics 2008*. Accessed at nces.ed.gov.

NATIONAL CONFERENCE OF CHRISTIANS AND JEWS (NCCJ). 1994. *Taking America's Pulse*. New York: NCCJ.

NATIONAL ITALIAN AMERICAN FOUNDATION. 2006. Stop Ethnic Bashing. *New York Times* (January). Accessed June 4, 2008, at www.niaf.org/news/index.asp?id=422.

NAVARRO-RIVERA, JUHEM, MARRY A. KOSMIN, AND ARIELA KEYSAR. 2010. *U. S. Latino Religious Identification 1990-2008 Growth, Diversity & Transformation*. Hartford, CT: American Religious Identification Project, Trinity College. Accessed at http://www. americanreligionsurvey-aris.org/latinos2008.pdf.

NELSEN, FRANK C. 1973. The German-American Immigrants Struggle. *International Review of History and Political Science* 10 (2): 37–49.

NEW AMERICA MEDIA. 2007. *Deep Divisions, Shared Destiny*. San Francisco, CA: New America Media.

NEWMAN, WILLIAM M. 1973. *American Pluralism: A Study of Minority Groups and Social Theory*. New York: Harper & Row.

NEWPORT, FRANK. 2011. *Very Religious Have Higher Wellbeing Across All Faiths*, January 6. Accessed at www.gallup.com.

NEW YORK TIMES. 1991. For Two, an Answer to Years of Doubt on Use of Peyote in Religious Rite (July 9): A14.

———. 2005b. Warnings Raised About Exodus of Philippine Doctors and Nurses (November 27): 13.

NIEBUHR, GUSTAV. 1998. Southern Baptists Declare Wife Should "Submit" to Her Husband. *New York Times*.

NORTON, MICHAEL I. AND SAMUEL R. SOMMERS. 2011. Whites See Racism as a Zero-Sum Game That They Are Now Losing. *Perspectives on Psychological Science* 6 (3): 215.

OFFICE OF IMMIGRATION STATISTICS. 2009. *Yearbook of Immigration Statistics: 2008*. Accessed at www.dhs. gov.

———. 2011. *Yearbook of Immigration Statistics: 2010*. Accessed at http://www.dhs.gov/files/statistics/ publications/LPR10.shtm.

OGBU, JOHN U. 2004. Collective Identity and the Burden of "Acting White" in Black History, Community, and Education. *Urban Review* 36 (March): 1–35.

—— AND ASTRID DAVIS. 2003. *Black American Students in an Affluent Suburb: A Study of Academic Disengagement.* Mahwah, NJ: Lawrence Erlbaum Associates.

OHNUMA, KEIKO. 1991. Study Finds Asians Unhappy at CSU. *AsianWeek* 12 (August 8): 5.

OLIVER, MELVIN L. AND THOMAS M. SHAPIRO. 2006. *Black Wealth/White Wealth*, 10th anniversary ed. New York: Routledge.

OMI, MICHAEL. 2008. Asian-Americans: The Unbearable Whiteness of Being? *Chronicle of Higher Education* 55 (September 25): B56, B58.

ORFIELD, GARY. 2007. *Historic Reversals, Accelerating Resegregation, and the Need for New Integration Strategies.* Los Angeles, CA: Civil Rights Project, UCLA.

——, AND CHUNGMEI LEE. 2005. *Why Segregation Matters: Poverty and Educational Inequality.* Cambridge, MA: Civil Rights Project.

PAGE, SCOTT E. 2007. *The Difference: How the Power of Diversity Creates Better Groups, Firms, Schools, and Societies.* Princeton, NJ: Princeton University Press.

PAGER, DEVAH. 2003. The Mark of a Criminal. *American Journal of Sociology* 108: 937–975.

——. 2007a. *Marked: Race, Crime, and Finding Work in an Era of Mass Incarceration.* Chicago, IL: University of Chicago Press.

——. 2007b. The Use of Field Experiments for Studies of Employment Discrimination: Contributions, Critiques, and Directions for the Future. *Annals* 609 (January): 104–133.

—— AND BRUCE WESTERN. 2006. *Race at Work: Realities of Race and Criminal Record in the NYC Job Market.* Report prepared for 50th anniversary of the New York City Museum on Human Rights. Accessed June 3, 2008, at www.princeton.edu/~pager/race_at_work.pdf.

——, ——, AND BART BONIKOWSKI. 2009. Discrimination in a Low-Wage Labor Market: A Field Experiment. *American Sociological Review* 74 (October): 777–799.

—— AND HANA SHEPHERD. 2008. The Sociology of Discrimination: Racial Discrimination in Employment, Housing, Credit, and Consumer Markets. *Annual Review of Sociology* 34: 181–209.

—— AND LINCOLN QUILLIAN. 2005. Walking the Talk? What Employers Say versus What They Do. *American Sociological Review* 70 (3): 355–380.

PALUCK, ELIZABETH LEVY AND DONALD P. GREEN. 2009. Prejudice Reduction: What Works? A Review and Assessment of Research and Practice. *Annual Review of Psychology* 60: 339–367.

PARISER, ELI. 2011a. *The Filter Bubble: What the Internet is Hiding from You.* New York: Penguin Press.

——. 2011b. In our own little Internet bubbles. *The Guardian Weekly* (June 24): 32–33.

PARK, ROBERT E. 1928. Human Migration and the Marginal Man. *American Journal of Sociology* 33 (May): 881–893.

——. 1950. *Race and Culture: Essays in the Sociology of Contemporary Man.* New York: Free Press.

—— AND ERNEST W. BURGESS. 1921. *Introduction to the Science of Sociology.* Chicago, IL: University of Chicago Press.

PARRILLO, VINCENT. 2008. Italian Americans. Pp. 766–771 in vol. 2, *Encyclopedia of Race, Ethnicity, and Society*, Richard T. Schaefer, ed. Thousand Oaks, CA: Sage.

PASSEL, JEFFERY S. 2005. *Unauthorized Migrants: Numbers and Characteristics.* Washington, DC: Pew Hispanic Center.

—— AND D'VERA COHN. 2009. *A Portrait of Unauthorized Immigrants in the United States.* Washington, DC: Pew Hispanic Center.

—— AND ——. 2011. *Unauthorized Immigrant Population National and State Trends, 2010.* Washington DC: Pew Research Center.

PASTOR, JR., MANUEL, RACHEL MORELLO-FROSCH, AND JAMES L. SAAD. 2005. The Air Is Always Cleaner on the Other Side: Race, Space, and Ambient Air Toxics Exposure in California. *Journal of Urban Affairs*, 27 (2): 127–148.

PEARSON, BRYAN. 2006. Brain Drain Human Resource Crisis. *The Africa Report* (October): 95–98.

PELLOW, DAVID NAGUIB AND ROBERT J. BRULLE. 2007. Poisoning the Planet: The Struggle for Environmental Justice. *Contexts* 6 (Winter): 37–41.

PERRY, BARBARA, ED. 2003. *Hate and Bias Crime: A Reader.* New York: Routledge.

PEW FORUM ON RELIGION AND PUBLIC LIFE. 2008b. *U.S. Religious Landscape Survey: Religious Beliefs and Practices: Diverse and Political Relevant.* Washington DC: Pew Forum on Religion and Public Life.

——. 2010. *Growing Number of Americans Say Obama Is a Muslim.* Washington, DC: Pew Forum.

——. 2011. *The Future of the Global Muslim Population.* Washington, DC: Pew Forum.

PEW RESEARCH CENTER. 2010. *Blacks Upbeat about Black Progress, Prospects.* Accessed at http://pewsocialtrends.org/2010/01/12/blacks-upbeat-about-black-progress-prospects.

PINCUS, FRED L. 2003. *Reverse Discrimination: Dismantling the Myth.* Boulder, CO: Lynne Rienner.

——. 2008. *Reverse Discrimination.* Pp. 1159–1161 in vol. 3, *Encyclopedia of Race, Ethnicity, and Society*, Richard T. Schaefer, ed. Thousand Oaks, CA: Sage.

POLZIN, THERESITA. 1973. *The Polish Americans: Whence and Whither.* Pulaski, WI: Franciscan Publishers.

PORTES, ALEJANDRO. 1998. Social Capital: Its Origins and Applications in Modern Society. *Annual Review of Sociology* 24: 1–24.

────── AND ERIK VICKSTROM. 2011. Diversity, Social Capital, and Cohesion. *Annual Review of Sociology* 37: 461–479.

POWELL-HOPSON, DARLENE AND DEREK HOPSON. 1988. Implications of Doll Color Preferences among Black Preschool Children and White Preschool Children. *Journal of Black Psychology* 14 (February): 57–63.

PRESTON, JULIA. 2007. Polls Surveys Ethnic Views among Chief Minorities. *New York Times* (December 13).

PRESTON, JULIA. 2010. On Gangs, Asylum Law Offers Little. *New York Times* (June 30): A15, A19.

PRYOR, JOHN H., SYLVIA HURTADO, LINDA DEANGELO, LAURA PALUCKI BLAKE, AND SERGE TRAN. 2010. *The American Freshman: National Norms for Fall 2010*. Los Angeles, CA: Higher Education Research Institute, UCLA.

PURDY, MATTHEW. 2001. Ignoring and then Embracing the Truth about Racial Profiling. *New York Times* (March 11).

QUILLIAN, LINCOLN. 2006. New Approaches to Understanding Racial Prejudice and Discrimination. Pp. 299–328 in *Annual Reviews of Sociology 2006*, Karen S. Cook, ed. Palo Alto, CA: Annual Reviews Inc.

RAYBON, PATRICIA. 1989. A Case for "Severe Bias." *Newsweek* (October 2): 114: 11.

RESKIN, BARBARA F. 1998. *The Realities of Affirmative Action in Employment*. Washington, DC: American Sociological Association.

RICH, MEGHAN ASHLIN. 2008. Resegregation. Pp. 1152–1153 in vol. 3, *Encyclopedia of Race, Ethnicity, and Society*, Richard T. Schaefer, ed. Thousand Oaks, CA: Sage.

RICHMOND, ANTHONY H. 2002. Globalization: Implications for Immigrants and Refugees. *Ethnic and Racial Studies* 25 (September): 707–727.

ROBERTS, SAM. 2011. Little Italy, Littler by the Year. *New York Times* (February 22): A19.

ROBINSON, MICHELLE. 1985. *Princeton-Educated Blacks and the Black Community*. Senior Honors Thesis, Princeton University. Accessed July 9, 2009, at http://obamaprincetonthesis.wordpress.com.

ROBNETT, BELINDA AND CYNTHIA FELICIANO. 2011. Patterns of Racial-Ethnic Exclusion by Internet Daters. *Social Forces* 89 (no. 3, March): 807–828.

ROEDIGER, DAVID R. 1994. *Towards the Abolition of Whiteness: Essays on Race, Politics, and Working Class History (Haymarket)*. New York: Verso Books.

──────. 2006. Whiteness and Its Complications. *Chronicle of Higher Education* 52 (July 14): B6–B8.

ROOF, WADE CLARK. 2007. Introduction. *The Annals* 612 (July): 6–12.

ROSE, ARNOLD. 1951. *The Roots of Prejudice*. Paris: UNESCO.

RUSK, DAVID. 2001. *The "Segregation Tax": The Cost of Racial Segregation to Black Homeowners*. Washington, DC: Brookings Institution.

RYAN, WILLIAM. 1976. *Blaming the Victim*, rev. ed. New York: Random House.

SAAD, LYDIA. 2006. Anti-Muslim Sentiments Fairly Commonplace. *The Gallup Poll* (August 10).

SAKAMOTO, ARTHUR, KIMBERLY A. GOYETTE, AND CHANGHWAN KIM. 2009. Socioeconomic Attainments of Asian Americans. *Annual Review of Sociology* 35: 255–276.

SASSLER, SHARON L. 2006. School Participation among Immigrant Youths: The Case of Segmented Assimilation in the Early 20th Century. *Sociology of Education* 79 (January): 1–24.

SAULNY, SUSAN. 2011. Black? White? Asian? More Young Americans Choose All of the Above. *New York Times* (January 29): A1, A17–A18.

SCHAEFER, RICHARD T. 1976. *The Extent and Content of Racial Prejudice in Great Britain*. San Francisco, CA: R&E Research Associates.

──────. 1986. Racial Prejudice in a Capitalist State: What Has Happened to the American Creed? *Phylon* 47 (September): 192–198.

──────. 1992. People of Color: The "Kaleidoscope" May Be a Better Way to Describe America than "the Melting Pot." *Peoria Journal Star* (January 19): A7.

──────. 1996. Education and Prejudice: Unraveling the Relationship. *Sociological Quarterly* 37 (January): 1–16.

──────. 2008b. Nativism. Pp. 611–612 in vol. 1, *Encyclopedia of Social Problems*, Vincent N. Parrillo, ed. Thousand Oaks, CA: Sage.

────── AND WILLIAM ZELLNER. 2011. *Extraordinary Groups*, 9th ed. New York: Worth.

SCHWARTZ, ALEX. 2001. *The State of Minority Access to Home Mortgage Lending: A Profile of the New York Metropolitan Area*. Washington, DC: Brooking Institution Center on Urban and Metropolitan Policy.

SCOTT, JANNY. 2003. Debating Which Private Clubs Are Acceptable and Private. *New York Times* 7 (December 8): 5.

SEMPLE, KIRK. 2010. Immigrants Find Voting Can Come at a Cost. *New York Times* (October 17): A28.

SENTENCING PROJECT. 2008. *Felony Disenfranchisement*. Accessed January 30, 2008, at www.sentencingproject.org/IssueAreaHome.aspx?IssueID=4.

SHANKLIN, EUGENIA. 1994. *Anthropology and Race*. Belmont, CA: Wadsworth.

SHAPIRO, THOMAS M. 2004. *The Hidden Cost of Being African American: How Wealth Perpetuates Inequality.* New York: Oxford University Press.

————. 2010. *New Study Finds Racial Wealth Gap Quadrupled Sing Mid-1980s.* Boston, MA: Institute on Assets and Social Policy.

————, TATJANA MESCHEDE, AND LAURA SULLIVAN. 2010. The Racial Wealth Gap Increases Fourfold. Research and Policy Brief (May) of Institute on Assets and Social Policy, University of Michigan.

SHARON, SUSAN. 2010. Ten Years After Somalis Begin Arriving, Littleton Looks Back. *Maine Public Broadcasting Network* (January 29). Accessed April 12, 2011, at www.mpbn.net.

SHERIF, MUSAFER AND CAROLYN SHERIF. 1969. *Social Psychology.* New York: Harper & Row.

SHERWOOD, JESSICA HOLDEN. 2010. *Wealth, Whiteness, and the Matrix of Privilege: The View from the Country Clubs.* Lanham MD: Rowman and Littlefield.

SHIN, HYON B. AND ROBERT A. KOMINSKI. 2010. Language Use in the United States 2007. *Census Brief ACS-12.* Washington, DC: U.S. Government Printing Office.

SIGELMAN, LEE AND STEVEN A. TUCH. 1997. Metastereotypes: Blacks' Perception of Whites' Stereotypes of Blacks. *Public Opinion Quarterly* 61 (Spring): 87–101.

SIMPSON, CAM. 2009. Obama Hones Immigration Policy. *Wall Street Journal* (July 29): A6.

SIMPSON, JACQUELINE C. 1995. Pluralism: The Evolution of a Nebulous Concept. *American Behavioral Scientist* 38 (January): 459–477.

SKRENTNY, JOHN D. 2008. Culture and Race/Ethnicity: Bolder, Deeper, and Broader. *Annals* 619 (September): 59–77.

SLAVIN, ROBERT E. AND ALAN CHEUNG. 2003. *Effective Reading Programs for English Language Learners.* Baltimore, MD: Johns Hopkins University, Center for Research on the Education of Students Placed at Risk.

SMITH, TOM W. 2006. *Taking America's Pulse III. Intergroup Relations in Contemporary America.* Chicago, IL: National Opinion Research Center, University of Chicago.

SOCIETY FOR HUMAN RESOURCE MANAGEMENT. 2008. *2007 State of Workplace Diversity Management.* Alexandria, VA: SHRM.

SOLTERO, SONIA WHITE. 2008. *Bilingual Education.* Pp. 142–146 in vol. 1, *Encyclopedia of Race, Ethnicity, and Society,* Richard T. Schaefer, ed. Thousand Oaks, CA: Sage.

SONG, TAE-HYON. 1991. *Social Contact and Ethnic Distance between Koreans and the U.S. Whites in the United States.* M.A. thesis, Western Illinois University, Macomb.

SOUTHERN POVERTY LAW CENTER. 2010. *Ten Ways to Fight Hate: A Community Response Guide.* Montgomery, AL: SPLC.

STARK, RODNEY AND CHARLES GLOCK. 1968. *American Piety: The Nature of Religious Commitment.* Berkeley, CA: University of California Press.

STEINBERG, STEPHEN. 2005. Immigration, African Americans, and Race Discourse. *New Politics* (Winter): 10.

————. 2007. *Race Relations: A Critique.* Stanford, CT: Stanford University Press.

STEINHAUER, JENNIFER. 2006. An Unwelcome Light on Club Where Legends Teed Off. *New York Times* (September 23): A8.

STERN, NUCOLAS. 2007. *Review on the Economics of Climate Change.* London: HM Treasury.

STONE, EMILY. 2006. Hearing the Call—In Polish. *Chicago Tribune* (October 13): 15.

STONEQUIST, EVERETT V. 1937. *The Marginal Man: A Study in Personality and Culture Conflict.* New York: Scribner's.

STRETESKY, PAUL AND MICHAEL LYNCH. 2002. Environmental Hazards and School Segregation in Hillsborough County, Florida, 1987–1999. *Sociological Quarterly* 43: 553–573.

SULLIVAN, KEITH. 2005. Desperate Moves. *Washington Post National Weekly Edition* (March 14): 9–10.

SZE, JULIE AND JONATHAN K. LONDON. 2008. Environmental Justice at the Crossroads. *Sociology Compass* 2.

TAKAKI, RONALD. 1989. *Strangers from a Different Shore: A History of Asian Americans.* Boston, MA: Little, Brown.

TAYLOR, PAUL, ET AL. 2010. *Marrying Out: One-in-Seven New U.S. Marriages is Interracial or Interethnic.* Washington, DC: Pew Research Center.

TAYLOR, STUART, JR. 1987. High Court Backs Basing Promotion on a Racial Quota. *New York Times* (February 26): 1, 14.

————. 1988. Justices Back New York Law Ending Sex Bias by Big Clubs. *New York Times* (June 21): A1, A18.

TERANISHI, ROBERT T. 2010. *Asians in the Ivory Tower: Dilemmas of Racial Inequity in American Higher Education.* New York: Teachers College Press.

THOMAS, OLIVER. 2007. So What Does the Constitution Say about Religion? *USA Today* (October 15): 15A.

THOMAS, WILLIAM ISAAC. 1923. *The Unadjusted Girl.* Boston, MA: Little, Brown.

———— AND FLORIAN ZNANIECKI. 1996 [1918]. *The Polish Peasant in Europe and America* (5 vols.), Eli Zaretsky, ed. Urbana, IL: University of Illinois Press.

THREADCRAFT, SHATEMA A. 2008. Welfare Queen. Pp. 1384–1386 in vol. 3, *Encyclopedia of Race, Ethnicity, and Society*, Richard T. Schaefer, ed. Thousand Oaks, CA: Sage.

TOMASKOVIC-DEVEY, DONALD AND PATRICIA WARREN. 2009. Explaining and Eliminating Racial Profiling. *Contexts* 8 (Spring): 34–39.

TOUGH, PAUL. 2004. The "Acting White" Myth. *New York Times* (December 12).

TOWNSEND, SARAH S. M., HAZEL R. MARKOS, AND HILARY BERGSIEKER. 2009. My Choice, Your Categories: The Denial of Multiracial Identities. *Journal of Social Issues* 65 (1): 185–204.

TURE, KWAME AND CHARLES HAMILTON. 1992. *Black Power: The Politics of Liberation*. New York: Vintage Books.

TURNER, MARGERY AUSTIN, FRED FREIBURG, ERIN GODFREY, CLARK HERBIG, DIANE K. LEVY, AND ROBIN R. SMITH. 2002. *All Other Things Being Equal: A Paired Testing Study of Mortgage Lending Institutions*. Washington, DC: Urban Institute.

TYSON, KAROLYN. 2011. *Integration Interrupted: Tracking, Black Students, and Acting White After Brown*. New York: Oxford University Press.

———, WILLIAM DARITY, JR., AND DOMINI R. CASTELLINO. 2005. It's Not "a Black Thing": Understanding the Burden of Acting White and Other Dilemmas of High Achievement. *American Sociological Review* 70 (August): 582–605.

UNITED NATIONS HIGH COMMISSION ON REFUGEES. 2008. *2007 Global Trends: Refugees, Asylum-seekers, Returnees, Internally Displaced and Stateless Persons*. Geneva: UNHCR.

UNIVERSITY OF NORTH DAKOTA. 2008. *B.R.I.D.G.E.S.* Accessed July 8, 2008, at www.und.edu/org/bridges/index2.html.

USDANSKY, MARGARET L. 1992. Old Ethnic Influences Still Play in Cities. *USA Today* (August 4): 9A.

U.S COURT OF APPEALS. 2008. *Chicago Lawyers' Committee for Civil Rights Under Law, Inc. v. Craigslist, Inc. For the Seventh Circuit*. No. 06 C 657 (February 15).

U.S. ENGLISH. 2010. *Welcome to U.S. English, Inc.* Accessed June 9, 2010, at www.us-english.org/inc.

WAGLEY, CHARLES AND MARVIN HARRIS. 1958. *Minorities in the New World: Six Case Studies*. New York: Columbia University Press.

WALLERSTEIN, IMMANUEL. 1974. *The Modern World System*. New York: Academic Press.

WARK, COLIN AND JOHN F. GALLIHER. 2007. Emory Bogardus and the Origins of the Social Distance Scale. *American Sociologist* 38: 383–395.

WARNER, W. LLOYD AND LEO SROLE. 1945. *The Social Systems of American Ethnic Groups*. New Haven, CT: Yale University.

WATERS, MARY. 1990. *Ethnic Options. Choosing Identities in America*. Berkeley, CA: University of California Press.

WEBER, MAX. 1947. *The Theory of Social and Economic Organization* [1913–1922], Henderson and T. Parsons, trans. New York: Free Press.

WEINBERG, DANIEL H. 2007. Earnings by Gender: Evidence from Census 2000. *Monthly Labor Review* (July–August): 26–34.

WELCH, WILLIAM M. 2011. More Hawaii Resident Identify as Mixed Race. *USA Today* (February 28).

WESSEL, DAVID. 2001. Hidden Costs of Brain Drain. *Wall Street Journal* (March 1): 1.

WEST, DARREL M. 2010. *Brain Grain: Rethinking U.S. Immigration Policy*. Washington, DC: Brookings Institution Press.

WICKHAM, DE WAYNE. 1993. Subtle Racism Thrives. *USA Today* (October 25): 2A, 15, A1, A26.

WILKES, RIMA AND JOHN ICELAND. 2004. Hypersegregation in the Twenty-First Century. *Demography* 41 (February): 23–36.

WILLIAMS, KIM M. 2005. Multiculturalism and the Civil Rights Future. *Daedalus* 134 (1): 53–60.

WILLOUGHBY, BRIAN. 2004. *10 Ways to Fight Hate on Campus*. Montgomery, AL: Southern Poverty Law Center.

WINANT, HOWARD. 1994. *Racial Conditions: Politics, Theory, Comparisons*. Minneapolis, MN: University of Minnesota Press.

———. 2004. *The New Politics of Race: Globalism, Difference, Justice*. Minneapolis, MN: University of Minnesota Press.

———. 2006. Race and Racism: Towards a Global Future. *Ethnic and Racial Studies* 29 (September): 986–1003.

WINERIP, MICHAEL. 2011. New Influx of Haitians, But Not Who Was Expected. *New York Times* (January 16): 15, 22.

WINSEMAN, ALBERT L. 2004. *U.S. Churches Looking for a Few White Men*. Accessed July 27, 2004, at www.gallup.com.

WINTER, S. ALAN. 2008. *Symbolic Ethnicity*. Pp. 1288–1290 in vol. 3, *Encyclopedia of Race, Ethnicity, and Society*, Richard T. Schaefer, ed. Thousand Oaks, CA: Sage.

WITHROW, BRIAN L. 2006. *Racial Profiling: From Rhetoric to Reason*. Upper Saddle River, NJ: Prentice Hall.

WITT, BERNARD. 2007. What Is a Hate Crime? *Chicago Tribune* (June 10): 1, 18.

WORKING, RUSSELL. 2007. Illegal Abroad, Hate Web Sites Thrive Here. *Chicago Tribune* (November 13): A1, A15.

WRONG, DENNIS H. 1972. How Important Is Social Class? *Dissent* 19 (Winter): 278–285.

WYATT, EDWARD. 2009. No Smooth Ride on TV Networks' Road to Diversity. *New York Times* (March 18): 1, 5.

WYMAN, MARK. 1993. *Round-Trip to America. The Immigrants Return to Europe, 1830–1930*. Ithaca, NY: Cornell University Press.

YANCEY, GEORGE. 2003. *Who Is White? Latinos, Asians, and the New Black–Nonblack Divide*. Boulder, CO: Lynne Rienner.

YINGER, JOHN. 1995. *Closed Doors, Opportunities Lost: The Continuing Costs of Housing Discrimination*. New York: Russell Sage Foundation.

YOSSO, TARA J. 2005. Whose Culture Has Capital? A Critical Race Theory Discussion of Community Cultural Wealth. *Race Ethnicity and Education* 8 (March): 69–91.

YOUNG, JEFFREY R. 2003. Researchers Change Racial Bias on the SAT. *Chronicle of Higher Education* (October 10): A34–A35.

ZENG, ZHEN AND YU XIE. 2004. Asian-Americans' Earnings Disadvantage Reexamined: The Role of Place of Education. *American Journal of Sociology* 190 (March): 1075–1108.

ZIMMERMAN, SETH. 2008. *Immigration and Economic Mobility*. Washington, DC: Economic Mobility Project.

ZOGBY, JAMES. 2010. *51% Expect Major Terror Attack This Year and 25% Plan to Fly Less* (February 4). Accessed March 2, 2011, at http://www.zogby.com.

# Photo Credits

# Name Index

# Subject Index